Conditioning for Dance

Eric Franklin

Human Kinetics

Library of Congress Cataloging-in-Publication Data

Franklin, Eric N.
   Conditioning for dance / Eric Franklin.
       p.   cm.
  Includes bibliographical references and index.
    ISBN 0-7360-4156-7 (soft cover) – ISBN 0-7360-4156-7
    1. Dance. 2. Physical fitness. 3. Dance–Physiological aspects. 4.
Imagery (Psychology) I. Title.
   GV1588.F73 2004
   792.8–dc21
                                       2003012254

ISBN: 0-7360-4156-7

The Web addresses cited in this text were current as of July 1, 2003, unless otherwise noted.

Acquisitions Editor: Judy Patterson Wright, PhD; **Developmental Editor:** Julie Rhoda; **Assistant Editor:** Carla Zych; **Copyeditor:** Joanna Hatzopoulos Portman; **Proofreader:** Cheryl Ossola; **Indexer:** Nan N. Badgett; **Graphic Designer:** Nancy Rasmus; **Graphic Artist:** Kim McFarland; **Photo and Art Manager:** Dan Wendt; **Cover Designer:** Keith Blomberg; **Photographer (cover):** © Jose Luis Pelaez, Inc./CORBIS; **Photographer (interior):** Franz Öttl; **Illustrators:** Sonja Burger and Eric Franklin; **Printer:** Sheridan Books.

Human Kinetics books are available at special discounts for bulk purchase. Special editions or book excerpts can also be created to specification. For details, contact the Special Sales Manager at Human Kinetics.

Printed in the United States of America   10 9 8 7 6 5 4 3

Human Kinetics
Web site: www.HumanKinetics.com

United States: Human Kinetics, P.O. Box 5076, Champaign, IL 61825-5076
800-747-4457
e-mail: humank@hkusa.com

Canada: Human Kinetics, 475 Devonshire Road, Unit 100, Windsor, ON N8Y 2L5
800-465-7301 (in Canada only)
e-mail: orders@hkcanada.com

Europe: Human Kinetics, 107 Bradford Road, Stanningley
Leeds LS28 6AT, United Kingdom
+44 (0) 113 255 5665
e-mail: hk@hkeurope.com

Australia: Human Kinetics, 57A Price Avenue, Lower Mitcham, South Australia 5062
08 8277 1555
e-mail: liaw@hkaustralia.com

New Zealand: Human Kinetics, Division of Sports Distributors NZ Ltd.
P.O. Box 300 226 Albany, North Shore City, Auckland
0064 9 448 1207
e-mail: blairc@hknewz.com

Acknowledgments

I thank the late André Bernard for showing me how to use imagery in a deeply meaningful way, and to his memory I dedicate this book.

Thank you to all of the dancers, dance educators, and choreographers that have attended my classes over the last years. Through continued dialogue with my students I have been able to create a book that serves their specific needs. I thank Zvi Gotheiner, who provided me with insights into conditioning that are truly meaningful for dancers. I would also like to acknowledge Bonnie Bainbridge Cohen's great teachings and all the wonderful educators at the school of Body–Mind Centering®.

Thank you to the Hygenic Corporation, makers of Thera-Bands, especially Hermann Rotinghaus in the USA and Ludwig Arzt in Germany, for their support in making this book possible.

Photographer Franz Öttl created the beautiful exercise shots in a very short period of time with great sensitivity to dance and attention to detail. Thanks also to my models, Mucuy Bolles, Sheila Joy Burford, Verena Tremel, and Russ Warfield. A big thank you also to my illustrator Sonja Burger, with whom I collaborated to create the many drawings that adorn this book.

I thank my family, who patiently endured my many writing hours.

At the American Dance Festival I thank Martha Myers and Donna Faye for their continued support throughout the many years I have been associated with this wonderful place for dancers to learn and develop. A thank you also to Jan Dunn, Karen Wells, and Morten Dithmer for their support of my work.

Finally I thank my editor at Human Kinetics, Julie Rhoda, for her excellent work on this book. I greatly appreciate her patience and endurance, her great attention to detail, and her insight into the subject matter. I also thank acquisitions editor Judy Patterson Wright. Her coaching and insights on the structure and content of this book made this project possible.

Contents

Foreword

Eric Franklin's books should be in the hands of all dance students, teachers, and performers from the beginning of their study. *Conditioning for Dance* is no exception. It is an eye-opening tour of the conditioning topography, both a Baedker and a Berlitz course addressed specifically to the needs of dancers. Franklin reinvents the traditional how-to book in this field, integrating his extensive scientific knowledge with the principles of major somatic systems (especially ideokinesis). Thus, he is able to merge these approaches in his system of training for dancers and to offer readers a comprehensive experience in the exercise sequences and concepts he presents. He does this, moreover, with the eye and sensibility of one who has a wide background as a dancer and visual artist. It is a landmark in our field.

Franklin fully integrates traditional components of strength, flexibility, and cardiorespiratory fitness with somatic perspectives. He emphasizes the importance of alignment in all movement sequences—exercises and dance steps—describing the biomechanics of alignment (a more mobile term than "placement") and explaining its effect on the execution of dance sequences. The importance of mental presence, concentration, awareness, mental imagery and practice are addressed, and Franklin discusses the role that cognitive as well as neuromuscular patterns play in the development of a dancer's performance.

Throughout my reading of this book, I found myself nodding in affirmation of Franklin's thoughts: "Exercise is an ongoing dialogue between mind and body." "Training is not an end in itself; it cannot stand alone, without feeling and expression." Such reminders that dance is an art, not just a pleasant form of exercise should resound through every dance studio. These words are not free-floating sentiments. The author brings you full-circle back to the anatomy and physiology that grounds them; this information supports and prepares you for the experiential sequences that follow. The eye is informed as well as the body–mind by his witty, inspiring drawings. I found myself trying the exercises as I read them, enjoying a kind of interactive experience.

Insights, information, and wisdom pop up throughout the book, such as the reminder that "Flexibility and strength must be entrained with presence of mind and body to create an inspiring performer." Mindless grippers of the barre, and lifters of weights beware! Read on and you will find innovative interventions for particular technical problems: simple readjustments in preparing for a plié, a pirouette or a jump. There is a special emphasis on new ways to amplify Thera-Band exercise with breath and images. All of these will allow the dancer more ease, grace, and *joy* (that underused word in training) in moving and dancing.

Having spent a large portion of my professional life studying dance science and somatics, and through teaching at the American Dance Festival (ADF) and Connecticut College, pioneering their acceptance in dance training, I am thrilled to see this book in print. Franklin has been on the ADF faculty (a "pied-piper" teacher if ever there was one), and his originality was evident as an early participant in my Choreolab there. He presents his ideas with just the right touch, rhythm, aesthetics, clarity of mind, and imagery that he espouses in his classes and his training system. *Conditioning for Dance* is a "good read" in the bargain, something we don't usually expect of such volumes. It's a helpful companion to keep by your side as you train and dance.

—Martha Myers

Preface

Years ago when I was training to be a dancer, I noticed someone working out before a class. He was struggling with what looked like an old bicycle tire. It turned out that I was not mistaken; the dancer was using the tire to strengthen certain muscles that he felt were not sufficiently trained by the class itself. Later I encountered an age-old German invention, the "Deuser-Band" which was basically a refined bicycle tire, thin and very resistant; you could hardly pull it apart. Dancers were wrapping these bands around their legs to help them improve turn-out by forcing the inner thigh muscles to stretch, assuming a supine position with the legs split apart. This position was quite painful, but many dancers felt the results were more important than comfort, or even safety.

I thought that there must be a better way to achieve more turnout, but I had not yet seen what I was looking for: a portable resistance method to increase my strength as a dancer. I began to search for something broad and more elastic that I could stretch around my feet to practice pointing them against resistance; the tire simply would not stretch enough. A friend of mine pointed a out store in the center of Zürich that sold plastic products. The man there cut a piece of what looked like an oversized rubber band, and suddenly I had my own complete home resistance exerciser. I started devising many different exercise routines using the band to strengthen my legs. The band was adaptable in length and elasticity, and it could be attached to the body, so my exercises simulated familar dance movements. Along with the resistance bands, I started using a variety of balls to roll around on and balance on. The balls provided a means of releasing tension and increasing flexibility without constantly forcing my body into akward positions. I started to notice that my lack of flexibility was related to knotty, tense muscles. If I exercised with the balls before my rubber band workout, I felt more limber and was able to increase my range of movement. Moreover I noticed an immediate increase in my strength when dancing.

When I started teaching at the American Dance Festival (ADF) in 1991, I had already established an exercise routine using the elastic bands and small, 4-inch balls. The exercises were received with great enthusiasm by my students at ADF, and the newly available Thera-Bands and the rolling balls became very popular with them. As the years passed and I learned more about conditioning and resistance training, I was able to develop more sophisticated exercises. Based on the principles of dance medicine and science, exercises were added or altered to engage a more complete range of muscles and to meet the specific needs of dancers. I adapted the exercises to the age, training level, and dance styles of the participants and included imagery to ensure the correct alignment and movement initiation for every exercise. I taught my conditioning routines to dancers at such diverse places as the Guangdong Modern Dance Company in China and the Royal Ballet School in London. My students kept asking me to write about the exercises, so I started collecting the exercises in a notebook, which planted the seed for this book.

The result of years of practical experience combined with scientific and anatomical analysis, this book emphasizes practical exercises, mind–body relationships, and conditioning routines. The aim is to provide immediate benefits to dancers as well as to offer them the chance to create a focused buildup of strength and flexibility. Many of the exercises are also suited for non-dancers who are simply interested in improving their overall fitness. The approach is learning by doing, experiencing, and imaging and through personal insight. A key focus is to help the dancer become kinesthetically aware of how he can create great dance technique in his own body. Instead of forcing technique on the dancer, technique is built from the inside out to create an injury-free and artistically successful career.

The first part of the book builds the foundation for the exercises you will find later in the book that are specific to dance technique. Chapter 1 describes the basic principles of resistance training and dance conditioning. Chapter 2 focuses on imagery, the mind–body connection, and how to apply those principles to resistance training. You'll use this information throughout the rest of the book as most exercises use imagery to fine-tune coordination and increase awareness of the body's movements. Chapter 3 then shows you how to improve balance by improving body coordination and doing playful exercises with balls. Chapter 4 focuses on how to improve flexibility through imagery, touch, movement awareness, and stretching. And chapter 5 works on conditioning alignment and the pelvic floor, important areas of focus for dance technique.

Chapters 6, 7, and 8 then introduce key muscles to target for strengthening and balancing the core muscles, the arms, and the legs, respectively. In chapter 9, I address three of the main concerns of dancers; turns, jumps, and turn-out; and I show how to improve these three skills using kinesthetic awareness and conditioning techniques. The book culminates in a 20-minute Thera-Band workout that combines the principles covered throughout the book into a full body workout.

All the chapters contain insights into how to create lifelong dancing skills that give you power without hurting your body. These methods illustrate how much more you can achieve if you allow your body's intelligence to help you.

Throughout the book I have often used ballet terms because they provide the most standard description of many basic dance positions; however, readers who are not coming from a ballet background may need some of these terms defined. Many exercises start in a ballet first, third, or fifth position. In the first position, the heels touch and the feet are turned out. In the third position, the feet are together and one heel is in front of the other. In the fifth position, one foot is in front of the other, and the heel of the front foot is at the base of the big toe of the back foot. In a perfect fifth position, the feet touch the inner border of the back foot to the outer border of the front foot. Fifth position is not part of the modern dance repertoire.

Battement (from French) means "to hit." In the battement the leg initially slides along the floor to the front, side, or back and then extends out in the chosen direction. The leg then reverses direction and returns to the original position. There are different types of battement such as *battement tendu* (often shortened to *tendu*). In battement tendu the tip of the foot does not leave the floor after foot is stretched out. *In the battement tendu dégagé* (often shortened to *battement dégagé*, or *dégagé*), the tip of the foot does leave the floor. A modern dance brush is usually similar in outward form to a battement dégagé, starting from the first or a parallel position, though there may be differences in the quality and timing between a brush and a battement dégagé.

In the *battement fondu* both knees are bent and the gesture foot points in front of the supporting leg's ankle. In the *battement fondu développé* both the supporting and gesture leg are extended to the front, side, or back. In the *battement jeté* and *grand battement* the gesture leg is rapidly swung forward (or to the side or back) to at least 90 degrees elevation. Again there are great qualitative and rhythmic differences in these high leg gestures among ballet, modern, and jazz dance styles.

The *grand battement développé,* or *développé,* is also known as the dancer's extension. This is performed from fifth position in ballet by slowly lifting the turned out gesture leg, the pointed foot moving up the front of the supporting leg. The gesture foot moves through the passé position with the pointed gesture foot directed at the knee of the supporting leg. The gesture leg then extends to the front at a level of 90 degrees or higher. The gesture leg then returns along the same path to fifth position. In modern dance and other styles this movement is also performed in parallel to the front.

Mind–Body Conditioning

A few years ago while teaching at the Ballet School of the Zürich Opera, I was help-ing an experienced dancer with her pirouettes. She could perform three to four of them quite predictably, but her head slightly tilted to the side and her pelvis tended to drop forward toward the end of the turns. I pointed out these observations to her and she tried again, but her pirouettes did not improve. These misalignments were hardwired into her movement patterns, so merely being aware of them was not going to help her turn perfect pirouettes. She asked me what she should do to turn better pirouettes. I told her that she required some additional force but that it would do her little good within the movement pattern that she was currently exhibiting. How-ever, she could go beyond her current level if she were ready to relearn the alignment for her pirouettes. Because muscles are strengthened within the coordination that you use them, we first needed to discover better coordination before we strengthened her pirouettes.

To help this dancer to experience the connection between her strength and coordina-tion, I asked her to first perform a simpler movement. I provided her with imagery and initiation skills to improve the coordination of her arabesque, and, after a few exercises, she felt it was stronger—the leg was able to go higher. Lifting the leg higher was a result of better coordination, but keeping the leg in the same position in the context of a dif-ficult dance step would require conditioning.

Another dancer became very interested in what we were doing after seeing the first dancer's increase in leg elevation. She asked that I coordinate her arabesque as well. As I worked with her on the arabesque, I also helped to release tension in her shoulders. Her leg went higher, but she noted that the position felt unusual. She had been practicing crooked arabesques with her shoulders tensed, so her muscles had become stronger to support crooked arabesques with tense shoulders. For her, exhibiting better align-ment and less tension made the movement feel weak because she had become used to compensating for misalignment and tension with strength. In the stress of class or performance a dancer often reverts to a dance position that feels comfortable even when it is an inefficient way of performing the movement.

If a dancer can't perform a step, he is sometimes told that he simply is not strong enough to do it. What looks like a lack of strength in individual muscles may actually be inefficient technique such as poor alignment, imbalance, lack of flexibility, or improper movement initiation. The point is, if you increase the strength of individual muscles without considering your whole body coordination, you cannot achieve better technique. So if you increase strength in a misaligned body, you will strengthen the misalignment.

Conditioning the dancer as an athlete and as an artist is a mind–body exercise—strength, balance, flexibility, alignment, and imagery training need to come together as a balanced whole. If the dancer is able to break the cycle of misaligned movements and strengthen proper ones, he can not only become more skilled but also reduce his risk for injury. To reap the greatest benefits from and create a clear focus for the exercises, follow these general conditioning tips that are emphasized throughout this book:

- Get used to practicing better ways of doing familiar movements. Train your senses, inform your body about correct alignment and movement initiation, and constantly find ways to improve technique. Don't waste your time practicing old habits that will take great effort to unlearn.

- Become skilled in using imagery and mental practice. Visualize and feel in your body a new idea—a new image—during training. Contemplate an image before you go to sleep—a flowing psoas muscle, a floating first rib—so that when you sleep your brain will keep working on the idea and will build the information into your next day's training.

- Seek help from an experienced teacher in dance or somatics—somebody who not only knows how to dance but how to help your body to dance with more ease.

- Observe your thought patterns and think positively. Are your thoughts supporting your goals as a dancer? Don't dwell on your fears and anxieties; such thoughts are a recipe for failure. Rather, use images and sensations of where you want to be and how you want to dance, combined with positive expectations and emotions. Seek out the teachers that help you on this track. Don't suppress problems; dwell on solutions. Put your best mental and physical energy at the service of your best image as a dancer, and watch yourself progress in leaps and bounds.

- Increase your flexibility in a balanced fashion. Discover new ways other than stretching to improve your flexibility. If you do stretch, make sure you are supporting balanced muscle action and are proceeding carefully.

- Perform strength training routines that are well structured and that engage your muscles in balanced movements that apply specifically to dance. Think of strength training as part of dance training; perform the exercises as if they were a dance.

- Learn how to improve your alignment without increasing tension. Alignment and flexibility skills go hand in hand. Discover how improving your alignment allows you to use your full flexibility and balance potential.

Flexibility and strength alone do not make you an artist. Dancers may insist that their technical difficulties with a particular movement come from a lack of strength and that the right strengthening routine is all they need. But then, two minutes and a little coaching later, they find they are able to perform the once-difficult step easily and expressively. To improve a movement, a dancer may only need information on how to coordinate joints and muscles along with a new awareness, a new image, and a clear physical sensation. Emphasizing physical skills at the expense of becoming aware of space, rhythm, phrasing, and the best way to create good coordination with your body's specific structure can distract a dancer from artistic expression. Technique is not an end in itself; it cannot stand alone, without feeling and expression. Flexibility and strength training are just a part of performance skill; such training should be done with presence of mind and body to create an inspiring performer who can master all the steps efficiently and with ease.

Many people who condition their bodies separate sensation from training. If you go to any gym where people are watching television screens or reading books while exercising, you'll notice that they don't show much interest in perceiving the body's processes and its reaction to exercise or in building a new awareness within the body while exercising. In such a case, the mental and physical processes are on two different tracks, so the mind and body are increasingly separated. Anyone benefits if the mind is present with the body while exercising. For a dancer, this connection is an absolute must. A dancer needs to experience each exercise she does as having an effect on the whole body, not just on the muscle or body area she is training. By actually noticing and feeling the changes an exercise has on the whole body, you can make training more effective.

Whole-Body Conditioning for the Artist

If you look at the variety of classes confronting the dancer, you'll notice that there is no consensus about what total conditioning for dance entails. Exercises are often based on habit rather than on what is really useful for the individual dancer and his skill level. Recently I was surprised to see a group of young dancers pour into a new style of dance class (I had never heard of the style before) and perform exercises that closely resembled those of a jazz warm-up from the 1980s. The style of clothing had changed, but the exercises stayed the same.

Nevertheless, in most classes dancers get very strong, mostly because they are talented and they fine-tune their bodies to a level that is unheard of in most other movement disciplines. In addition, many dance teachers have intuitively recognized the need for more balanced training and have updated their classes by combining traditional exercises with current conditioning trends. They recognize that a dancer's specific conditioning needs are not covered by flexibility and strength training alone. Dance conditioning also needs to achieve a highly developed sense of balance, timing, rhythm, and orientation in space as well as a measure of cardiovascular fitness. The exercises throughout this book develop each of these areas.

Bursts of intense exercise performed in less than one minute are called anaerobic. Running, swimming, or any continuous exercise that increases heart and lung (cardio-respiratory) activity for several minutes or more is termed aerobic exercise. Dance training is mostly anaerobic in nature—made up of shorter bursts of movement—and, by itself, usually does not have the cardiorespiratory benefits of aerobic training. It is therefore advisable to build some aerobic exercises into your conditioning routine and warm-up if you do not cross-train (more on warming up and cross-training follow). Being aerobically conditioned gives you more mental and physical stamina during a performance or a long rehearsal.

Jean-Pierre Egger, a trainer of several world champion athletes, once pointed out to me that dancers tend to jump higher than his track and field athletes who are much more muscular than dancers. "The extra muscle does not help my athletes jump higher than the dancers; they [the dancers] must be doing something right," he said. This *something* involves presence and awareness in training and a constant preoccupation with how to dance with greater subtlety and ease.

A growing number of fitness instructors are recognizing the importance of the mind–body connection. Ever since the publication of Deepak Chopra's *Ageless Body,*

Timeless Mind (1993) and Bill Moyers' *Healing and the Mind* (1993), interest in the relationship of the mind and body has been growing rapidly. Even so, most of the mind–body approaches are focused on the mental aspect of the equation. It is often not clearly demonstrated how to access the intelligence of the body and enter into a true dialogue with equal emphasis on the pathways from mind to body and from body to mind. Surprisingly, as early as 1937, Mabel Elsworth Todd was expounding this balanced approach in her book *The Thinking Body*.

So what does it mean to incorporate mind–body principles into training? Following are some ways that holistic principles—allowing the mind to connect with the body's movements and conditioning—can make your training more effective.

- Every exercise will affect the whole body, not just the muscle or part you are training. When you notice and feel the changes an exercise has on the whole body, your training becomes more effective.

- All elements of conditioning—alignment, balance, flexibility, strengthening, and cardiorespiratory endurance—are interrelated. Change one element and it affects all the others, just as change in one joint influences all the other joints.

- Your state of mind influences the effect of an exercise while you train. The same exercise performed with a different awareness—a different mental image—has a different effect on the body. If, while you are doing stretching exercises, you are worried about an upcoming audition, for example, it will be difficult for you to relax enough to make the stretch effective. Calm breathing is a key to effective stretching, and a relaxed state of mind creates calm breathing.

- Mental presence and concentration are the solid foundation of mind–body training. Being present in movement means experiencing the moment-to-moment changes in shape and dynamics in every part of the body during the whole exercise. Your desire to be present in the movement helps you to create a more efficient movement, because you improve your concentration and focus, thus increasing the awareness of the sensory feedback mechanisms of the nervous system and leading to greater motor control.

- Your thought patterns are influenced by the physical structures you are identified with. Stress, for example, is identified with a certain state of (over-) alertness in the nervous and endocrine systems. Similarly, every thought that crosses your mind during exercise becomes a part of the overall mix of your mental training. So your every thought can influence the result of your exercise. Exercising is an ongoing dialogue between mind and body. This communication can manifest itself through sensation, feeling, or imagery.

Conditioning Concepts

Before we delve into specific dance conditioning exercises, it is useful to cover some basic conditioning concepts and terminology. Some of these principles are more relevant than others for dancers, but all are good to keep tucked in your mental dance bag as you improve your mind–body conditioning.

Principle of Specificity

In conditioning, the principle of specificity states that the adaptation of the body to training depends on the type of training you undertake. In other words, if you stretch, you are specifically working on enhancing flexibility. If you lift a heavy barbell eight times to exhaustion, you are maximizing your strength. If you lift a lighter barbell 30 times until you feel tired, you are gaining muscular endurance.

When applying the specificity principle to strengthening for dance training, you need to use strengthening movements that are similar to or the same as those of the dance steps you intend to perform. The Thera-Band® (www.thera-band.com) is ideal for dance-specific strength training (see chapters 8, 9, and 10) because you can use it to apply resistance to a variety of dance movements. But when you strength train using free weights or machine weights, you are most often not performing dance-specific exercises (though training in the weight room can make a dancer *feel* stronger, and thus it may have psychological benefits).

To benefit most from any conditioning, you must choose exercises that target the muscles you would like to strengthen, moving in as close to the coordination as will be required to perform them with increased strength. For example, to increase strength for a grand battement (a fast, high leg kick), you must consider three specificities:

1. A speed specificity: The movement should be fast.
2. A muscle group specificity: The movement should work the hip flexors as well as stabilize musculature.
3. A muscle action specificity: The muscle action needs to be concentric and eccentric and performed with the correct alignment.

So performing an isometric (nonmoving) resistance exercise for the hip flexors will not improve your grand battement, but performing a grand battement using a Thera-Band for resistance will.

The following chapters include some exercises that work on strengthening the abdominal muscles in a position that may not seem specific to dance. These conditioning exercises balance muscles, increase awareness of the body, or release tension and improve overall alignment. They also may have a therapeutic effect and address previously neglected aspects of your dance training. A good example of this type of conditioning is the exercise series for the iliopsoas muscles in chapter 6 (pages 124 to 139), which are aimed at releasing the lower back and hip joint and aligning the pelvis. As you'll learn throughout this book, such a conditioning routine is crucial for improving performance in all styles of dance. Many exercises and conditioning routines are most appropriate for certain styles of dance, depending on your individual goals. The following are three basic challenges facing any muscle:

1. The need for a brief spurt of maximal activation (e.g., lifting a partner over your head). This action requires maximal strength, usually defined as the maximum force that a muscle can exert in a single, all-out effort.
2. The need to be able to endure the same type of repeated exertion for a long period, as when running, cycling, or performing the same dance step again and again during a rehearsal. The type of strength required in this instance is called strength endurance or muscular endurance.
3. The need to be able to perform an action with great speed, as when jumping into the air for a double turn. This kind of effort is defined as the muscle's power, or speed strength.

As a dancer, you usually do not need the maximal strength of a weightlifter, just as you don't need the muscular endurance specific to a marathon runner. However, including an aerobic workout three times a week can be beneficial, especially if you pay attention to alignment and use imagery to move with sound biomechanics. (This recommendation is for adults only; training for young children should emphasize improving coordination and flexibility and having fun.) Aerobic training is also a good way to balance muscle strength. Swimming, cycling, or any sport activity that does not stress joints or is non-weight bearing is advisable. Other good cardiorespiratory training methods are jogging, running, fast walking, cross-country skiing, and hiking. Experiment to discover the most suitable exercise for you.

Adapt your conditioning routine to exercise and strengthen the movements that are common in the specific form of dance you perform, such as modern dance contractions, high leg kicks in jazz dance, or petit allegro in ballet. If you perform a variety of dance styles and you don't have time to include specific training for every style, perform a general conditioning routine with a specific warm-up adapted to the style of the day. If you are unclear about your needs, consult an exercise expert. Generally speaking, developing all the previously mentioned elements of strength with particular emphasis on muscular endurance and power, is advisable for most dancers and is duscussed in detail in chapters 9 and 10.

Principle of Progressive Overload

Begin conditioning gradually and build slowly, focusing on listening to your body. Easing into a conditioning routine smartly saves you time and aggravation, because you avoid injuries that occur from jumping into conditioning programs that your body is not prepared for. Listen to your body; if an exercise feels wrong or painful, don't do it.

Any conditioning program should start slowly, but it does need to eventually increase in intensity. If you do not gradually increase the stress on the musculature throughout your conditioning program, your strength level will reach a plateau. You need to increase the resistance over time to match the strength and conditioning gains of the muscle. This concept is called the progressive overload principle, and without it there is no training effect. To train for a marathon, you need to progressively increase the distance you run. In dance, this principle is mostly applied in the sense of neuromuscular control, strengthening, and the performance and mastering of increasingly difficult dance steps.

There are many ways to progress. You may increase the load on the muscle by increasing the intensity, volume, and the frequency of the exercise.

> **Intensity.** You can increase the intensity of strengthening work simply by using resistance from a partner, heavier dumbbells, or higher-resistance Thera-Bands. To increase your cardiovascular conditioning you need exercise that maintains 60 to 77 percent of your maximal heart rate (HRmax) for at least 15 minutes. You can calculate your HRmax by multiplying your age by .7 and subtracting that number from 208 (HRmax = 208 − [.7 × your age]).
>
> Another way to increase the intensity specific for dance is to increase the challenges to your coordination by trying new, more difficult exercises or steps. The next chapter includes some balancing exercises that require standing on balls; those exercises exemplify such a challenge. Any kind of exercise that increases the activity of a muscle in a systematic way will improve the muscle's performance.
>
> **Volume.** You can also increase the amount or volume of work by increasing the number of repetitions and sets of an exercise. Generally the higher the resistance (intensity), the fewer the repetitions (volume) you can perform. The more repetitions you require, the lower the resistance. If your aim is to increase maximal strength, perform fewer repetitions with greater resistance;

if your aim is to improve muscular endurance, perform more repetitions with less resistance. Once you have performed several repetitions of an exercise, you have completed one set. Research has shown that it is sufficient to perform one well-executed set of an exercise to gain strength. Additional sets do little toward gaining more strength (Westcott 1996, p. 34). You may, however increase the number of sets, up to three, if desired. The advanced dancer could perform a maximum strength set in the morning and a muscular endurance set in the evening.

Usually the quality of execution is reduced if resistance is too high. And in dance training quality is key. The exercises in this book emphasize more repetitions with less resistance, and they use imagery to increase the muscular endurance and qualitative movement gains of each exercise.

Frequency. A dancer must train at regular intervals to benefit fully from his training. Exercise frequency of three times a week is sufficient to increase strength and maintain fitness. Dancers often train more frequently than that, because the main focus of dance training is on being able to perform the complex movements required by choreographers. These movements cross all genres from semi-acrobatic to ballet, jazz, improvisation, and modern. In most cases dancers are not able to try all genres within one class, so they have to participate in several classes of different styles. Quite often the only class that teaches them the right style is the one taught by the choreographer whose company they aspire to be in. Many young dancers try to learn as many dance styles as possible, which leads to overtraining and burnout, but their more experienced colleagues have found their niche and focus on it. Many dancers would do better and have longer careers if they would follow these principles of frequency:

- Limit time spent in dance classes to three hours a day.
- Use more imagery and other somatic disciplines to hone technique.
- Practice a conditioning routine three times a week.

Neurogenic Versus Myogenic Change

The effect of overload is an increased effort by the nervous system to organize the muscle to overcome the resistance. Strength training helps to improve the coordination within and among the muscles. So the experience of increased power after moving your leg against the resistance of a Thera-Band does not necessarily have to do with building more muscle; it has more to do with the way the nervous system controls the movement. This type of change is called *neurogenic*. Strength training, at least initially, is the result of an improvement in the way the nervous system controls muscles. The activation of the individual fibers within the muscle is orchestrated with greater precision, and the individual muscles and joints learn how to coordinate in a more efficient fashion.

If you perform resistance training over a long period, especially at intensities near your maximum strength, you can also create *myogenic* change in the muscle. In this type of change, the protein structure of the muscle actually changes, so you build muscle mass.

Sometimes dancers are worried that strength training will make them look more bulky. However, the exercises in this book are not designed to create a significant increase in muscle mass. In fact, the opposite is more likely to happen—the muscles may become thinner and longer. Muscles make this adaptation to speed up the delivery of nutrients to them, a task that is easier when muscles are thinner. So your body will most likely look leaner, stronger, and more toned once you have completed the first few weeks of training.

Balancing Eccentric and Concentric Actions

Many dancers, despite training for many years, lack strength in certain muscle groups while their other muscle groups have been overloaded. For example, because pointing the foot is practically a nonstop action in dance, the muscles that perform it are strong, whereas the opposing muscles are often neglected and relatively weak. Even though inversion and eversion of the foot (moving the ankle to the inside and outside when standing) are frequent movements in dance, the muscles responsible for these movements are usually not trained in a dance class, and they remain dangerously weak for the required tasks. Often dancers become acquainted with certain steps and can perform them with minimal effort. If a dancer feels overconfident about her strength based on her mastery of a learned repertoire of steps, she may get injured when a choreographer introduces new, unexpected steps that require the use of muscles that are weak for her.

You can enhance training effects with a mixture of eccentric (lengthening) and concentric (shortening) training. A muscle is able to produce more force in an eccentric contraction, so for dancers, it may be beneficial to emphasize eccentric training because of the flexibility gains it achieves (Hather et al. 1991). This is especially true when the eccentric action is performed slowly, as in the iliopsoas exercises in the following chapters. But it is not a good idea to perform too many eccentric contractions consecutively. Anyone who has hiked down a mountain can tell you why: Your quadriceps feel sore because they are required to work eccentrically hundreds of times in a row. One of the best ways to emphasize eccentric work while achieving a good balance of concentric action is to take more time for the lengthening phase than for the shortening phase of an exercise. For example, when performing an arm curl with a dumbbell, use 4 counts to lower the weight and 2 counts to lift it.

Principle of Periodization

One of the best ways to ensure a progression in conditioning is to build the program around a three-phase system that allows for the gradual progression of overload mixed with periods of rest so that the body is able to regenerate both physically and mentally from the stresses of training. This principle is commonly called periodization.

1. Start with a *preparatory phase* in which you do low-resistance exercise and only light stretches. This phase can last between two and four weeks. It is an excellent time to tune in to the body and improve alignment and mental strength according to individual technique and fitness goals. Returning to a full rehearsal schedule or class load on the first day after a break or a vacation is not healthful for the dancer's body. It is understandable to want to get in shape as fast as possible, but a crash course will not speed up conditioning.

2. During the three- to five-week *build-up phase* you gradually increase the resistance and the number of repetitions you perform for each exercise.

3. During the *maintenance phase*, continue to condition to keep what you have gained. Although this phase takes much less work than building strength and flexibility, the duration depends on your activity as a dancer. If you are a professional dancer in a company, the maintenance phase should last as long as your performing season. If you are in a dance school or college, it should last as long as your semester.

Each of these three phases includes periods of rest. If you do not allow time for rest, the benefits of training will be diminished or even reversed because the body will become overtrained. To fully recuperate your body I recommend a two- to three-week break twice or even three times a year. This time is not wasted, often you come back to training with new insights into your dancing technique.

Just as you build up to your dancing season, you should allow a deconditioning phase when you will be taking a break or a vacation. During this resting phase you may not take class or rehearse, but you may continue some conditioning exercises. The ball balance exercises in chapter 3, the sitting Thera-Band exercise series in chapter 8, and the Thera-Band center barre exercises in chapter 10 are all portable exercises. In 20 to 30 minutes a day you can maintain a significant level of fitness that in turn will reduce the duration of the preparatory phase when you return to dancing.

Intensive class, rehearsal, and performance schedules can cause overtraining, exhaustion, and even depression if you don't balance them with proper rest and adequate sleep. Once you become overtrained, it takes longer to rebuild strength and stamina than when recuperation and rest periods are a regular part of your routine. During rest, you may feel as if you are not making progress. But if you do not rest, you will not benefit much from your conditioning routine, dance class, or rehearsal, because the nervous system will not be able to deal with new information.

You can greatly enhance improvements in technique by taking one or two days off each week between any regular dance classes or by doing a completely different physical activity, such as swimming, to rest dance-specific muscles. Alternating dance with another activity, or cross-training, helps the body to adapt and make progress because it gives the nervous system a rest from the usual activity patterns. A dancer's performance year should also include a few weeks of complete rest.

Constructive rest, as described in pages 234–242 of *Dance Imagery for Technique and Performance* (Franklin 1996), during midday or in the evening is also an excellent way to recuperate while reorganizing the body for improved dance technique. In constructive rest you use imagery to relax the breath, release tension, and reorganize the muscles, helping you expend less energy during class, rehearsals, and performances. (There will be more discussion of this topic in chapter 4). Many of the exercises in chapters 4 and 7 can serve as miniature break periods for rest and regeneration.

Warming Up

Start a class, rehearsal, or conditioning session gradually so that the body systems have time to adapt. During a warm-up, the heart rate changes, breathing accelerates, and muscle temperature rises. A warm-up should include some mildly aerobic, large-body movements such as the Thera-Band workout detailed in chapter 7, the Thera-Band Centre described in chapter 10, or the combined ball and band exercises in chapter 3. Beneficial warm-up exercises are ones that raise the pulse rate gradually and warm up and lubricate the joints to make them more fluid.

I remember being surprised at the nature of my first warm-up with a professional dance company in New York. Expecting the usual straight-into-a-hamstring-stretch-on-the-floor routine, we were instead told to jog in a circle and do jumping jacks. This was a straightforward way to accelerate the breathing, increase blood flow, raise tissue temperatures, and simply wake up and become alert. However, if a warm-up does not include movements similar to those used in the class, the dancer will probably not be properly warmed up for the class.

If the dance steps in a class, rehearsal, or performance require one side of the body to be very active while the other is stabilized, the warm-up should include at least some movements of this nature. If the steps emphasize a diagonal action through the body, the warm-up should include diagonal movement patterns. If a dance includes many turns or spirals, the warm-up should include similar movements. Some dances require balancing on the hands. The warm-up for these dances should include preparation for putting weight on your hands, such as handstands. If the warm-up closely matches the dance steps, the dancer will feel the dance movements more quickly.

Volianitis and colleagues (2001) suggest that in sport, you should divide the warm-up into three phases: "Getting the body ready (physiological), getting a feel (psychophysiological) and getting the mind ready (psychological)" (page 78).

One way to "get a feel" is to become aware of your body each day. Generally, dancers tune in to the changes in the body from day to day and even hour to hour. An experienced dancer should be skilled in using this awareness and adapting to it accordingly. For example, if the hip joints feel tighter today than they did yesterday, you know you should spend more time warming up the hip area today.

It may be helpful to begin the mental part of your warm-up on the way to dance class by tuning in to the body and scanning for tense areas that could use some coordination or extra attention. Use a favorite imagery to cue your body to function optimally. Imaging will also increase your mental alertness. If you are an experienced imager, you can realign your pelvis while just walking down the street. Imagine the movement of the pelvic bones or the lengthening of the hip flexors as the leg swings back and helps to lift the front of the pelvis. Just don't forget to pay attention to the street.

When I started dance training, stretching was still advocated as the main part of the warm-up. More recent evidence points to the fact that most flexibility is gained by combining mild stretches with activity that raises the temperature of the body (Volianitis et al, 2001, page 75).

Most of the Thera-Band exercises described in the following chapters both warm up and stretch the muscles of the body. Ideally, you should use a low-resistance band (red or green) for warming up and a higher-resistance band (blue or gray) for conditioning. The standing-on-ball exercise series in chapter 3 and the exercises in chapters 7 through 10 include many warm-up options using Thera-Bands. You may also choose to do some iliopsoas and pelvic floor exercises (see chapter 5) as part of your warm-up.

Young children require a warm-up before a dance class, even though they may be excited about getting into the dance immediately. Finally getting a chance to move after sitting in a classroom for hours, they will practice difficult steps the minute they walk into the dance space. Quite often this causes them to overstretch muscles. Sometimes children do not report muscle discomfort to their teachers, but if they are educated to be sensitive to something being "off," they will likely have fewer injuries later in their careers.

In *Dance and the Specific Image* Daniel Nagrin emphasizes the following warm-up points (Nagrin 1994):

- Early stretches are for waking up muscles, not for increasing flexibility.
- Progress warm-up exercises from slow to fast and from simple to complex.
- Limit the number of grand pliés, and keep them well controlled when performing them.
- Introduce jumps late in the exercise sequence, and do little jumps before big ones.

Consider eliminating grand pliés from a warm-up, because they are not specific to most dance styles and they place great strain on the knees. Eliminating them from a class warm-up may raise a few eyebrows, but it will also lengthen some dancers' careers by discouraging a movement that can lead to injury.

Cooling Down

Just as it is not a good idea to start exercise suddenly, it is dangerous to stop exercise abruptly. I have observed exercise and dance class participants as well as rehearsing and performing dancers back on the train home less than 15 minutes after a class is over. This abrupt switch from exercise to a sitting position causes blood to pool in the lower limbs, and the heart and all body systems to slow down too rapidly. Also, waste products accumulated by the muscles during exercise are not as easily removed from the tissue if there is no cool-down phase. The result is sore and tired muscles, achy joints, and less overall stamina the following day.

A proper cool-down may consist of recapitulating some of the movements that were taught in class, but in a more leisurely manner, winding down for at least five minutes. Once the body has slowed down, it is also good to do mild stretching, focusing on the main muscle groups that were used during the exercise sequence, class, or rehearsal. Dancers should not ignore their intuitive sense of what muscles need to be stretched after class, but they should be well informed about the most important stretches for their individual body build. Chapter 4 illustrates stretches that are essential to cooling down but are often missed.

I do not advise any deep stretching after class because the muscles need time to recover from the previous exertion. Postpone deep stretching for at least an hour after class has ended. Waiting an hour may be inconvenient, but it is likely to cause less muscle soreness the next day. As an alternative I suggest doing low-resistance Thera-Band exercises after class. They can be performed with great specificity, and they can improve flexibility as well as stretching does.

I particularly recommend using cool-down time to anchor some of the new positive feelings and technical insights gained during a class. The cool-down period offers a chance to get dancers to tap into the long-term memory loop. If no technical or artistic insights were gained from class or a conditioning routine, dancers should use this time to imagine having them in the future. Expectation is a powerful part of mental training. The more time you take to notice the positive changes in the body, the more positive changes will happen because the mental focus is reinforced.

Use the final part of the cool-down time for a brief constructive rest session (see pages 234–242 of *Dance Imagery for Technique and Performance*). Because the nervous system is alert after training, constructive rest works particularly well at this time.

There may be times during a rehearsal when a dancer has nothing to do but sit or lie on the floor. This may be problematic, because she needs to remain physically ready to dance, and this readiness is lost after a short period of inactivity. During these times, the dancer should stay mildly active with active stretches or nonstrenuous conditioning exercises. The tired dancer may prefer to rest, but suddenly starting and stopping activity causes more stress on the nervous and cardiovascular systems than when the dancer maintains a certain level of preparedness with some peaks of activity.

Using Thera-Bands for Conditioning

The Thera-Band is an approximately 6-inch-wide elastic band of various lengths created for exercise purposes such as training strength, flexibility, and relaxation. When you move your arm against the resistance of a Thera-Band for several repetitions, you will notice that it is much easier to lift your arm after the band is removed. This is the effect of reciprocal innervation.

When you train with a Thera-Band you need to either hold it in your hands, attach it to a part of the body such as under the foot, or attach it to an external fixture such as a secure ballet barre. There are three basic ways in which you can apply the resistance of the Thera-Band to the body:

1. Attach the band at a right angle (perpendicular) to the moving limb (figure 1.1a). This creates a great resistance to movement and is optimal for gaining strength because the force of the band can be fully exploited to create resistance.

2. The band may be positioned parallel to the limb and pulled inward (figure 1.1b). In this case resistance to movement is minimal, but this kind of pull increases a limb's muscle tone by stimulating pressure receptors in the joints. It is most often used in exercises for improving alignment and in cases of hypermobility (excess flexibility). Figure 1.1c shows an example of the band being used to increase tone for the upper body while deepening the plié and increasing stability using balls.

3. The band may be aligned on the same axis as the limb while pulling away from the body (figure 1.1d). If done with relaxed breathing and a slight shaking motion of the limb, this application can release tension in muscles and joints.

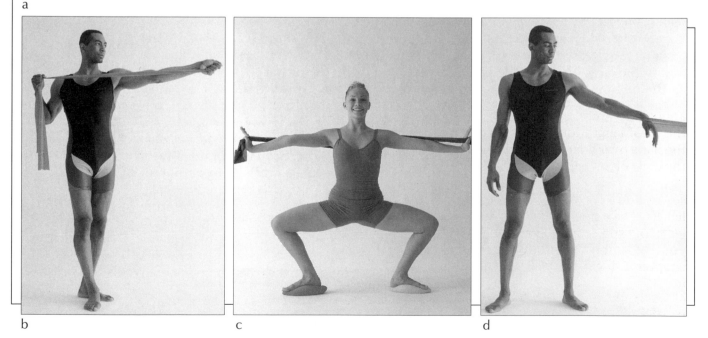

a   b   c   d

Figure 1.1 There are several ways to use a Thera-Band effectively for strength training: (a) attaching it at a right angle to the moving limb; (b and c) attaching it parallel to the limb; or (d) aligning it on the same axis as the limb.

Choosing the Proper Length

When you are exercising, the angle of the Thera-Band relative to the moving limb changes constantly and you rarely have the clear-cut situations just described. The limbs do not move linearly through space; they move in a curved path. Arms and legs are attached to the trunk by joints that create an arcing movement of the peripheral joints like the circling of planets around the sun.

Muscles can shorten to about half their length. It is unwise to perform an exercise that offers a lot of resistance when muscles have reached their maximal shortening capacity, because at that point they have little strength. Most muscles have maximum strength when they are slightly longer than their medium length. Ideally, this is the point at which you should give muscles the most resistance. You can come close to this point by organizing the length of the band during an exercise. Use a Thera-Band to try the following exercise for the deltoid muscle:

1. Place the foot firmly on one end of the band and hold the other end with the arm stretched to the side (figure 1.2a).

2. Adjust the length of the band so that it has no slack and is not overly tight.

3. Lift the arm (figure 1.2b). You will most likely feel quite a bit of resistance when the arm is facing diagonally upward.

4. Notice how the deltoid (the muscle of the upper chest) feels. It has to work hard while it is already shortened considerably. This kind of training tends to cause the muscle to cramp in an effort to create maximum force when it is already shortened.

5. Try the movement again, but start with the arm pointing down at an angle of 45 degrees.

6. As you pull upward and the band begins to stretch, you will feel significant resistance by the time your arm is horizontal to the ground. This position is much better training for the muscle. The earlier resistance results from the fact that the length of the band you are using is shorter to begin with.

For most of the exercises in this book we use a Thera-Band that is about 3.5 yards long. You can find the ideal length for you by placing the band over your head and having the ends of the band touch the floor on both sides of you. You can also do some of the exercises with a shorter, lighter-resistance band (1.5 yards in length), especially when exercising your feet and toes, as shown in chapter 7. Ideally, have two bands for daily use: one that is shorter (1.5 yards) for shorter and lighter resistance movements, and one that is longer with stronger resistance for the whole-body exercises.

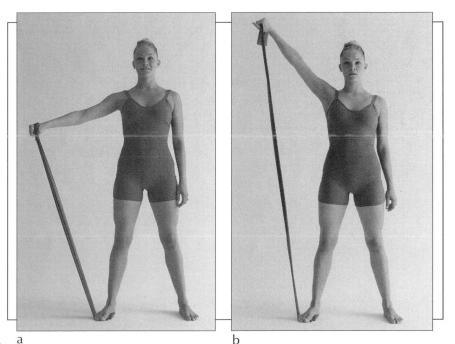

a   b

Figure 1.2 *a* and *b* You can easily determine the appropriate length of the Thera-Band for a particular exercise by adjusting it during the exercise.

Choosing the Proper Resistance

In addition to the length of the band you'll want to choose the proper resistance for specific exercises. Several factors influence the resistance of the Thera-Band. The longer the band, the less resistance it has because there is more elastic material that can stretch and adapt to the movements of the body. Thera-Bands differ in resistance according to their color.

Yellow = light resistance

Red = medium resistance

Green = heavy resistance

Blue = extra heavy resistance

Black = special heavy resistance

Gray = maximum resistance

There is also a gold Thera-Band, but it is so tough that I have not applied it in dance classes. This gradation of bands is an excellent way to gauge the optimal intensity for progressing in strength training. Start with a red or green band on any given workout and build to a blue or black band. After two to three months keep using a blue or black band for the warm-up and cool-down, and use a gray band for conditioning, but do not start by using a gray band if it feels uncomfortable. The black band is sufficient for maintaining the level of conditioning. Notice that if you try a blue band after working with a gray one for a while, you will feel little resistance, reflecting that the muscles are responding to the effects of overload training.

Choosing the Volume of a Workout

If you are using bands, you have two options for varying the repetitions and sets to achieve the desired type of workout. For the strength set, perform fewer repetitions using a shorter band (a tighter hold) to increase resistance, and for the muscular endurance set, perform more repetitions with a longer band (or a looser hold). You can also vary the sets by using the same length of band but two different resistances—a maximum-resistance gray Thera-Band for the maximum strength set and a medium-resistance red Thera-Band for the muscular endurance set.

Increase the number of sets if you are using the band for long-term conditioning. The Thera-Band exercise series in chapters 7, 8, and 10 are specifically suited for complete exercise sets. The exercises outlined in those chapters can also be performed as a circuit without any significant break between the individual exercises except perhaps to adjust the position of the band. Circuit training is specific for dance training because one movement flows into the next, similar to performing a dance combination. The Thera-Band centre workout in chapter 10 and the torso and arms series in chapter 8 are excellent circuit programs.

General Thera-Band Tips

Because many exercises in this book use Thera-Bands, I have included guidelines on applying them for the greatest effect. In conditioning classes, using a combination of small (3 to 4 inches in diameter) physioballs and Thera-Bands is quite effective for performing hundreds of exercises that train every muscle in the body. The whole exercise "machine" (balls and band) can fit neatly into a backpack and weighs only one pound! You are not limited by the movements of a machine. With the balls and band you can perform very creative, even choreographed movement that simulates your style of dance and provides the proper resistance.

- Before you start exercising, check your Thera-Band for cuts, broken edges, and holes. You don't want your band to snap apart while you exercise. This can be painful, not to mention dangerous for the eyes.
- Maintain the width of the band throughout the exercise. Keeping it straight can depend on how you tie the knot and how you loop the band around your body. If the band rolls up, it slides on your body and may feel as if it is pressing into the muscles.
- If you have hair on your legs, wear long pants and socks for most exercises so that hair does not become entangled.
- Attach the band in such a way that it does not constrict blood flow.
- If you attach the band to an external object such as a pipe or a barre, make sure that the structure cannot move. Never attach the band to a heater of any type, because the heat will weaken it.
- Don't get the band wet. It will be sticky and useless unless thoroughly dried.

Creating the Power to Move

How do you create more power for movement? How do you increase this power efficiently, without increasing your risk of injury? Power is a combination of coordination and strength. A dancer's coordination depends on alignment, sense of balance, spatial orientation, and ability to initiate movement efficiently. These factors are controlled by the nervous system. Without an increase in the efficiency with which the nervous system directs movement, muscular strength will not do much good. Misguided muscular strength can actually cause injury.

The exercises in this book will help to create an organized nervous system that supports good coordination, the basis of the power to move. The brain adapts to support what you do, listening to your every thought and recording your every move. The way you think about your dancing sets up the pattern for the development of your skills. If movements are uncoordinated, with a lot of tension, fear of reprimand from a teacher, and scorn from an audience, all of these elements combine to create a global gestalt in the brain that guides your overall image as a dancer. The intelligent dancer needs to become aware of the power of his every act, mental and physical. So many dancers are unaware of how little they use their available power for the desired movement. For example, many dancers strain upward, distorting the jaw and face and tightening the shoulders when they jump, even though the power is better directed into the floor, like rocket propulsion. Much of their power is lost to tension and distortion.

Once you start working with increased resistance from bands or weights, your coordination becomes even more important. Increased resistance calls on the nervous system to create powerful solutions to the movement at hand. If you are moving with faulty alignment and too much tension, the nervous system records it. In this case your training actually decreases your coordination as the strength is built into an undesirable movement pattern. The result is that you either do not have great power to move, or the power you have will hurt the body.

There is, however, a thin line between a sense of power and tension. A key to success is learning to distinguish the efficient movement path from one that is uncoordinated. We start this process by deciding never to train without focusing on making the movement more efficient.

chapter 2

Embodied Imagery

Have you ever had a thought that made you feel physical changes? Do you notice how much better you dance on a day when you are full of inspired thinking? If so, you have had a first glimpse of what the mind–body connection can do for you. Down to the smallest cell of the body, every mental act reverberates in your physical being, and every chemical and biomechanical process in your body helps weave the patterns of your thinking. If you are able to understand this interaction, you are ready to reach the highest peaks of your dancing skills.

As a dancer, how can you connect to the body's wisdom? Become attentive to the way you think about dancing, and you will be able to eliminate harmful thought patterns and replace them with positive reinforcement, which in turn will lead to better technique and expressivity. Learn how to sense the influence of your body image in the movements and actions of the muscles and joints. Any dance step or conditioning routine that you can do with presence of mind and body as well as a clear understanding of how the body works allows you to gain strength and flexibility much faster than mindless repetition of movement. Conditioning exercises will become more interesting, even pleasurable, because you more fully experience the muscles, joints, and organs and their optimal support of your movement.

Consciousness and Control

As every dancer has experienced, certain steps seem to flow more naturally some days than on other days. Often dancers try to master a step by relying entirely on *control*—that is, they remember what they did yesterday and try to control the movement today based on that memory. This method can be very frustrating, because often it does not work. The body and mind experience subtle changes and adjustments every day. Yesterday's strategy simply may not be suitable for today's body and mind. If you traveled on an airplane or had a long, exhausting rehearsal, your alignment may be different than it would be if you had taken a good dance class the previous day. Even nutrition influences the mind and body states. If you did not drink enough water the previous day, you may feel tired and achy. If you did not stretch or perform flexibility exercises the previous day, you may have certain restrictions to deal with. You may be in a new relationship that makes you very happy. This alone can completely change the way you experience your body. The reasons for change are infinite.

Zvi Gotheiner, choreographer and ballet teacher, suggests, "Replace control by consciousness. Without being aware of what needs to be done in a new way—every day, without being able to elicit fresh solutions, it is hard to develop technically." These daily solutions can only be found with an awareness of the body from moment to moment, noticing its responses to the images and thoughts in the mind and finding the subtle shifts and changes that are necessary to master the steps. By habitually putting consciousness before control, you make controlling the body's movement more flexible and alive, ready to respond to the realities of the moment. One of the aims of training is to *automate* movement. No one has to tell an experienced ballet dancer how to do a pas de bourrée. But if he does the step as an automaton, he certainly is not dancing. If your only resource is control, then you will dance through tension and habit. The more tension you develop, the less you feel the flow and rhythm, and the dance ends there.

Another way dancers try to gain control of movement is by building strength, thinking that stronger muscles will allow them to control the unruly parts of the body. Although strength training gives dancers stronger muscles, it does not necessarily give them better control of movement. Unless strength is built into a more efficient movement pattern, it can even do more harm than good for controlling movement. Rather, consciousness and specificity (as discussed in chapter 1) are the keys to successful strength training in dance. This is not to say that strengthening the abdominal muscles is not helpful for dance. Many dancers train the abdominal muscles for aesthetic reasons and to feel stronger and more confident about their appearance. These are viable reasons, but unless specificity and consciousness are also involved, incorrect application of abdominal strength may hamper technique. I have yet to see the dancer with tight shoulders and neck muscles reduce his tension level through doing sit-ups. He has problems turning because the neck is "locked," not because the abdominal muscles don't look like washboards.

Strength training to enhance control as a means to solve technical problems is popular, because it provides a targeted solution that seems to have tangible, visible results. Furthermore, using the mind–body connection as a resource for gaining conscious control or learning how to use imagery for this purpose takes more time and commitment than a typical strength training program. If the dancer trains the muscles consciously, he will achieve his technical *and* aesthetic goals and he will make long-term changes, creating more efficient movement patterns that will also reduce the chance of injury. No permanent changes take place until the brain actually records a more efficient movement pattern. To ensure a permanent change, the dancer must be actively involved and experience the changes in the body as they occur during his training and conditioning routine.

Dr. Rodolfo Llinas, chief of physiology and neuroscience at New York University School of Medicine, is one of the leaders of modern neuroscience and has spent over 40 years studying brain cells. Llinas does not believe that neurons are neutral actors that simply relay messages; he sees nerve cells as complex entities with their own point of view. This *point of view* is the perfect description of the body's experience with movement. By knowing the body's daily point of view, a dancer can dance much better. You can't dance with yesterday's body. Every step needs to be reexperienced with the viewpoint of the day, even if it has been performed a thousand times. According to ancient Greek philosophers, life's one certainty is *pantha rei*—everything flows, everything is always changing.

The Power of Imagery

Mental imagery may be defined as the "the cognitive rehearsal of an action without overt performance of the physical movements involved" (Moran 1996, page 203) or the "symbolic rehearsal of a physical activity in the absence of any gross muscular movements" (Moran 1996, 203).

Many kinds of imagery applications are used effectively to improve dance technique: ideokinetic imagery, programmed imagery, intuitive imagery, and mental simulation of movement. They are discussed in detail in the following sections.

Ideokinetic Imagery

Ideokinetic imagery, or ideokinesis, was developed by movement educators Mabel Todd, Lulu Sweigard, Barbara Clark, and André Bernard with the aim of using certain images to create improved neuromuscular coordination. Ideokinetic imagery differs from the imagery used in mental rehearsal. In sport mental rehearsal you imagine the actual movement that you intend to perform, accompanied by a realistic representation of the environment—what you will be seeing and hearing. In ideokinesis you visualize the desired changes in the alignment and tension gradients in your body, most often using metaphors. Among many other applications, ideokinesis helps the dancer improve alignment and balance the action of muscles around joints. This type of imagery is usually practiced in the hook-lying position, also called the constructive rest position: lying supine on the floor with the knees at right angles and the feet resting on the floor. (For a detailed discussion of the position see Franklin's *Dynamic Alignment Through Imagery*, pages 59–61).

Ideokinesis is well known for the nine lines of action within the body, proposed by Lulu Sweigard (figure 2.1). Visualizing these lines brings the body into an improved postural pattern (closer to the person's ideal alignment). The imagery can be roughly categorized into activating and releasing imagery for each line of action. The image serves either to create an increased tone or activity in certain muscles or muscle groups, or to release tension in certain muscle groups. For example, if you imagine the extensor muscles of the spine that run along both sides of the spine on the back of the body (erector spinae) sliding downward like many puffs of foamy bubble bath, you are using a tension-releasing image. If you imagine the line of action between the center front of the pelvis (pubic symphysis) and the middle of the spine (12th thoracic vertebrae) and think of a tightening rubber band between those two points, you are using an activating, tone-increasing image. In the latter case you are increasing the stabilizing tone of the psoas muscle.

By developing the use of imagery beyond the original scope of ideokinesis and the nine lines

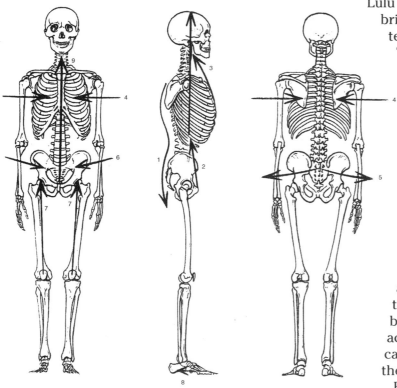

Figure 2.1 The nine lines of action in the body.

Adapted, by permission, from L.E. Sweigard, 1974, *Human Movement Potential* (New York: Harper & Row).

of action, you may also learn to work with skeletal musculature or organ musculature, because they can both be reached through imagery. For example, when visualizing the head resting on top of the spine (the atlas) or the nerves resting in their soft protective coverings (myelin sheaths), you use the image and sensation of weight to create change.

The rationale for lying down while using ideokinetic imagery is simple and effective: Because you are trying to develop *new* postural patterns, you do not want to engage *old* patterns. So when lying down (as opposed to standing, walking, or dancing), the body is relaxed and free from postural needs. If you stand, walk, or dance while trying to establish new postural patterns, you will cause conflicting messages in the nervous system, slowing the process of change. Sadly, this may be one of the reasons some people are turned off from imagery at an early stage—the teacher uses too much personal metaphoric imagery that the student can't embody in a movement. But once a dancer is skilled in using imagery while lying down, she can begin to use the imagery while moving.

Intuitive Imagery

Much of the imagery described in *Dance Imagery for Technique and Performance* (Franklin 1996) actually occurred to me intuitively during dance training. The mind of the body provides information on how to improve movement. This is similar to the premise of Mabel Todd's aptly named *The Thinking Body* (Todd 1937).

Another proponent of this concept of the body's mind states is Bonnie Bainbridge Cohen, founder of Body–Mind Centering® (BMC™), a technique that reeducates the body's movement patterns through imagery, touch, and movement. Some of the exercises in this book are based on her ideas.

When a choreographer presents an image to you and you use it, as is the case in ideokinetic imagery, you use imagery that comes from an external source and then try to experience it physically. With continued use of imagery, you will soon begin to spontaneously discover your personal, intuitive imagery, the images that are tailored to you.

Dance teachers can encourage a dancer's development of intuitive imagery. When teaching dance technique I often ask each dancer how he experiences the movement we are working to improve. Most often the dancer describes his experience as an image. This image is his personal starting point for change, his momentary experience of his dancing self. I then continue to work with him on this image, making suggestions about movement initiation, phrasing, or a new anatomical awareness, or I use touch to help him experience a more efficient or expressive way of performing the movement. I ask again about his experience with the movement, and most often the dancer's imagery has changed. It now supports his new embodiment of the movement. As a teacher I can then use this tailor-made image throughout the class or rehearsal to help the dancer reinforce his new, improved movement pattern.

Guiding students to create their own imagery has the advantage of authenticity. Through such guidance, the dancer eventually becomes his own coach, and imagery that improves his movement spontaneously arises when he needs it. This skill is a boon to the professional dancer, who may have to go for long periods without any external input. Sadly, failures are pointed out to dancers more often than successes are, potentially leading to stagnation or even a downward spiral in technique.

Candace Pert, cell biologist and discoverer of the endorphin receptor, sees the mind as located in every cell of the body. At a lecture I attended, she pointed out that every cell contributes to what we call the mind. Her studies have been published in many renowned scientific journals, and her fascinating story of discovery can be found in

The Molecules of Emotion (Pert 1999). When you develop your intuitive imagery, you have a dialogue with the cells of the body. Through detailed attention to the body, the mind of the cells becomes a felt reality, and the intelligent support system behind every tissue and movement becomes available to you. You can fully use the inner resources of the body to improve technique.

Seed Imagery

I have coined the term seed imagery to describe the starter images that teachers can supply to students to help them develop their own intuitive images as training proceeds. To work effectively, a seed image needs to be accessible to a dancer. For example, to help with leg extension I may suggest to a dancer, "Imagine the pelvic half on the gesture side as a wheel rotating backward to lift the leg. Think of the ball of the femur (upper leg bone) resting in the socket." As a teacher I know that both these images help the dancer release restrictions and lengthen muscles. I may support the imagery by touching the hip joint, outlining the imaged movement of the pelvic half, or resting my hand on the sacrum to ensure that the dancer does not tuck in the pelvis. These seed images then drop away as the dancer comes to experience the leg extension in her own way.

Unfortunately, society has not been very helpful in fostering the spontaneous imagery process; we mostly speak about our bodies when we experience a negative sensation such as pain or discomfort. People are not too surprised to hear you say that you feel a bit stiff and tired or that your knee hurts. But to state that your spine feels like a glittering string of pearls or that you feel energy shooting up the center of your body seems comical to all but the most experienced imagers. Reinforcing the imagery process is key to helping any dancer develop her imagery skills. Outside of dance class there may not be much opportunity to practice imaging.

Mental Simulation of Movement

If you imagine yourself performing a dance step, you are using imagery to simulate the actual movement situation. Dave Collins, professor of sport psychology at Edinburgh University, calls this imagery mental simulation of movement (MSM).

For MSM to work best, you should create vivid imagery that includes the physicality of the movement (how it feels to move), the environment (what the surroundings are like), task orientation (which steps are required), and emotion. For example, using MSM for a performance, you should feel yourself moving in a realistic way, see the surroundings, hear the people watching you, and notice your reactions and interpretations of all of these sensations to create a realistic image of the event. You may feel the air brushing against your body, hear the sound of your take-off and landing, and even imagine your breathing pattern. In most classes I have observed that dancers do not use the time between performing their steps to image them. They simply wait at the side or practice the actual movement, if space allows. A dancer can vastly accelerate his technique improvement *and* memorize his steps if he uses this time for imaging through MSM.

When practicing MSM, try to reflect the movement you are trying to image on a physical level. The ideokinetic constructive rest position is not ideal for mental rehearsal aimed at improving a vigorous dance step. While lying on the floor, your state of arousal, breathing, and heartbeat do not relate to the movement you are imaging. Constructive rest imaging is aimed at inner body reorganization, whereas MSM is best for rehearsing the movement you want to perform.

Applying Imagery Effectively

There are many approaches to learning dance, and no one method works best for everyone. But certain activities can improve the speed of any dancer's progress and reduce the chance of injury. These activities include performing solid overall conditioning; properly warming up before each session; taking rest periods within and between sessions; and being in a supportive environment in which teachers, mentors, and parents provide educated coaching both on the technical and psychological level and nurture the dancer's skill and self-esteem.

A dancer also needs sufficiently varied movement instruction. He must be shown how a movement should look, hear the movement described with words and imagery, and be helped to feel and visualize the movement he is to perform. Margaret Skrinar (Shell 1986) notes that kinesthetic and visual instructions are not used sufficiently in dance class. She points out that "teaching methods combining all types of cues are more effective than using only one type" (page 190).

Throughout this book I emphasize the changes in how you feel during a movement that result from an exercise. Awareness of these changes trains your kinesthetic sense and makes it a more accurate tool for guiding you to improved body coordination. Some of the exercises use touch to enhance the effect and to deepen the experience. I suggest also using brief exercises interspersed during dance classes or conditioning routines to improve the kinesthetic experience. Having fresh insight based on the felt sense leads to an understanding that replaces a thousand words. There is evidence that this inner perspective greatly enhances the effect of imagery (Holmes and Collins 2001, page 88).

If a dancer can visualize what he actually looks like on the inside, anatomically, he can better relate what he feels to this structure and function. Some dancers spend years repeating deleterious movement patterns without knowing it. Within minutes of receiving some anatomical information and kinesthetic cues, they are able to self-correct years of improper movement with the help of their newfound awareness. I do not propose that anatomical visualization skills solve all of a dancer's problems, but they can empower any dancer by giving her a greater range of choices when working on problems of technique, performance, and choreography.

Also, anatomical visualization skills make it easier for a dancer to pick up movement instructions because he can match the words of a teacher or choreographer with an accurate anatomical image. Visualizing the muscle group that is being trained during conditioning makes the exercise more effective because the timing, speed, and range of the motion can be done with increased precision. Recent research shows that strength can be increased through visualization techniques, even without any movement at all. Still, technical training, conditioning, and anatomical knowledge will not in themselves make a dancer. To fully benefit from the exercises in this book, consider them as part of continuously fine-tuning the body. No amount of anatomical knowledge or number of conditioning exercises can compensate for a simple lack of inspiration.

To avoid the pitfalls of using imagery and to apply it specifically and effectively for dance, students and teachers should do the following:

> **Keep the imagery dynamic**; the desired result in itself may not be the best image. For example, I've often heard teachers or choreographers say, "pull up," meaning "lengthen" or "lift." A dancer certainly does not want to slouch, but to achieve a natural sense of length in the body she needs to be shown how joints and body structures interrelate to create lift without tension. Saying "pull up" often results in the opposite effect and the dancer tenses the muscles rather than lengthens them.

Use simple, understandable images, and avoid burying them with too many instructions. Using too many images is overwhelming and can make any dancer think he is incapable of using imagery.

State imagery in the positive. Images always lead you to what you are imaging. A teacher of mine once directed the class to divide into three groups so that we would have "more space to fall over." After hearing that description, I saw myself and everyone in my group falling as we moved. The teacher actually intended to have us divide so we would have plenty of space to *dance*.

Translate the imagery into movement. Don't separate yourself from the image you are trying to create. Try, as much as possible, to become what you are imaging on all levels of the experience. The teacher should embody the imagery he is teaching, making it easier for the student to experience it. Even if the teacher does not fully demonstrate the step, he should aim at being as musical and expressive as possible. The more a dancer is surrounded by the qualities that make a good dancer, the sooner he will mirror it in his own body.

Focus on movement enjoyment. I've heard a teacher teaching pirouettes remark, "Don't think of pirouettes; dance up into the turn." This is a good strategy. Instead of focusing on the anxiety and apprehension that may surround the word *pirouette,* focus squarely on the inner physical experience. You could say, "Dance the balance" for any other step that is surrounded with anxiety. Using this language helps you to focus on the main reason you are here—for the joy of dancing. It is also an excellent way to create an inner physical image of a difficult step before you actually perform it.

Use rhythm. Rhythm holds a key place in imagery for dance. I remember being completely confused by the arrhythmic demonstration of steps by some dance teachers. I simply could not form an image or an inner feeling of the dance until the teacher demonstrated the movement with music. Other teachers made it so easy to learn the step by demonstrating rhythm, not just shape and position. If the imaged dance step involves music or rhythm, keep it at a realistic speed and vividly image its musicality and phrasing.

Maintain a calm center and conscious control. In an effort to make fast progress, dancers can become tense. It becomes difficult to use the power of the mind when you are not centered within yourself. When practicing MSM, for example, maintain a realistic level of alertness. Think of dancing as unfolding on two levels within your being: Find a still center, and then let the dance unfold around it with virtuosity. Stay grounded and keep a calm center, even in the fastest and most complex steps. Developing a calm center is challenging, but with practice it can be done, and the payoff is in your improved technique.

Be prepared to move from visual to physical. Just as rhythm is important in imaging and learning steps, so is the ability to switch from outer to inner focus. One of the keys of learning a step rapidly is developing an inner feeling of the outer shapes you are seeing. Turn the outer visual impression into your own physical experience. The next time you learn a step, emphasize your inner experience; don't just stay outside with what you are seeing. Not only will you learn faster, but you will also perform the step with increased physicality. Once you have learned the step, take a moment to review it in real time, with the inner feeling and rhythm including your perspective (what you see) when you are dancing.

A teacher must develop the opposite skill as well, moving from physical to visual. She must convey to her student the steps she is feeling in her own body. By observing the student, the teacher then notices whether the student's movement corresponds to the feeling she is trying to convey. Use imagery to make the inner feeling more real. Most dance teachers do this intuitively, but using a systematic approach can benefit the students. The teacher may ask herself, *What physical feelings am I trying to convey with the steps I am showing? Is the movement smooth and silky, or is it hard-edged and sharp?* Even though it may seem apparent to the teacher, it may not be so to the student.

Focus on goals, not problems. Instead of trying to fix something that is wrong with a movement, emphasize the sensation for which you are striving. Focusing on the problem is one of the biggest stumbling blocks in using imagery. Rarely do I experience dance classes where the teacher provides the dancer with pertinent information on what he needs to do and the most important aspect on which to focus at the moment. Yet, in most cases it is not helpful to inform a dancer what he is doing wrong. Instead, dancers need to hear in a supportive way what to do to get better. Without a feeling of safety and belonging, the dancer will tighten up and lose his ability to improve. If the dancer loses his spontaneous curiosity about how to improve his technique, the learning process will be endangered. If a student is criticized in front of the whole class, he may feel inadequate and uncomfortable; such feelings are most harmful to progress. Students learn best when they know they are accepted with all of their momentary challenges. Without making mistakes, how can anyone learn?

Apply imagery with sufficient intensity, clarity, and power, and it will work better. Beware of strong negative emotions such as fear, anxiety, and anger because these emotions are powerful image enhancers. For example, if you are scared of something, you usually imagine the feared event with much clarity. You visualize what you don't want to occur, and you hear what you fear hearing. If you use the same intensity, clarity, and power in a positive sense, your imagery will work fabulously. Try saying to yourself, *I already know how to dance; I just need to allow it to happen from within.*

Be sincere about wanting to change deleterious movement patterns and thus ready to face the problems you may encounter in the process. This is the basic message Mabel Todd, author of *The Thinking Body* (1937), conveys in her writings. We can change if only we are willing to do so. This sounds much easier than it is, because our behavior, no matter how harmful, may feel natural to us. Tell a dancer to imagine relaxed shoulders while dancing and the reaction may be, "But if I do that I don't feel like I am dancing powerfully."

If the dancer associates shoulder tension with the initiation of powerful leg movements, she will feel something is missing or lacking once the shoulders are relaxed. Getting through the phase of bodily reorganization takes courage. If the dancer persists, she will find that she will ultimately develop more power in her leg movements if the shoulders are relaxed.

Remember, choose safety from injury over aesthetics. It is interesting that even the knowledge of harmful patterns often does not lead to their rejection. If the dancer is creating a large portion of her turn-out by twisting the knees and feet, this will damage the joints. If you help a dancer to find safer alignment, you may also reduce turn-out, as seen from the perspective of the foot. This reduction may be only momentary until safer options of increasing turn-out have been explored. Some dancers nevertheless keep turning out excessively to maintain the momentary aesthetic, regardless of the consequences to their joints. Consequences are in the future, and the emotional reward of having good turn-out in the present may be too powerful a temptation. Teachers play a role in helping dancers realize that they can achieve their goals faster and maintain their career longer if they use a healthy dance technique.

Remain receptive. While you use imagery, create a sense of openness to the change the image brings. Predetermining the result of the image hinders its free flow. Using imagery without being open to change and ready to adapt and accept a new way of perceiving yourself and the way you move prevents the benefits from taking hold in the body. Allow the new image and its accompanying feelings to sink in.

Be consistent. Imagery works best if it is used consistently. It may take weeks and months of repeated practice to most efficiently image the coordination of the pelvis and legs in a plié, especially if you were previously using tension and excess force. Train with a sense of limitless time. The constant feeling of competition and speed exhausts body and mind. Use at least one image in every dance class, and see how it affects your technique. Even seemingly simple images such as shoulders melting or toes sensing the space can revolutionize your technique if applied consistently.

Developing Your Personal Imagery

As suggested earlier in this chapter, personal imagery is the most powerful imagery. No image suggested from another person is as tailored to your needs as the imagery you discover through personal experience. With practice you will find that you have an inner teacher, ready to guide you on the path to better technique. The path you ultimately choose is unique, and it may vary from day to day and from situation to situation. The powerful images happen to you. You do not make them; they arise when your whole mind–body system has prepared the groundwork for them and you are ready to receive them. The following section provides some ideas for developing your personal imagery. All the ideas I describe are simply starting points, seed imagery, for your own personal exploration.

Focus Selectively

To experience the body, you need to calm the inquisitive mind. If the mental chatter is too loud, it is difficult to sense what is going on within the body. The sensory nerves constantly provide the spinal cord and brain with a barrage of information on the status of muscles, joints, and organs. Little of this information is brought to your conscious awareness; most problems are solved at an unconscious level. Most of the information is suppressed by the nervous system to avoid mental overload. Just imagine what it would be like if you noticed everything going on in your muscle fibers, organs, glands, and vessels at all times. It would be distracting, and even immobilizing.

Nevertheless, to move the body in a precise way, you need to learn how to become selectively conscious of these sensations. Metaphorically speaking, you must have the choice of placing yourself in the middle of the incoming flow of sensory information and change your movement habits based on that information. It is as if you are stepping into the middle of a ray of light at will instead of being at the side of it and receiving only peripheral and random illumination.

Let's say you want to know more about the joint that connects the base of the spine (the sacrum) to the pelvic bones (the inominates) at the back of the pelvis—the ilio-sacral joint. This joint plays a central role in body coordination, as it is the interface between the lower and upper body. You may have a visual picture, or a feeling about its location, but you do not perceive enough in this area to receive precise information. By focusing intently on the joint and remaining there with your concentration, you may suddenly have a clear experience of its exact spatial orientation, the length and width of the joint surfaces, and the relative level of the left and right iliosacral joints. You may notice that in performing a pirouette the joints are not on the same level. Now that you can experience them, you can correct this misalignment and feel surprise at how your balance improves.

How is it possible that you did not have this sense before? The answer is simple: It takes time and practice to create a detailed awareness of the body's inner geography. You can use selective focus to make certain areas or relationships in the body clearer, thereby enabling you to correct imbalances. If the same imbalance is corrected manually by a teacher positioning you, the result may not be permanent. Unless your nervous system can record the change in the joint, the effect of the manipulation will be short-lived. Touch is very valuable, but it needs to bring out the same kind of clarity in the body as does your own concentrated focus. The person being touched needs to have a sufficiently trained sensory system that can visualize and sense minute changes in the body that are brought out by touch. To create permanent change, he must repeat those minute changes once the touch is not there.

Following is an exercise to help you step into the body's stream of information. You can do it in a resting position or during a familiar and nonchallenging dance movement.

Choose an area of the body you would like to know something about, and focus on it without straining to visualize it. Just be there in a meditative way and wait for something to happen. Imagine that you are at the center of the sensory information coming from this area. Bathe yourself in this information. It is as if you have opened a book with blank pages and you are waiting for this part of your body to write some information into that book. If the book is already full of writing, there is no place for new information. Eventually (and this may take a long or a short time, depending on your capacity to be focused and calmly receptive) you will receive an image, an idea, or a sensation. The key here is patience.

You could, for example, focus on your feet as you plié. Do your feet feel adaptable and elastic, or stuck and rigid? What are the changes that happen when you move down and up in a plié? Do the feet feel the same in the downward and in the upward movement? How is the weight falling through your feet? Do you feel any bones, joints, or muscles adjusting? What is the image you have of your feet? Do the bones feel heavy or light? You could then move to another part of the body: How does the neck feel when you perform a plié? Does it also adjust? Does it feel supple and relaxed? Are there tension spots? Do you feel muscles changing length or do they stay the same? Watch the top of the neck just under the skull. Do any of the sensations here relate to what is happening in your feet as you perform a plié? Try to be as detailed as possible in your sensing.

If you practice this exercise resolutely, you will discover that the body provides you regularly with an area to focus on and shows you places that are out of balance or need a change in quality. It is as if a screen is suddenly turned on in the mind, and something is brought to your attention: The spine could lengthen like this, the heels could release like that, the shoulders are imbalanced like that. You can then either enjoy and pursue the new perception, or you could correct the misalignment. These events that allow you to correct your alignment are a key in conditioning. As soon as you do any of the exercises for increased strength provided in this book, you will also reinforce the sensory signals to the central nervous system. If strong signals arise from an imbalanced body structure, they will be reinforced in the nervous system, causing an increased imbalance in strength.

Start With an Image or Phrase

If your own imagery is the best, how do you avoid getting stuck in your own standard set of images? Use other people's imagery as a starter, or use anatomical imagery you find in a book to enrich your repertoire of inner sensations and movement qualities. I provide several images in the following chapters (as well as in my four other books) to help. Another way to develop images is to look at a drawing or a picture of the anatomical structure you want to experience. Try to feel it in your body and visualize it with the mind's eye. Kinesthetically move about the structure, trying to sense its size and dimensions. What is above it, below it, behind it, beneath it? What does the surface feel like? What is its weight and color? Is it moving in any way? How is it changing as you watch it? What happens if you place the mind's eye within this structure? Imagine that you are absorbing the sensation of this specific place into your whole body, as if you were a sponge absorbing water. Record your sensations and any images that may emerge in a journal so that these can be starting points for continued discovery.

You can perform this exercise with a sentence or a phrase. Find a situation that you would like to improve in your body. For example, you want tension-free shoulders. Find a phrase that gives you the feeling of moving in the direction of this goal, such as *My shoulders are flowing away from my neck*. Repeat this phrase often in the mind's voice. Feel that you are moving into the center of the experience of tension-free shoulders. Suddenly you may notice that you don't have to repeat the phrase any more, because the shoulders are releasing by themselves.

Use Touch

Touch can greatly enhance the effectiveness of your conditioning routine. You can use touch on yourself while exercising or just before you execute an exercise, or you can ask a partner to help you. Touch can help your training in the following ways:

- It can help you clarify the exact location, origin, and attachment of a muscle or muscle group on which you are focusing.
- It can relax tired or tense muscles after a workout.
- It can increase the effectiveness of a stretching exercise.
- It can increase the circulation to a muscle or muscle group.
- It can increase the rate at which the muscle warms up.

Use touch to help enhance your experience. First, decide on the area you want to experience. Try to delineate the outlines of its structure through touch. For example, if it is a bone, trace it with a finger. How does light touch or a stronger touch affect the experience? What kind of touch relates best to this area of the body? Do you use the same kind of touch to feel an organ as you use to feel a bone? Use touch to help the area move and to support its movement. Use touch to jiggle the area, enliven it, or resist its movement. Project your sense of touch into the very cells of the tissue.

I provide information on how to use touch during specific exercises throughout this book. But I suggest trying the following experiment with a partner first to get a feel for how touch can help. Hold a one- to five-pound weight in each hand. The weight should be equal on both sides. If you don't have any weights, use two books of equal weight. Let your partner put his hands on the front and back of your right arm. Flex and extend your arms and notice which arm gets tired first. Most likely the arm that is being touched will have more endurance and will feel more flexible and less fatigued after the exercise.

You can experience another interesting touch experiment with abdominal strength and endurance: Place the hands on the abdominal muscles while performing abdominal curls. You will notice that the exercise feels less strenuous and that you have more muscular endurance than when you do not place the hands on the muscles.

Use Movement

You can also use movement to enhance your imagery experience. Try this experiment: Begin by deciding on a part of the body to experience. Imagine this area initiating movement. To initiate movement does not mean that the rest of the body does not move; it means that the first inkling, the causative agent for movement, resides within this place. Choose an easy place from which to move, such as the elbow. Then try something unusual. For example, try initiating movement from an organ such as the right kidney. What is the difference in sensation? Finally, practice initiating movement at different speeds.

Another way to enhance personal imagery through movement is to take an experiential walk. Go for a walk with the sole purpose of noticing. As you walk, notice which areas of the body you are drawn to with your perceptions. Stay with one area until your attention is drawn to another place in the body. Notice the images that arise and how they affect your walking. Are there any places that feel resistant to movement? Which areas feel free and flowing?

You may find that you are automatically attracted to an area of the body where a sensation or an image arises. You may notice that you can move differently, with a new quality or with less effort. This change may occur several times during the course of a day, or even during a dance class or a conditioning routine. This spontaneous dialogue between the mind and the body tells you that the self-correcting mechanisms of the body are coming alive.

Use the Breath

Use the breath to find a place in the body that you would like to explore. Be in that place with the breath only, while the mind remains quiet and receptive. Notice how breathing affects this area. Does it create movement there? Does it change the sense of space you have in this area? Breathe into the right arm for a few minutes. Imagine that you can fill the right arm with the breath. Watch the breath flow in and out. Compare the sensation between the right and left arms. Do they feel the same? Go to another place in the body and fill it with breath. Try guiding the breath to exotic places such as the space under the kneecap, or the sutures (firm joints) of the skull.

Script the Experience

Scripting, or interviewing, is a process used to create accurate mental simulation of movement. The interview is an excellent tool for developing realistic, personal imagery with the help of another person.

Consider this scenario: A teacher wants to help a dancer with a performance by giving her the most realistic imagery experience of what will actually happen so she will not be surprised by any aspect of the performance and will go through it with ease. The teacher sits down with the dancer and interviews her about all the aspects of the event: the environment; what she sees, hears, and feels; her reactions to these sensations; and the meaning these sensations have for her at the moment they unfold. The teacher writes down all of this information.

Once the script is complete, the teacher narrates the script back to the dancer so that she can experience the actual event as realistically as possible. When you try this exercise, if the actual performance stage is nearby, by all means explore the sound, the look, and even the smell of the stage to make the situation feel real. Keep working on the script until the dancer feels that what she is imaging is her true experience. If appropriate, add some performance ambience in the form of audience coughing, applause, and latecomers opening the theater door, as well as the dancer's reaction to these types of disruptions.

Use Self-Talk and Positive Expectation

The thoughts in your mind have a great influence on your performance. Peak performers have learned to keep this stream of thought in the positive, self-motivating range. Some dancers get worried when confronted with this idea, because they are so tuned in to the self-perfection and the self-critique that goes with it. There is nothing wrong with trying to achieve perfection and analyzing your technique, but there is something wrong with an ongoing inner monologue of self-criticism. I have observed dancers whose faces have a constant apologetic look on them and whose body language reveals their dissatisfaction with their moment-to-moment performance. I have heard dancers react to a demonstration of difficult steps with "that's hard," "no way," or "I can't do it." Interviewing these dancers confirmed that the mind was supplying them with a constant barrage of negativity.

When dancers begin to turn the negative self-talk into positive self-talk, they can experience a turnaround in their dancing. Some dancers start thinking positive and self-encouraging thoughts, and their technique improves instantly. They jump higher the minute they let go of self-criticism. Their muscles have become more elastic and resilient, because they are not bracing for the next negative comment. Their new motto is *What I can't do today, I will master tomorrow;* or *I am up to any challenge.*

The last image you have in mind, the last thought you have before you perform a movement, is very important for a successful performance. If you think, *Easy, balanced head on spine,* not necessarily in words, but as a feeling image that takes a split second to move through your body, you will most likely have a better result than if you think, *My neck is so sore today.* Notice what happens when you select a thought that works for you and let it flash through your mind just before you start a movement. It could be the feeling of being grounded, being aligned, being relaxed, or breathing.

Don't fall into the trap of trying positive ideas for a few minutes and then, if you don't experience instant results, falling back into negative thinking. If you have been a negative self-talker, you may think this reversal is strange or even a lie. But if recognizing your improvements and others' positive reactions to your dancing is a lie, then why bother dancing at all? It is better to be overly positive than to be overly negative. Surround yourself with the perfume of your positive thoughts, create a cushion of positively reinforced ideas (not illusions) that surrounds you at all times, and you will start noticing a difference. Keep in mind that no matter where you stand now, improvement is always possible and easier if supported by your strong intention and imagination.

chapter 3

Reflexive Balance

Balance is one of the most important dance skills, yet it eludes so many dancers. The body balances ingeniously in a variety of positions with every step we take. When you are in centered alignment, with the bones well stacked and the muscles well coordinated, you actually need less overall muscle activity to stay that way than when you are misaligned. So if you are a dancer currently attempting to improve your balance by simply engaging more muscles, you are doing the opposite of what occurs during aligned balancing. Aligned balance feels like less effort.

To improve balance, you first need an awareness of what you are doing while trying to balance. You achieve this awareness through observing yourself and becoming increasingly in tune with your habitual way of performing a movement, leading you to reach your goal of effortless balance in all situations.

Let's look at an example of what movement patterns mean for balance. If you are trying to relevé in an attitude position and you are falling over or you cannot maintain the position, you may be moving your body in parts as opposed to one complete, well-aligned unit. To relevé and move up onto demi-pointe or pointe position, you need to first plié the supporting leg. If the right shoulder moves more than the left shoulder and the spine twists, the body uses tension in some body parts to compensate for a lack of balance in that leg. As you relevé, this tension makes it difficult to feel the whole body moving uniformly upward; one side of the back and one arm move up faster than the other, and again you have to compensate to stay balanced. Compensation is complex and much more difficult than experiencing the whole body as one. Moreover, as you fall off balance, you are already pondering what went wrong this time, making you even more worried and tense the next time you have to balance.

You cannot improve balance through conditioning alone; but through increased conscious awareness of your strength, you can perform a balanced movement with minimal effort. The fear of not being able to balance when required is ironically one of the reasons dancers struggle with balance. In several exercises in this chapter you will perform dance movements while balancing on small balls (sometimes with your eyes closed). Challenging your balance in such extreme ways improves your overall balance and makes balancing easier. These exercises will build your confidence as you learn how easy it can be to balance. The key to success will be to transfer your experience from the exercises to an actual dancing situation, getting as close as possible to the reality of being on stage with lights glaring in your face and a large black space in front of you where the audience is awaiting a grand performance.

Reflexes and Righting Reactions

Primitive reflexes are the underpinning of all movement. They are movement responses to stimuli that are very much in the foreground when, as children, we learn to move and walk. Brush a feather over a baby's foot, and he bends his toes and retracts his leg; tickle the side of his back, and he bends toward that side.

Righting reflexes or reactions are what bring the head into alignment with the spine or the whole body axis into alignment with gravity. These reflexes reorient us toward our center so that we know where we are in relation to our axis and can respond to other stimuli efficiently. Righting reactions are controlled by the numerous sensory organs in the neck muscles (muscle spindles) and the balance organs of the inner ear (vestibulum) and the eyes (optical righting). Try to selectively eliminate the optical righting reflex by closing your eyes while performing a difficult task, and feel how much you rely on this mechanism. For dancers it is especially important to train the vestibular and neck righting mechanisms. The exercises in this chapter will provide ways to do that.

Equilibrium responses are complex reactions to difficult rebalancing situations. It is not easy to discern stimulus from reaction with equilibrium responses—the movements are just too complicated. For example, let yourself fall forward and automatically the foot moves forward to break your fall. It is wonderful to feel that you can turn off your thinking and just let your body ride on the equilibrium responses. They are taking care of our equilibrium needs as a mother takes care of her baby.

Balancing the Balance Organs

The body has many ways to sense its balance and movement (figure 3.1). Most of these sensory mechanisms respond to changes in length and pressure and tension in the joints, tendons, skin, and muscles in the form of reflexes. As briefly discussed earlier, the eyes and vestibular organs in the ears also contribute to balance.

The plantar grasp reflex causes the foot to grasp an object that stimulates the sole of the foot. This reflex is integrated, or not as obvious in the adult as it is in the child. The toe-spreading reflex is another important reflex for dance. Placing weight on the balls and toes of the feet causes the toes to spread. This action surprisingly increases the tone of the muscles of the torso. This reflex ensures that the spine lifts away from the floor as soon as the feet experience the floor's counterthrust. Should the spine collapse when the feet hit the floor, you could not land from a leap. Many dancers unfortunately wear dance shoes and ballet slippers that are so tight, the toes can hardly move, impeding this reflex. Under normal circumstances, the reflex aids your sense of lift without effort. If a dancer tunes in to the function of the balance organs, he will also tune in to his reflexes to improve his balance and experience a feeling of lightness and lift in the body without strain.

The vestibular organs are made up of two distinctive parts: the labyrinth, named after three rings located in all three planes, and the sacculus and utriculus, which sense your relationship to gravity. Within the sacculus and utriculus, there are little sensory hair cells, or cilia, that float in a gelatinous substance called the otolithic membrane.

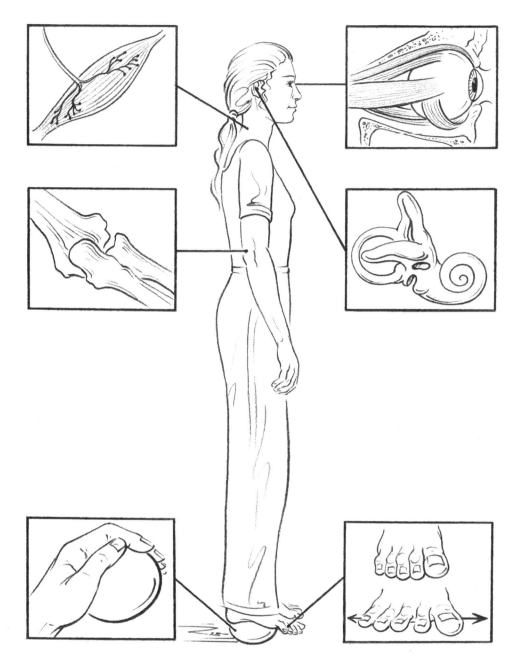

Figure 3.1   Sensory mechanisms the body uses to determine balance and movement.

Perched on top of this substance are the otoliths, small structures that look like little stones. When you move the head into a new relationship to gravity, the relatively heavy otoliths tend to displace the otolithic membrane with the cilia. The bending of the cilia informs the central nervous system how your head is positioned in space.

If you habitually hold the head in a misaligned position, the nervous system gets used to this imbalance and stops informing you about the problem. If a teacher corrects your alignment, the correct position may feel wrong to you, because you have gotten used to the incorrect one. It will not feel right until you have readjusted your sensory organs—including the eyes.

The eyes are mirrors of the soul, a direct link to the brain that is visible on the surface of the body. You can touch the space with the eyes, just as you can touch it with the body. The eyes may initiate movement and enhance your ability to balance. Try sensing your eyes as a primordial mouth that takes in images from the outside and mirrors them within its own sphere.

You can train your eyesight to help improve your sense of balance and space. Generally speaking, women have better peripheral vision, while men's eyes are better at seeing things in a narrow focus. The theory behind this fact is that prehistoric women needed to have an eye on everything going on around them, such as children and sudden danger, while men needed to observe animals moving in the distance (Pease 2001).

1. When you look in front of you, do you feel as if the eyes are on the same level as each other? Check in a mirror to see if your feeling and fact are the same.

2. While you look in front of you, can you also observe what is going on next to you?

3. Hold the arms out to the sides, and move the fingers. How far back can you hold the arms and still see the movement?

4. Balance on one leg and notice your eye movements. Do you fix the eyes on an object to help you control your balance? Move the eyes around and notice how easy or difficult it is to balance.

5. Imagine that the eyes are like a spotlight, and they illuminate everything they look at. (This exercise is also good for checking head alignment in various positions.)

6. Imagine that the whole face is one big eye, so you can see with the whole face, not just with two eyes.

7. Place eyes on various parts of the body, such as the back of the head or the soles of the feet. As you dance, what do these eyes see?

8. See a beam of light coming from the top of the head. If you are well aligned, a spot precisely above your head should be lit up.

9. Place the right hand over the right eye. Imagine the warmth of the hand relaxing the circular muscles around the eye. Think of all the circular muscles around the mouth relaxing as well. Think of the eye resting in its socket. The eye is filled with a clear fluid. Feel the weight of the eye as a fluid-filled ball resting in its socket. Now remove the right hand, and notice the difference between the shoulders. The right shoulder probably feels more relaxed and is lower than the left shoulder. Perform an extension to the side or front with the right leg. Perform the same movement with the left leg. You may notice that you are more flexible on the same side where you relaxed the eye. Eye tension influences flexibility in other areas of the body, so repeat the exercise with the left eye.

Balancing Muscles

The muscles are sensory organs that contribute greatly to the ability to balance. To understand how muscles create coordinated movement, let's take a short trip through evolutionary history.

The human body consists mostly of muscles created to move the body against resistance. This resistance can be the body's own weight, elastic tissues within it, or some external force such as water or the kitchen door. In the primal oceans the movement of unicellular organisms was primarily a result of the currents in the surrounding water. Access to food was a result of a chaotic game of chance encounters between nourishment and the cell. The enticing morsels at the mouth of a river were forever out of the cell's reach because of the currents moving it away from its desired breakfast. Not until cilia—the outboard motors of the cell, the small hairlike projections swaying like a field of windswept wheat—were developed could the cell move about.

We still have cilia-like structures in our own body removing dust from the lungs and waving food along the intestinal canal. Cilia are powered by muscular molecules that form the tiny building blocks of the large muscles. Ciliar movement in the unicellular organism was far too weak to counter the strong currents of the primordial soups surrounding the cell. More sophisticated cellular machinery had to be concocted, or the cell would be forced to stay forever geographically restricted. As the cells united to form larger structures such as sponges and jellyfish, they also began to develop muscles. So enters the myosin molecule, capable of performing bending and straightening movements with the miniaturized power of an awe-inspiring samurai bowing before his lord. Together with other filaments, the myosin creates a miniature contractile unit, the sarcomere—the basic building block of muscle.

Once muscles arrived on the stage of the early oceans, propulsion was close at hand. The next step was to create a body form that could use a shortening and lengthening mechanism to create movement through water. This body form arrived with a cord lined by muscle cells that allowed for alternate contraction on either side.

Snakelike, wavy creatures began to roam about, currents were overcome, new territories were explored for their rich harvest in food that in turn enabled the organism to build larger bodies with stronger muscles. Poking their heads out of shallow seas, the first terrestrial creatures were about to test the power of their muscles. It would be a while before any animal was capable of lifting its belly off the ground. Even today, millions of years later, our babies replay this drama. The art of elevating their bodies upward is a challenge they meet with endurance and grace. Without delicately controlled muscles, they would never move or balance on their legs. From all this information about evolution, we can derive some of the primordial mind states of muscle: contraction and expansion, moving out into space, sensing our movement, and cushioning our falls.

Now, let us look at some of the events governing muscles in the larger perspective. Muscles work in pairs or groups that balance each other's function—agonists and antagonists (figure 3.2). Despite their names, these groups should be looked at as one team, not fitful foes trying to inhibit one another's game. When a muscle on one side of a joint

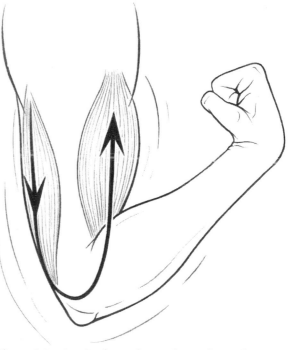

Figure 3.2 A pair of muscles work together. When one contracts the other must let go to support the movement of a joint.

contracts, the muscle on the other side needs to let go to create movement at that joint. If two muscles are helping to create movement, and if we think of both those muscles as being part of the same arc in the desired direction, the movement will be easier to perform. The term antagonistic muscle then seems a misnomer; rather than antagonize, the actions support one another. Anatomical nomenclature does not necessarily make for good movement imagery.

When a muscle is stretched, its natural tendency is to protect itself with a shortening reflex called a stretch reflex. If stretching continues beyond a certain point, the muscle will tear. Shortening the biceps and brachialis muscles to bend the elbow causes the triceps, which stretches the elbow, to lengthen. In this case the shortening muscles reflexively send instructions to their partners to calm down or inhibit the stretch reflex. Without this so-called reciprocal inhibition, movement would not be possible. In other words, the biceps and the triceps and all opposing muscle groups are in a constant dialogue. The measuring devices for such changes in length are the muscle spindles that run alongside the regular muscle fibers.

Muscle spindles are specialized fibers surrounded by connective tissue. This connective tissue is slightly removed from the fibers and filled with fluid to create the typical spindle shape. These spindles are able to detect the amount and speed of lengthening that occurs in the muscle with the help of nerve endings surrounding the spindle fibers. If the muscle is stretched rapidly, the spindles are also stretched, stimulating the sensory endings surrounding the spindle fibers, and resulting in an increased contraction of the whole muscle. The spindles cause this contraction by sending the signal to contract through the spinal cord to the regular fibers within the same muscle. This way, the muscle is not overstretched and damaged.

With the help of the spindle, muscle can act as an adjustable spring. If you land from a jump, the muscle is stretched, the spindles are stimulated to contract the muscles, and up you go again into the next leap.

The muscle spindle measures the length of the muscle as well as how fast the muscle changes in length. If we take a closer look at the fibers located in the spindle, we notice a difference between the middle and end parts. The end parts have striated muscle and therefore are able to contract like regular muscle. In other words, the device that measures the length of the muscle is able to change its own length. This means that it can adjust its sensitivity to being stretched. Let us assume that you are about to perform a series of small jumps. Just by thinking about it, you may be setting your spindle sensitivity and preparing your muscles for the action. In a sense the springiness of your muscles can be adjusted by your thinking. One of the effects of imagery is that it presets the spindle sensitivity in a certain way. We all have experienced the fact that when we are afraid, the muscles tighten up and make movement difficult and irregular. Tightening occurs because of changes in the muscle spindles through complex connections to our emotional centers in the brain. On the other hand, a calm and confident state of mind helps us move in a smooth and well-controlled fashion.

Imagery can set the tension level of the muscles though the activity of the muscle spindles. Once you are aware of this fact, you may be much more selective about the kind of imagery you use while dancing.

1. Stand in parallel, then take one step forward and move the same foot back again. Notice the feeling in your whole body as you perform this shift of weight.

2. Now imagine there is a soft, warm, sandy beach in front of you. Imagine being barefoot, and take a step forward into the silky sand. Notice how the muscles react to this image. It may be that the joints are a touch more flexible and the muscles are apt to be a bit softer.

3. Move the foot back into the starting position and conjure a less appealing scene, such as sharp rocks spread between you and the beach you need to get to. Take a step forward with bare feet onto the rocks, and notice how the muscles react (even though it is only an image). Knowing that you should not push down on the rock, the muscles are tighter to begin with.

4. Practice with imagery that makes balancing easier. Is it easier to balance if you think that the feet are deep in the sand?

Less Stress, More Balance

Because muscle spindles are influenced by your level of stress, your state of mind greatly influences your muscle coordination. The more you worry about your technique and ability to perform a step, the more your spindles are in a state of oversensitivity, causing opposing muscle groups to restrict each other's movement. Recent research has found that there is a link between stress and injury in dance (Smith et al 2000). Therefore, to improve your technique, try to find a feeling of relaxed focus to achieve improved function of the muscles as sensory organs.

Often dancers are surrounded by stress concerning their technique relative to other dancers. Ironically, if you could actually let go of this idea even for a moment, you would notice an immediate boost to your technical facility. If you feel calm and nothing can bother you, your balance is better. No physical exercise can replace mental balance. During dance class or in a rehearsal, use self-talk (see chapter 2). Say inwardly, *I am moving with complete confidence. I feel at ease, and I perform all steps effortlessly,* and notice how this self-talk affects your movement. Even if you initially feel that these statements don't reflect your current state of mind, try them on for size. You may suddenly notice that they begin to fit.

3.3 BALANCING THE NECK

The large muscles of the back and the muscles of the neck are highly relevant for balancing, because they contain many muscle spindles.

The latissimus dorsi is the largest expanse of muscle in the body, and it helps balance the back. Even though this muscle covers a large part of the back, is not a true back muscle. It originates on the connective tissue on the lower part of the back (thoracolumbar fascia) and the iliac crest. It attaches to the top front of the upper arm bone (humerus). It can extend, adduct, and medially rotate the arm and can pull the arm down and back from an elevated position with great power. It is related to two other muscles, one under the shoulder blade (the subscapularis) and one that connects the shoulder blade to the arm (the teres major). Because this muscle is so large and wide its position greatly affects your balance. Due to the attachments to the lower back and pelvis, tightness in the muscle tends to tilt the pelvis forward when the arms are elevated, making balance and turns more difficult. If you can feel the left and right latissimus dorsi lengthened, flexible, and working equally, your balance and the scope of your arm movements will greatly improve. This does not mean that the latissimus dorsi actually lifts the arm. This job is taken care of by the deltoid and the muscles that rotate the scapula (trapezius and serratus anterior).

1. Notice your sense of length (eccentric action) and width in the latissimus dorsi as you move the arms.

2. Imagine both sides of the latissimus dorsi being equal in expanse and activity. Feel the width of the muscle enveloping the back.

3. Stretch the arms up over the head and move them behind you. Externally rotate the arms so the palms face to the back and the elbows are pointing forward. Now feel the lengthening of the latissimus dorsi from the pelvis up to the arm. Remain in the position for half a minute breathing freely. Then take your arms down to the side and notice the feeling of width and support in the back.

4. Stand on one leg. Notice that you are more balanced when you can feel both sides of the latissimus dorsi.

5. The latissimus dorsi spirals as it attaches into the top front of the upper arm bone. Imagine this spiral continuing into the biceps of the arm and the flexors of the wrist and fingers. Think of this spiraling flexor chain of muscles lengthening into space to create more support for the arms.

6. Think of the muscle supporting the arm from below. Imagine the muscle thrusting upward against the upper arm bone.

7. Imagine curtains sliding out under the arms, creating more width and breadth in the back.

The pyramid is a stable and solid structure. Not surprisingly, some muscular arrangements in the leg are pyramidal—long and thin, three-sided, with their edges created by the belly of a muscle. The muscles of the sartorius-gracilis-semitendinosus pyramid have a common insertion on the inside of the top of the lower leg (tibia), also called the pes anserinus (goose's foot).

1. Locate the pes anserinus muscle on the top of the right shinbone (tibia). You can best find it by following the front bony edge of the shin up to a bony knob just below the knee. Move your fingers an inch to the inside on the shin bone and you will be on the pes anserinus. Often the area feels tender to the touch. Rub it lightly with your fingers.

2. The sartorius is one of the muscles that inserts at the pes anserinus. It is the longest muscle in the body, and it originates at the anterior superior iliac spine (ASIS), the bone on the front of the pelvis that sticks out bit and can hurt if you are ever required to roll on the floor.

3. Rub the right ASIS for a moment, then glide your fingers down around the front of the leg to the inside top of the right shin bone. The muscle's path spirals.

4. The gracilis originates on the lower part of the pubic bone. This place is difficult to touch, but you can rub the front of the right pubic bone and send the mind's eye back and down to the actual origin. Then glide your fingers down the inside of the right thigh to the pes anserinus.

5. The semitendinosus originates at the sit bone. Touch the right sit bone, then glide the finger down the inside of the leg (you may have to switch hands) to the pes anserinus.

6. Now that you have touched origin and insertion of all these muscles, balance on your right leg.

7. Visualize the triangle created by origins of the sartorius, gracilis, and semitendinosus muscles as you balance on the leg. Together with their insertion they create the geometric shape of a pyramid standing on its head (see figure).

8. Now balance on the left leg. You may notice that the side on which you have awareness of these three muscles is much more stable.

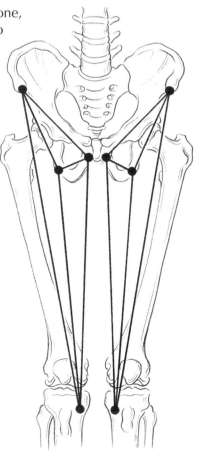

3.5   LENGTHENING MUSCLES

If you have ever ridden a horse and attempted to turn to the left, you have likely noticed the principle of muscle pairs working together. To turn to the left, you must shorten the rein on one side and lengthen the rein on the other. If you just shorten one side without giving way on the other, the horse's neck gets compressed. The same principle applies to lengthening muscles—to lengthen one, you must shorten the other. If the muscles at the front of the upper arm (biceps and brachialis) contract, and the muscles at the back of the upper arm (triceps) lengthen, the elbow bends.

1. Focus on the muscles on the front of the upper arm. Bend the arm and think of these muscles contracting to create the movement. How does this feel?
2. Explore whether the movement feels different if you focus on the action of the antagonistic muscle (the triceps) on the back of the upper arm.
3. Imagine the triceps lengthening to make the elbow bend (see figure 3.2). How does this movement feel?
4. Compare the sensation of shortening the front of the arm to bend the elbow with the sensation of lengthening the muscle at the back of the arm to bend the elbow. Does the lengthening imagery of the antagonist make the movement feel easier and smoother? Does it help to create more flexibility in the elbow?

3.6   BALANCING TURN-OUT

Balanced muscular strength helps create better turnout. This book provides many exercises to help improve turn-out, including a special section in chapter 6. In this exercise, you use the lengthening of the antagonist image to improve your battement tendu. This type of imagery has been successfully used by dance teachers for many years.

1. From first position, perform a battement tendu (brush) to the front. Think of the muscles on the front of the hip joint shortening to achieve this action.
2. Now think of the muscles of the back of the leg lengthening to achieve the same goal. Notice what feels easier.
3. Touch the inner hamstrings (semitendinosus and semimembranosus muscles).
4. Slide your fingers diagonally downward from the right sit bone to the top and inside the right shin bone. Repeat this gliding touch several times until you can visualize the direction of the inner (medial) hamstrings.
5. Perform a turned-out battement tendu with the leg you touched. Think of the inner hamstring increasing the distance between the sit bones and the inside of the shin bone.
6. After practicing these ideas for several battement tendus on one leg, compare the practiced leg with the unpracticed one. In the unpracticed one you may feel that more effort is required to initiate the leg movement, especially in the hip flexor muscles in front and above the hip joint.

Balanced Body Halves

One important part of creating balance is using the muscles of the two halves of the body equally. Of special concern are the body wall muscles that are not directly involved in moving limbs, but serve to make the torso and pelvis a container forming the core muscular structure (figure 3.3). The main body wall muscles are the pelvic floor, the abdominals, the intercostals, the quadratus lumborum, and the scalenes. Before a baby can use his limb musculature he is quite adept at rolling and initiating movement from his body wall musculature. If we can become aware of the body wall as a primary source of support and movement initiation, the body aligns, and the limb musculature releases excess tension. Often we dance with too much tension in the limb musculature, because we are not aware of the support that the body wall can provide. The psoas major, latissimus dorsi, and other muscles connect the body wall with the limbs.

They are, in a sense, mediators, important for both core stability and limb movement. The levator scapulae and the serratus anterior are body wall muscles that have transformed to help in the movement of the arms. If these muscles are imbalanced in length and tension, it is difficult for the limbs to function in a balanced way. The following imagery exercises focus on the scalenes and levator scapulae.

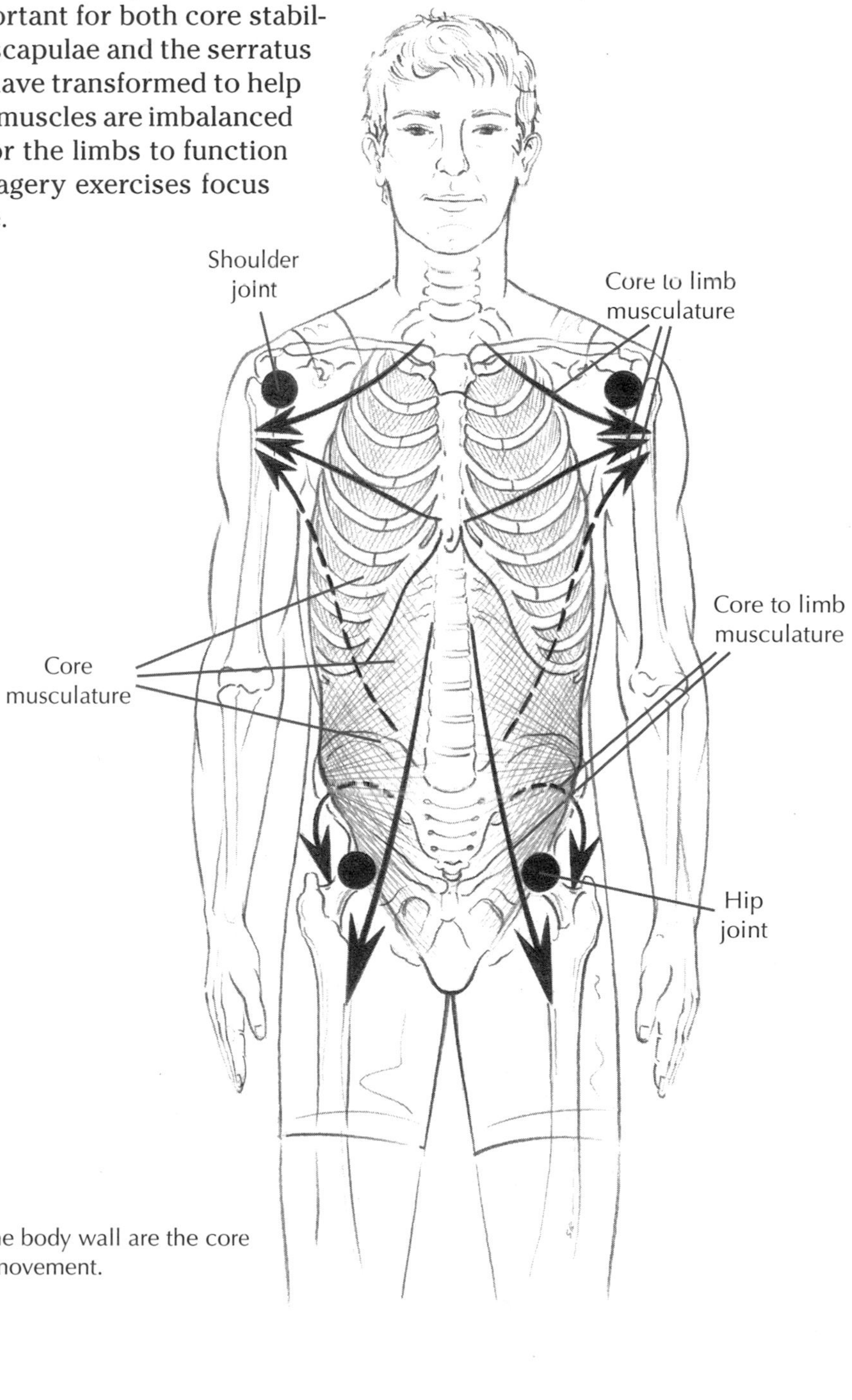

Figure 3.3 The muscles of the body wall are the core of the body that supports all movement.

3.7 BALANCING THE SCALENES

The scalenes connect each side of the cervical spine with the top ribs (see figure). In fact, the upper thoracic ribs are like hoops suspended from the neck by these muscles. There is also a scalene that connects the transverse process of the axis (second vertebra) to the first rib. If these muscles have different lengths and tension levels on the left and right sides of the neck, the head and torso will be off balance. Once you enliven these muscles, you sense a release in shoulder and neck tension, your turns are more centered, and the pectoralis major and minor muscles of the chest lengthen, effectively removing the tendency to round the shoulders.

1. Touch the bone behind the ears (the mastoid). To feel the scalenes, slide your finger down the sides of the neck below the mastoid. Do the muscles feel equally thick on both sides of the neck?

2. Slide your fingers down the sides of the neck one more time, and think of the first rib hanging from the sides of the spine and then dropping a little lower, causing the scalenes to stretch and come alive. Feel the activity of the scalenes equally on both sides of the neck.

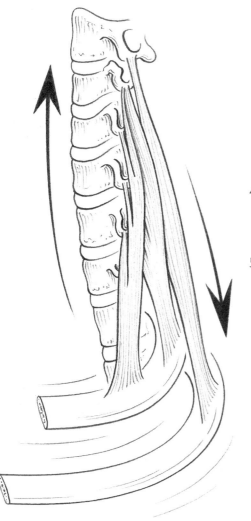

3. Imagine the individual ribs suspended from each other by the muscles between the ribs (intercostal muscles). Think of both sides of the rib cage suspended from the neck in a balanced fashion. Imagine the continuation of the body wall from the ribs through the quadratus lumborum in the back, from the abdominals at the sides and front of the body, and all the way to the pelvic floor. If this imagery and touch make the neck feel longer and the shoulders lower, you are on the right track. You may also notice a release in tension in the pectoralis major and minor muscles as well as the rhomboids between the shoulder blades.

4. Imagine the first rib becoming horizontal, and then feel wind blowing up the front of the spine and lifting the ribs from underneath. This image eases the pull of the anterior scalenes and increases the length of the posterior ones.

5. Practice some turns, and try to feel the first rib hanging equally from the top of the spine. Create a balanced feeling on both sides of the rib cage as you turn.

In the accompanying figure you can see that the scapulae are hanging from the top of the spine by the levator scapulae. If one of these muscles is shorter than the other, it will lift the scapula on that side and cause an unequal positioning of the shoulder girdle. You can touch the points described in the following exercise on your own, but it is easier if you have a partner help you.

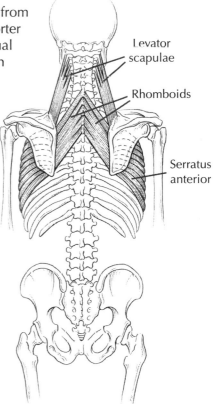

Levator scapulae

Rhomboids

Serratus anterior

1. Have your partner trace the shoulder blades so you can get a sense of this bone's location.
2. Then have your partner find the inner top edge of each scapula where the levator scapulae attaches.
3. Have him glide his fingers up the sides of the neck to a point just below the mastoid process. This is where the levator attaches to the transverse processes of the atlas.
4. Repeat this gliding motion from scapula to atlas three times as you think of balancing the muscles.
5. Imagine these muscles having equal length as you seek to balance them.

BALANCING THE NECK TRIANGLE   3.9

The upper spine is crucial for balance and alignment. You have already touched the mastoid process, the bony protuberance behind the earlobe. You will now visualize some of the muscles originating from this point. They are the sternocleidomastoid, the longissimus capitis and the splenius capitis (see figure). The sternocleidomastoid extends to the sternum and clavicle, and the longissimus capitis and splenius capitis extend to the back of the spine.

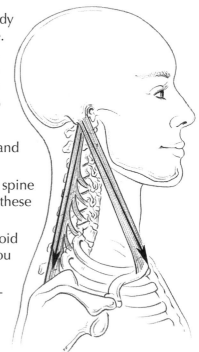

1. Glide your fingers from the mastoid process to the sternum and clavicle.
2. Glide your fingers from the mastoid process to top of the thoracic spine in back. The mastoid forms the point of a triangle created by these muscles.
3. Perform some dance steps while feeling the movement of the mastoid process. Do you feel them on the same horizontal plane when you turn?
4. Visualize the design of the muscles in the body as an aid to sensing the relationship of the head to the spine and sternum.

3.10 BALANCING THE QUADRATUS LUMBORUM

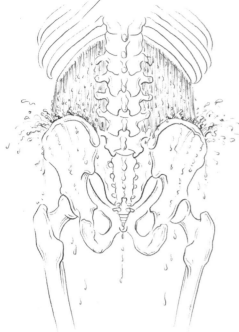

The quadratus lumborum extends from lowest floating rib of the back to the top edge of the pelvis called the pelvic crest. It also has attachments to the transverse processes of the lumbar spine. Acting on one side, the quadratus lumborum laterally flexes the trunk to the same side. When standing on one leg, it keeps the pelvis from dropping on the unsupported side. Working together, both sides can extend the lumbar spine. The quadratus lumborum balances the relationship between the back ribs and the pelvis.

1. Touch the lowest ribs on both sides of the body. You can feel them just above the pelvic crest.

2. Use your thumb to press down on the top of the pelvic crest, moving from the back near the spine to the side of the body.

3. Visualize the quadratus lumborum as sheet of rain. Think of the twelfth rib as a sprinkler providing this downpour on to the pelvic crest (see figure). Both ribs provide an equal shower of water.

3.11 BALANCING THE SPINAL–HAMSTRING CONNECTION

The spinal muscles can be felt as linked to the hamstrings. Some of the spinal muscles attach to the sacrum, and strong ligaments connect the sacrum to the sit bone (sacrotuberous ligaments). These ligaments form connective-tissue connections to the hamstring muscles. You can create a powerful sense of balance by visualizing connection of the head to the back of the leg through these muscles and ligaments.

1. Have a partner glide his hands down your back, starting from the skull and ending at the heels.

2. Repeat the gliding three times.

3. With this sense of top-to-bottom connection down the back, visualize a muscle-to-connective-tissue connection from the head to the knee and on to the heels.

4. Visualize two balanced muscle chains at each side of the spine and two each at the back of the leg (see figure).

5. Relevé on both feet in first or second position, and notice how the image helps align, balance, and ground you at the same time.

The spine exhibits a double S shape. The first inverted S extends from the bottom of the skull to the end of the thoracic spine. The second encompasses the lumbar spine, sacrum, and tail. This shape has the advantage of making the spine resilient and flexible without losing its ability to bear weight. To create a sense of center and alignment, the curves of the spine need to balance each other. If one curve is exaggerated or too flattened, the others, too, will suffer. Balance becomes easy when the spinal Ss are harmonized (see figure).

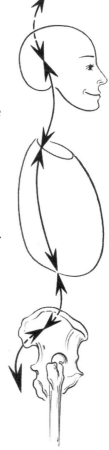

1. Visualize the double S shape of the spine. At the neck the spine curves forward slightly. The thoracic spine curves backward. The lumbar spine curves forward. The sacral spine curves back. The tail curves forward.

2. Imagine all the curves of the spine balanced on top of each other. Feel them finding their optimal depth and length.

3. Think of the spine as a harmonious wave, and notice the continuation of the wave upward and downward. Above the cervical spine the imaginary spine curves forward; so does the imaginary continuation of the spine below the tail.

4. In the downward phase of a plié imagine the spinal curves deepening just slightly. Imagine the spinous processes, the bumps on the back of the bones of the spine, floating up. In the upward phase of a plié imagine the spinal curves lengthening. Drop the spinous processes down to support this action. The spinal curves are in constant dynamic change in response to limb action.

5. Notice how it feels to perform a balance with a fabulously balanced, dynamic spine.

Balancing on Balls

One way to improve a skill is to practice it in an increasingly challenging way. You can do this with dance steps during a dance class. But if your balance is not progressing, or if you feel anxiety surrounding your ability to balance, choose a method that is playful and takes your skill to a higher level by training all your balance organs. Then, when you return to your dance, you will find that you have improved, seemingly without effort.

With this in mind, I recommend using two balls of 4 inches in diameter to practice balancing. Any type of air-filled ball around that size will do, as long as each ball is of equal size, is strong enough to stand on, and is resilient. (See the resources list at the end of this book for information on where to find such balls.) A pair of balls this size have the following advantages for balancing:

- They keep each foot's movement individual and three-dimensional.
- They support the feet under the arch to stimulate certain reflexes important for your balance. It takes a few days longer to learn balancing on balls than it does balancing on a board, but it is worth making that additional effort for dance-specific balance.
- The feet being stimulated by the ball increases the tone in the trunk muscles, which helps your balance. This increase in tone is amplified by the spreading of the bones that occurs when the foot presses on a ball (Roberts 1995, page 117). If the spine is more erect and balanced, the shoulders can relax as superficial tension melts away.
- The elastic balls pushing against the feet elicit an extensor thrust reaction, a downward thrust of the leg against the floor. This thrust gives you a sense of lift without effort.
- Standing on balls also stimulates the optical and vestibular righting reactions and trains the muscle sensory organs of the neck and the whole body. The result is a more effortless feeling of balance and alignment when you get off the balls or perform a dancing balance.
- The balls are light in weight and small enough that you can carry them in your dance bag.

When learning how to balance on balls, start slowly and build gradually, and stimulate one foot at a time with a ball. If you don't have a ball, use a tightly rolled towel or a high-quality hot water bottle. If you put warm water in the hot water bottle, you will have a quite agreeable wintertime warm-up.

1. Place one foot in front of the other, and put the arch of the front foot (the center of the foot) on the ball (figure a).

3. Rock forward and backward, rhythmically transferring your weight on and off the ball (figure b). As you shift your weight on the ball, imagine the toes and heel melting downward over it.

4. Swing the arms forward as you transfer your weight forward, and swing them backward as you rock back again.

5. Exhale as you shift your weight onto the ball. The latter two actions serve to release tension as you learn to balance.

6. After about 20 repetitions, take the foot off the ball and place both feet next to each other. Lift one leg, then the other. Balance in passé retiré position. Notice the difference in balance, stability, and relaxation between the sides of the body.

7. Repeat on the other side.

8. Think of the weight of the body resting on the ball.

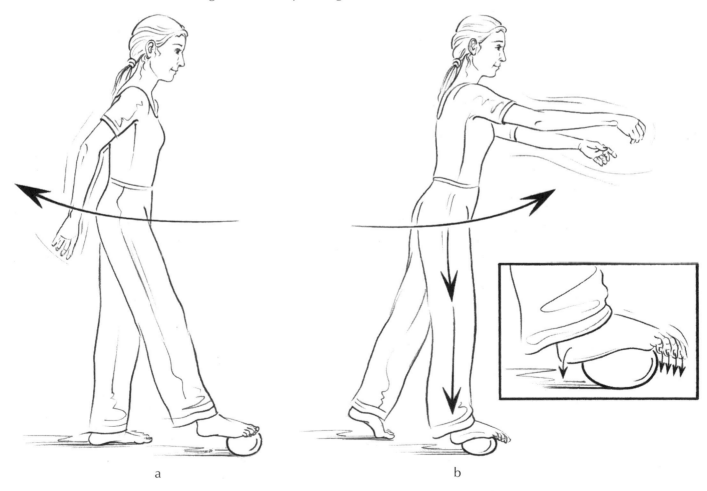

a

b

3.14 STANDING ON TWO BALLS

Once you have practiced with each foot individually, try to stand on both balls at the same time. This exercise seems difficult at the beginning, but with regular practice, you can master it within a week.

1. Place your feet on both balls and try to balance.
2. Hold on to a barre, or practice with a partner to start (see figure).
3. Try to let go of your partner or the barre, and balance on your own.
4. Imagine the muscles of the back releasing downward and the central axis lengthening.
5. You should be able to balance without outside help after practicing daily for about a week.

3.15 STRENGTH AND BALANCE

Use a Thera-Band or free weights while standing on balls for an effective strength and balance workout that exercises both the upper and lower body while improving your balance. The following is one example of such a combination strength and balance exercise.

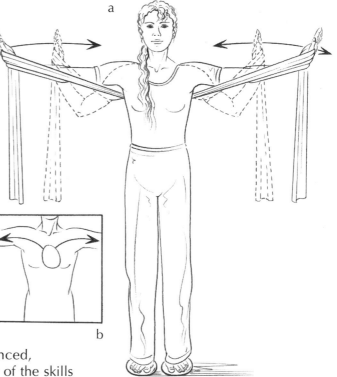

1. Stand on the balls holding both ends of a band around the back and under the arms.
2. Stretch the arms out to the sides and slowly release them back in; repeat the action eight times (figure *a*).
3. Think of pushing out from the center of the chest. You may even try initiating the movement from the heart (figure *b*).
4. Move the arms up to a 45-degree angle. Perform small circles with the hands eight times to the front, eight times to the back.
5. Bring the arms back in, drop the band, and rest the arms.
6. Repeat the sequence, only this time extend and flex the arms and legs simultaneously.
7. Notice your alignment, balance, and tension level after the exercise. You may feel stronger, more balanced, and more flexible all at once. Many of the skills you require when dancing are being trained in one exercise.

After two or three weeks of balancing practice have passed, try this exercise to increase the challenge.

1. Stand on the balls and lightly bounce to rhythmically bend and stretch the legs.
2. Lift the shoulders and inhale; slowly lower the shoulders as you exhale.
3. Place the hands behind the head (figure a). Send the breath into the neck.
4. Visualize the cervical spine lengthening, but do not actively try to make a long neck.
5. Drop your arms at the sides, and notice the length in the neck.

6. Place the hands on the neck again.
7. With the hands on the neck, rotate the upper body four times to the right and then to the left.
8. Move the hands up along the neck until they are placed at the back of the head.
9. Very slowly flex the cervical and upper thoracic spine (figure b). Allow for a gentle lengthening of the neck. Imagine the tailbone lengthening in the opposite direction.
10. Slowly extend the spine, drop the arms at the sides, and get off the balls.
11. Notice the effortless feeling of alignment, stability, and the length of the neck and the whole spine. Try an upper-body rotation and a spinal flexion, and you may notice an increase in flexibility and ease of motion.
12. Practice a few easy dance balance positions.

a

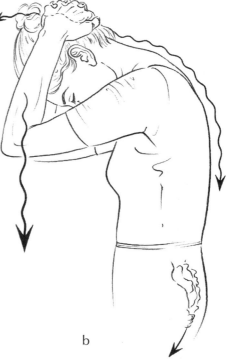

b

3.17 SPINAL EXTENSION BALANCE

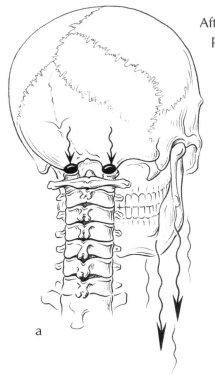

a

After practicing for several weeks, balancing on balls should feel easy. At this point you can add some more difficult moves to your repertoire. By closing the eyes, for example, you eliminate the optical righting reflex and have to rely on other sensory organs. This exercise is very helpful, because overuse of the eyes for balancing can spell disaster when faced with black nothingness instead of a rehearsal mirror on performance nights. This exercise also benefits all back-arching actions.

1. Stand on two balls with the arms relaxed at the sides.
2. Close the eyes, and try to maintain balance. Can you move the arms into various positions with the eyes closed?
3. Open the eyes.
4. Visualize the point where the head rests on top of the spine. Two miniature ball joints (condyles) at the bottom of the skull rest on two hollow facets at the top of the spine. The vertebra at the top of the joint is the atlas (figure a). Feel the jaw relaxing to increase your awareness of the skull's weight resting on the atlas.
5. Nod the head forward and backward, and feel equal weight on the two facets.
6. Extend the cervical spine, and lift the breastbone upward, as if it were being pulled by an imaginary string (figure b). Look at the ceiling. Try to maintain the position for 30 seconds.
7. Widen the space between the vertebrae as if your intervertebral discs were expanding like squeezed marshmallows that have just been released and are coming back into shape. Think of the spinous processes drooping downward (figure c).
8. Bring the head back to the neutral position.
9. Step off the balls and notice alignment.
10. Try a backward arch while standing. You may notice that your flexibility has improved.

c

The following workout is designed to raise your heart rate while training balance and strength. If there is limited space for warming up, this exercise fits the bill. It also strengthens many major muscles such as the deltoids, the serratus anterior, the gluteals, and the erector spinae.

1. Stand on two balls. Loop the proper length and resistance of Thera-Band (see chapter 1) under the upper legs (figure a). It is easiest to first position the band under the legs, then stand on the balls.

2. With each end of the band in one hand, stretch the arms in front of you.

3. Bend the legs and lift the outstretched arms upward. As you bend the legs, exhale and think of the gluteal muscles lengthening (figure b). As you lift the arms, think of the levator scapulae and rhomboid muscles lengthening (figure c).

4. Stretch the legs and lower the arms. Inhale as you stretch the legs, and think of the spine lengthening.

5. Repeat the sequence 12 times, then rest for 30 seconds.

6. Reposition the band, and stretch the arms forward.

7. Lower the arms while you bend the legs, and lift the arms while you stretch the legs.

8. Repeat the sequence 12 times, then let go of the band and keep doing the same movement for an additional three minutes without it.

9. To add cardiovascular spice to the exercise, touch the floor when the legs are fully bent.

a   b   c

chapter 4

Relaxed Flexibility

Rhythm, flow, alignment, and freedom of movement are key dance concepts relating to the level of tension and flexibility in your body. For example, the trapezius muscle connects the head to the spine and shoulder blades. When it is habitually shortened, it pulls the head back and the shoulder blades back and up. To experience the central axis and liberate the legs, you need to free this muscle. It is difficult to turn pirouettes or to balance well if the trapezius is tight, but a tight trapezius is common in many dancers.

To be free of tension is not just a nice feeling; it is essential to good dancing. This chapter aims to help you experience the relationship between flexibility and tension and improve technique by reducing tension. It also describes the basic principles of safe stretching and explains how to enhance stretching with imagery. It addresses key areas of the body that experience tension, such as the shoulders and neck, and describes the role of organs in flexibility.

The aim of flexibility training is to increase the range of motion (ROM) available in the joints and other structures of the body to give you a sense of freedom and spaciousness in all your movements. The exercises in this chapter also can help you feel unrestricted in your dancing and show you how to let go of tight, seemingly locked places in the body. Whenever two adjoining parts within the body can move relative to each other, you have created more flexibility. These parts or surfaces are by no means restricted to joints. You can also create more flexibility by moving organs relative to each other.

Flexibility training also contributes to the overall maintenance and health of the body by aiding the sufficient flow of blood through the tissues and the lubrication of the joints. Also, a strong connection exists between balanced flexibility, stability, and injury reduction.

I will discuss two kinds of flexibility:

1. *Static flexibility* is the ROM the joints permit when performing a nonmoving stretch. Emphasis is not on ability to move. Your static flexibility depends on the structure of the joints, the lengthening capacity of the muscles, and the elasticity of the connective and other surrounding tissues.

2. *Dynamic flexibility* is how much of this measured ROM you can actually use while dancing. You need dynamic flexibility when you perform a leg extension (développé). This flexibility may or may not correlate to your static flexibility.

Increases in static flexibility do not necessarily translate into an increased dynamic range of motion. Your flexibility can only be fully exploited in active movement if you have enough strength and coordination to move the limbs into the positions the joints permit. The body may be structured and stretched for flexibility, but the nervous system may not be coordinating the muscles, bones, and joints in a way to exploit it. Someone who has comparatively little static flexibility can still move flexibly if her movement is well coordinated by the nervous system.

Several years ago, a dancer in one of my ballet classes came to me frustrated about her turn-out. She showed me how flexible she was in various positions, and she noted that other dancers with the same level of flexibility had much more turn-out while dancing. She thought that her flexibility did not translate into an appropriate level of turn-out. So, I asked her to perform a plié. Watching her perform it, I recognized that her static flexibility was fine, but the problem was in her dynamic flexibility. She created tension in the way she coordinated her pelvis, legs, and spine, eliminating much of the flexibility she had gained through stretching. I detected these problems by observing the moment-to-moment alignment of her legs, pelvis, feet, and spine. If the knees, for example, move front and back during different phases of the descent and ascent from a plié, the dancer is not letting proper joint coordination and balanced muscles create the alignment but is instead using a variety of tension strategies, such as gripping the gluteus and quadriceps muscles. Other sure signs are feet that roll in or out and inconsistent pelvic alignment. Having performed tension strategies to control movement for a long time, the dancer is unaware of their negative effect; these habits are now automated. Imagery and kinesthetic cues based on touch can change these patterns in a short period of time. The patterns will remain changed if the dancer incorporates them into her body image.

According to ideokinesis (see chapter 1), optimal flexibility is a product of good alignment and the resulting muscular balance. Good alignment reduces the stress placed on muscles and increases elasticity. By transferring the body's weight in a centered way through bones and joints, muscles are relieved of holding patterns that inhibit flexibility. In faulty alignment, too much weight is held by the musculature, increasing tension and reducing flexibility.

The opposite holds true as well: If you have balanced flexibility, you are more stable, because weight transfer is centered through the joints. Balanced flexibility creates stability, but stabilizing with tension reduces flexibility. All the dancers with whom I have worked have improved their flexibility by applying these principles. But certainly the flexibility–alignment connection warrants increased research. Ultimately, flexibility also depends on many additional factors such as individual genes, differences between men and women, and even nutrition.

The Flexibility–Tension Connection

Reducing tension is about increasing your flexibility and your power to move. Why is this so? The most obvious reason is that excess tension causes you to hold the joints and structures more rigidly than necessary to perform a given movement. A less obvious reason is that all tension needs to be compensated with countertension, leaving with you less net strength with which to move. Each area that is held excessively taut in the body disrupts your alignment, breathing patterns, and balance. Once you release excess tension in the area, many of the places that you have been trying to stretch out will increase in flexibility as if touched by a magic wand.

When I first started to experience the connection between tension and flexibility, it came to me as a revelation. I always thought that my back was inflexible, especially in extension. One day I released my shoulders with the help of imagery and touch, and in an instant my range increased beyond what I ever had thought was possible. My spine was instantly more flexible, just through thinking differently. This experience led me to realize that my problem was not just a short muscle, but the way I had been using the whole body.

These ideas are similar to those put forward by many somatic disciplines, such as Feldenkrais®, Alexander Technique, Body-Mind Centering® (BMC™), and ideokinesis. Throughout this book I have chosen ideokinesis, Body-Mind Centering, and my own technique, the Franklin-Methode®, now named the Franklin Method®, as three somatic techniques that can be easily embodied within the traditional shapes and movements of all dance styles.

A muscle is composed of connective tissue, muscle fibers, blood vessels, and nerves. When you stretch, all of these elements are required to lengthen. Bone and joint structure are limiting factors. The resistance you feel when stretching a muscle most likely emanates from the connective tissue and not the actual muscle. Inflexibility is very much a matter of tight connective tissue (Alter 1988, page 31). Consistent, regular stretching stimulates the connective tissue cells to adapt to the increased length that you require (Albrecht, Mayer, and Zahner 1997, page 23). Great care must be taken when performing stretches because overstretching can be harmful for nerves. Blood vessels are tubes, and if they are stretched they become more narrow, reducing the flow of blood to the muscle and the nerves it contains (Van den Berg 1999, page 230). This can result in reduced message conduction in the nerve, or in the extreme, a tearing of the nerve fiber.

Nerves and blood vessels are somewhat protected by the fact that they usually run through the muscle not in a straight line but as a wave. An envelope of connective tissue with wave-shaped fibers surrounds most nerves. Stretching first straightens the waves and stretches the connective tissue before the nerve itself is stretched. A nerve that is stretched more than 15 percent will likely be damaged (Van den Berg 1999, page 227).

Chronic muscle tension is equally deleterious. If a muscle contracts with 20 percent of its maximal contraction force, blood flow is interrupted due to the rise in pressure within the muscle. Muscle tension that is maintained over a long period of time causes severe restriction in blood flow and damages the muscle (Van den Berg 1999 page 177). These facts must be taken into consideration when stretching tense musculature.

Since there are many contradictory statements in the literature, I advise you to use great caution when stretching. One interesting study found that inflexible people can suddenly become very flexible while asleep under narcosis. As soon as they wake up and the brain is alert, muscles tense up and flexibility is again limited (Albrecht and Gautschi 2001, page 27). This points out that flexibility resides to great degree in the controlling brain and with its resident image of our flexibility. By changing this image we can change our flexibility; this is a fact that I have observed countless times when teaching. Thus, I recommend that we view stretching as just one flexibility-enhancing method alongside many somatic techniques for improving alignment, releasing tension, and creating muscular balance.

Tension may cause a sequence of events that can seriously disrupt your technique. For example, many dancers hold tension in the tongue and jaw, disturbing the alignment of the cervical spine and increasing tension in the shoulders and abdominal muscles to counterbalance: A dancer goes off balance in turns and other movements, and he tries to compensate by lifting or holding his breath. This action causes even more tension, and soon all ease and flow leaves his movement, and he becomes frustrated. Tension also reduces the flow of blood to the muscle, causing a lack of oxygen and accumulation of toxins, resulting in fatigue and muscle aches.

Unless you can detect a harmful movement pattern, you cannot change it. What you can't feel, you can't change into a new feeling. Get into the habit of watching for minute changes in your tension level as you move.

Jaw–Neck Connection

1. Focus on the neck while moving the head forward and backward.
2. Clench the jaw, shut it tight, and move the head forward and backward again. Notice how the jaw affects the tension level in the neck.
3. Rotate the head to the left and right. Then clench the jaw and notice how this affects the rotation of the head.

Neck–Jaw–Jump Connection

1. Perform a few jumps from both feet. Notice how elastic the legs feel.
2. Clench the jaw and jump again. Do the legs feel stiffer?
3. Rub the hands together and place them on the neck. Imagine the neck being soft like gelatin.
4. Send the breath into the neck and drop the shoulders.
5. Remove the hands and shake the arms.
6. Jump up and down and notice how the jumps feel when the neck is relaxed.

Hand–Shoulder Connection

1. Lift the right arm and move it around while noticing the flexibility of the shoulder.
2. Make a fist with the right hand and notice how this affects shoulder flexibility. Release the hand, shake it, and move it around again to feel the freedom in the shoulder's movement.
3. Repeat this exercise on the other side.

Shoulder–Spine Connection

1. Rotate the torso to the right and left. Feel the flexibility of the spine.
2. Lift the shoulders and rotate the torso again while noticing what happens to the mobility of the spine.
3. Slowly drop the shoulders and rotate the torso to the right and left. Discover how shoulder positioning and tension relate to spinal flexibility.

Shoulder–Leg Connection

I have often seen dancers who are very flexible in a stretching position but have low legs when they dance because of shoulder tension.

(continued)

1. While standing, lift the right knee by flexing the hip joint. Then lower the leg.
2. Tighten the shoulders, lift them up a bit, and lift the right leg again. You may notice that the movement in the right hip joint is more restricted.
3. Drop the shoulders, relax them, and lift the leg again. If you are warmed up, perform a high leg kick (grand battement) with lifted shoulders, and notice the restriction in the hip joint.
4. Lift the shoulders and drop them slowly, and as they arrive at the lowest, most relaxed point, perform a grand battement with the leg. The leg will go higher and move with more freedom in the hip joint.

Spine–Hip Joint Connection

Another factor affecting the flexibility of the hip joint is the length of the spine. If the spine is compressed and shortened, hip joint flexibility is reduced.

1. While standing, imagine a force pushing the head down, compressing the spine.
2. With this image in your mind, swing one leg forward, and notice especially the effect on the hip joint and the hamstring muscles at the back of the leg.
3. Imagine the head floating upward and the tailbone dropping down. Imagine that the spine is a flexible chain of pearls.
4. Swing the leg once again and see if you feel any difference in ease of motion and flexibility in the hip joint and hamstrings.

4.2 LEARNING TO SELF-OBSERVE

Ideally you use minimal effort to achieve any given movement. In this case, you engage only the necessary pathways in the nervous system, freeing up the body systems for efficient coordination. The first step is to discover your tension patterns through self-observation, with the help of simple exercises or a skilled teacher or body therapist. Many of these patterns and their compensations become a part of the whole body feeling, the body image of the dancer. Nothing will change until you experience an alternative that will improve technique.

Learn to disidentify with the way you currently move, and look at your movement objectively. Go into self-observation mode to aid your technique. I am not proposing disembodied dancing, but allowing for a shift in focus. If you are faced with an intractable technical difficulty, this exercise can lead to great insights about what is wrong and what you can do about it.

1. While dancing, notice whether you hold the neck or tighten the tongue and jaw.
2. Try to move without such tensions; watch the body for signs of tension. Initially this may feel odd, because the old way of moving felt natural.
3. Now observe other areas of the body: the lower back, heels, and shoulders.
4. Stick with this method until the easier way to move starts feeling natural.

The preceding exercises show that tension in one part of the body affects the range of motion in another. The following exercise exemplifies the connection between feeling your weight and feeling your flexibility. Dancers are often concerned with lengthening their bodies; by trying to lengthen, they are actually creating distortion. In my experience length happens once you liberate and organize the structures of the body. One of the best ways to lengthen the spine, for example, is to use imagery with the pelvic floor and relax the jaw (see also chapters 5 and 7).

1. Stand in second position.
2. Lift the left arm and bend the torso to the right, lifting the body up to make yourself long.
3. Come back to the center position, and feel your weight on the floor. Notice the feet relaxing, melting, and spreading on the floor, and breathe freely. You are not collapsing, you are just experiencing how the body's weight cascades into the floor instead of nurturing the idea of holding yourself up against gravity.
4. Lift the left arm and bend to the same side again. Imagine a long curve in the spine while still feeling the feet grounded on the floor.
5. Notice the change in ROM. Do not forget that you are also creating more strength with this approach, even though you may feel more relaxed. By increasing your range you strengthen the muscles supporting that new range. If your movement is restricted, your strength gains are also restricted by the need to support these less flexible positions.

PAY ATTENTION TO WHAT YOU WANT ⬛ **4.4**

Flexibility is not just a question of getting tissue to lengthen, but also of adjusting the nervous system to create a new sense of length while you move. When teaching the nervous system new ways to move, *what you experience gets reinforced*. If you start a flexibility program by paying attention to where you cannot move, you will allow the nervous system to record the opposite of what you want to achieve. Experiencing limitations may be valuable as an analytic tool, because you are figuring out what areas of the body need to work. However, I do suggest focusing on feeling and imaging flexibility and not on limitation.

As Zvi Gotheiner points out, the key to permanent increases in flexibility is not just to do regular flexibility exercises, but to create a body image that contains an increased flexibility self-image.

1. Perform an extension à la seconde with the right leg and then the left leg.
2. Stand and visualize the extension to the right. Imagine the leg going higher than where it was when you just extended it in active movement. Be precise about your feeling as you strive to lift the leg higher. You may be surprised that it is suddenly going higher, you may feel more effort in the supporting leg, and you may notice how you are trying to keep the shoulders relaxed. In other words, make the situation as real as possible. Repeat the imagined extension to the right three more times, moving the leg higher up with each try.
3. After a minute or two try the extension to the right again, and notice whether it feels any different.
4. Repeat steps 2 and 3 on the left side.

Muscle Sliding and Flexibility

Imagining a muscle sliding is an excellent way to increase flexibility in that muscle without forcing it to lengthen. When muscles contract, they don't actually become shorter from a microscopic point of view. According to the sliding filament theory of muscular contraction, muscles become shorter when the filaments that make up the muscle—actin and myosin—slide together.

To understand the action of muscle filaments, imagine a rowing boat with oars (figure 4.1, *a* and *b*). The boat with its rowing team is the myosin filaments, and the oars are the heads of the filaments. The water is the actin. As the paddles push back on the water, the boat moves in the opposite direction of the water, shortening the distance to the finish line. In reality the situation is more three-dimensional, with the myosin surrounded by six actin filaments.

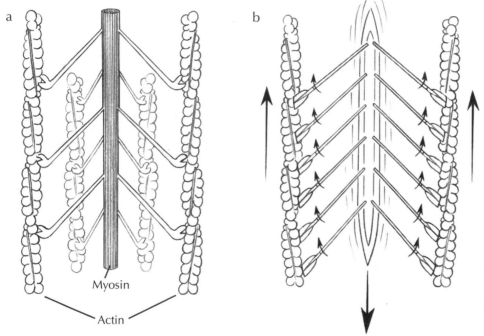

Myosin

Actin

Figure 4.1, *a* and *b* The action of the muscle fibers lengthening and shortening can be thought of as similar to the action of a rowboat's oars pushing against the water.

If you zoom out to take a larger picture of muscle contraction, you can imagine the myosin boats sliding into the actin docks when the muscle as a whole shortens, and the boats sliding out of the docks when the muscle as a whole lengthens. The key to this image is that neither the boat nor the dock shortens; the proteins that make up muscle do not shorten, but the muscle as a whole certainly does. Also, when the filaments slide together the tendon, which connects the muscle to the bone, stretches. When the filaments slide apart, the tendon slackens somewhat.

You can dance and improvise with ease while the muscle cells experience this sliding. This mind-set differs from the more traditional contractile approach. Compare the sliding to the idea of slippery, well-lubricated joints, and you enter a mindset that liberates the musculoskeletal system. Well-lubricated joints, created by the sliding of millions of filaments, support every movement.

Let's apply muscle sliding to specific muscles. If you place a hand on the upper arm, you touch the biceps and beneath it the brachialis muscle. These muscles are good models for using the image of sliding filaments. Through this exercise you will experience both ease of motion and increase in flexibility.

1. While standing, place the left hand on the biceps of the right arm.

2. Feel the muscle beneath the hand as you flex it by bending the elbow.

3. Now imagine the filaments of the muscles sliding together (figure 4.2a) as you bend the elbow and sliding apart (figure 4.2b) as you extend it.

4. Repeat this action a dozen times very slowly so you have time to clearly visualize the muscle action. Imagine you are in the muscle, and feel the sliding. You can support your imagery with your breathing.

5. Let both arms hang at the sides, and notice any differences in how each one feels.

6. Flex and bend both elbows and notice the feel of the muscle action. Bend both elbows maximally, and notice which side is more flexible. You may notice that the arm where you visualized the sliding of the filaments feels smoother, and the elbow on that side is more flexible.

7. Repeat the exercise with the other arm.

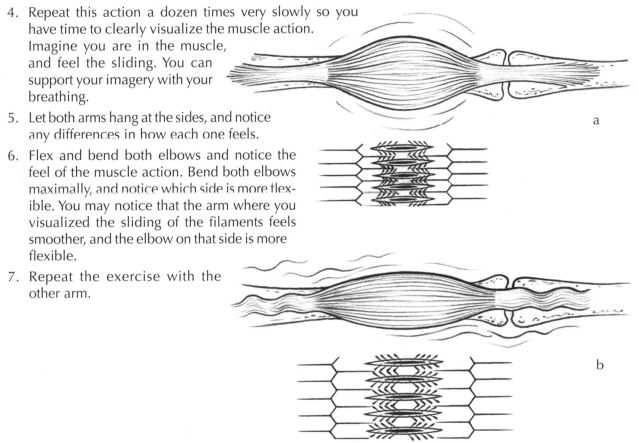

a

b

Figure 4.2, a and b   The elements of each muscle fiber do not shorten during contraction, but the fibers slide together like a boat pulling into a dock.

The following exercise leaves you with a feeling of openness in the chest and more flexibility in the shoulders. The pectoralis major muscle connects the upper arm with the clavicle, breastbone, and upper ribs. It can bring the arm forward powerfully as exemplified in boxing and karate. It also is active in lowering the arm against a resistance or in raising the body upward in push-ups. If this muscle is tight, the shoulders round forward. Muscle sliding is an effective way to release tension and increase flexibility in the pectoralis major and surrounding muscles.

1. Put the right hand on the left pectoralis major muscle on the inside of the left shoulder and the outside of the breastbone.
2. Raise the left arm horizontally in front of the body (figure a).
3. Move the arm to the back, and imagine the filaments sliding apart (figure b). For increased concentration, close the eyes.
4. Move the arm forward again and think of the filaments sliding together.
5. Allow breathing to support the action. As you inhale, move the arm backward, and as you exhale, move it forward again. Feel the sliding as slippery. For example, use the image of soap lather.
6. Move the arm forward and backward about a dozen times, then let the arms hang at the sides.
7. Notice any differences between the sides. The left shoulder may feel more to the side of the body, and the right more forward. Simply moving the right shoulder back to match the left shoulder will not feel comfortable. Stretch both arms out horizontally to the front. The left arm may feel longer than the right.
8. Move both arms horizontally to the back, and notice which side feels more flexible. If you move both arms the same distance, the side you did not image may feel relatively inflexible and tight. If you move both arms the same distance, the shoulder on the side you did not image may not feel comfortable at all. Touch and imagery can improve flexibility.

The pectoralis minor is also affected by this exercise. It connects the coracoid process of the shoulder blade with the front of the rib cage. Its action is to push the scapula downward. If you lower the elbow while bringing the arm in front of you during the previous exercise and imagine the shoulder blade dropping downward, you will emphasize the shortening action of the pectoralis minor. If you lift the elbow up again as you move the arm to the side, you will increase the length of the pectoralis minor.

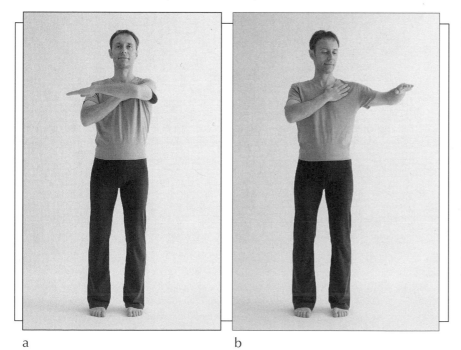

a   b

The coordination, flexibility, and alignment of the plié are key to dance, because the plié is involved in the initiation, transition, or final phase of almost every dance step. Although many muscles are involved in performing a plié, the bulk of the work is accomplished by the gluteals and the quadriceps muscles. As you move downward in a plié, these muscles act eccentrically to lower the body weight. By visualizing the sliding of the filaments in these muscles, you can increase the range, stability, and strength of the plié.

1. Perform a plié on one leg with the gesture leg in a coupé position at the ankle (working foot resting next to the ankle) on each side. Notice the ease and range of movement.

2. Stand on the right leg in a moderately turned-out position.

3. Visualize the gluteals and the quadriceps muscles. Notice the direction of the muscle fibers, and think about how they lengthen when you plié.

4. As you start to plié on the right leg, feel the synchronous lengthening of the right gluteals and the right quadriceps muscle. Feel the filaments sliding apart smoothly and continuously until you reach the bottom of the plié (see figure).

5. Without stopping, reverse the action and slowly move up again. If you have been habitually dropping into your plié, this movement will feel like hard work, a sign that you are now building a lot of strength. Visualize the pelvic crests on the top of the right and left sides of the pelvis becoming level.

6. Place the right hand on the right gluteals to help in visualizing the muscle action.

7. Repeat the plié eight times, and try to achieve maximum smoothness and continuity of action.

8. Once you have finished the exercise on the right side, compare the depth and ease of the plié in the right and left legs, then practice the exercise eight times with the left leg.

9. Practice lowering and raising the body in other positions as well, such as with the leg extended in second position.

10. Practice this visualization daily until you can create a natural smoothness in the lowering and lifting of the body weight on one leg.

IMPROVING TURN-OUT WITH TOUCH AND IMAGERY

Many dancers wish to improve their turn-out, and most can do so without strain if they learn to use the muscles' full potential. The following exercise uses a sponge image and the sliding filament image to increase turn-out for passé retiré and high leg extensions. The two-step procedure involves increasing circulation to the area and then imaging movement in the muscles. These two actions combined create a surprising increase in the hip joint's ROM.

1. With the left hand, hold on to a ballet barre or another stable, similar-height object. Shift your weight to the left leg, so the right leg is supported only by the ball of the foot.

2. Place the right thumb in front of the greater trochanter of the right leg. The other fingers of this hand reach around to the muscles behind and around the greater trochanter. These muscles are the gluteals and beneath them the deep external rotators of the leg.

3. Squeeze the muscles with the hand, and release your grip slowly, imagining the muscles melting.

4. Squeeze the muscles again. Slowly let go, and imagine the muscles as a sponge filling with warm water (see figure). Imagine the water spreading to all corners of the muscle, spreading it out and creating space.

5. Repeat the action of squeezing and letting go three more times with your preferred imagery of melting the muscle or warm water filling the sponge.

6. Leave the hand where it is, and bend the right knee. The ball of the right foot should stay on the floor with the heel lifted.

7. Visualize the muscles that move the leg to the side (abduction) and turn it out—the gluteus maximus and the deep rotators.

8. Turn the leg in by moving the knee to the front and toward the other leg. Visualize the muscles under the hand sliding apart.

9. Turn the leg out, and think of the muscles sliding together.

10. Repeat the movement and image six times.

11. Now it's time to savor the results of your efforts: Perform a passé développé with the right leg. Notice your range of turn-out and the flexibility in the hip joint.

12. Turn around and hold on to the barre with the other hand, and perform a passé with your left leg. Notice the difference in ease of motion and turn-out. Does the hip hike more on this side? Are the muscles working harder to achieve the position on the left?

13. Repeat the exercise on the other side. For more exercises to improve your turn-out, see chapter 9.

Most dancers want higher legs, but they do not know that straining to lift the legs higher is exactly what keeps them from getting there. In this exercise, you will explore the relationship between higher leg extensions and shoulder tension, organs, and touch. You will notice that you cannot gain full flexibility in the legs unless you release shoulder tension and get in touch with the inner space of the torso.

1. Perform a leg extension (développé) to the front and side with the right leg, and notice how high the leg goes and how free the hip joint feels.

2. Perform a grand battement or a high leg kick with the same leg to the front and side. Notice how free the leg feels and how high it goes. You may also try an arabesque to the back.

3. Place the left hand on the right shoulder and squeeze the trapezius muscle next to the neck.

4. Slowly let go of the muscle, and imagine it melting. Repeat the same action and image at another spot on the shoulder muscle (figure a).

5. Now imagine the trapezius as a sponge filled with water. Squeeze the sponge (shoulder muscle) to empty it. As you let go again and the sponge expands, feel warm water filling it, penetrating every bubble and space in the sponge.

6. Repeat the squeeze and release with the sponge image four times.

7. Drop the arms to the sides and shake the hands.

a

8. Now perform a développé and a battement with your right leg to the front and side, and notice any changes in ease of motion. Compare the feeling to the same movement with the left leg. Also perform an arabesque with each leg.

9. Place the left hand on the front of the body just below the ribs (at the liver) and the right hand at the back of the body at approximately the same level (near the right kidney) (figure b).

10. Send the breath into the kidneys, and imagine the kidneys relaxing.

11. Imagine the kidneys as warm water bottles. As you exhale, visualize the kidneys moving up, and as you inhale, visualize them moving down, following the motion of the diaphragm.

b

12. Remove the hands and shake them out. Notice the difference in feeling between the right and left sides of the body. Lift the right arm and then the left up over the head, and notice the difference in shoulder flexibility.

13. Perform a développé and a grande battement with the right leg to the front, side, and back, and compare the feeling to the performance of the left leg. You may notice more ease of motion or more elevation of the right leg.

14. Another intriguing comparison is the change in elasticity in the leg for jumping. Perform a few hops on the right leg and then on the left leg, and you may notice more bounce and less muscular effort on the right side.

15. Repeat the shoulder and kidney touch on other side of the body for balance.

4.10 ACHIEVING MORE RANGE

You can improve the range of movement in a joint by balancing the action of the flexors and extensors. Being more aware of the flexors than the extensors (or vice versa) in a specific joint results in overuse of some muscles and imbalance in the joint, a common cause of overuse injuries. This exercise balances the flexors and extensors of the hip joint.

1. Focus on the hip flexors and extensors. You do not need to be specific—just think of the muscles in front and in back of the hip joint. The supporting leg can be in a comfortable, slightly turned-out position as you swing the right leg forward or backward.

2. When you swing the leg forward, the muscles at the front of the hip shorten (i.e., the filaments slide together; figure a).

3. When you swing the leg backward, the muscles at the front of the hip lengthen (i.e., the filaments slide apart, figure b).

4. Focus on this event during several leg swings.

5. Now see whether you can swing the leg forward and backward while lengthening both the extensors and flexors at the appropriate moment. Image the filaments sliding apart.

6. As you keep swinging the leg, image the flexors and extensors shortening at the appropriate moment. Image the filaments sliding together.

7. Finish by imaging the filaments lengthening for a few more swings with the right leg.

8. Rest for a moment. Then swing the right leg as high as you comfortably can. Compare the action to the swing of the left leg:

   • Have you gained some range in the right hip joint?

   • Have you improved your balance if you use the right leg as the supporting leg?

   • Do you have more clarity and flow in the right leg in general?

9. Repeat the movement and imagery with the other leg.

a

b

Relaxing the Shoulders

Tension-free shoulders and neck muscles are important for dancers. They aid in ease of motion, a more aesthetic line, and increased stamina, and last but not least, they feel good. One of the most surprising results of releasing shoulder tension is increased flexibility in the legs.

Tension in the upper and lower body are related. The shoulder and hip joint mirror each other's flexibility. As long as you have tense shoulders, you will never achieve the full flexibility potential in the hip joints.

Some of these interactions are based on homology. The deltoid muscle of the shoulder, for example, is homologous, or related in function, to the gluteals of the pelvis. The gluteals extend and abduct the hip joint, while the deltoid powerfully abducts and contributes to extension of the shoulder joint. A constant level of chatter goes on between the nerve cells that control the muscles in the body. Much of this interchange happens unconsciously in the spinal cord and brain. In this way, a change in one area of the body is instantly communicated to other areas. Mechanical linkages also exist throughout the connective tissue, which is like a large net. If you make a knot in any corner of the net, the rest of the net will be tighter as well.

Tension-free alignment in the upper body allows the legs to develop full power. If the shoulder and neck are relaxed (not slumped!), the thrust of the legs is directed through the most efficient path, and a lower center of gravity improves balance. These benefits can only be appreciated once you have experienced them, at which point they may instantly boost your technique. Once you have released shoulder tension and increased flexibility, you can gain more strength, because muscles shorten and lengthen to a greater degree if the joints have greater range. This greater range, in turn, increases the training effect on the muscles.

Practice a dance step before and after each of the following exercises to notice any improvement in ease of movement. Do not be surprised if the movement seems more difficult initially. Remember: It takes time for the nervous system to adapt to new organization. Dancing with relaxed shoulders will reward you with more freedom and plenty of power to move.

4.11 GOODBYE, SHOULDER TENSION

This simple and effective exercise releases shoulder tension, particularly in the trapezius and levator scapulae muscles. In fish, the trapezius serves to elevate the gills. In humans, it still relates to breathing, but in a completely different sense: the more relaxed it is, the deeper the breathing.

The trapezius consists of a descending, a horizontal, and an ascending part (see figure). These parts need to have balanced action to allow for good placement of the scapula. The descending and ascending parts contract to rotate the scapula when the arm lifts above the horizontal plane. The levator scapulae attaches to the inner top corner of the scapula and connects the scapula to the cervical spine. You feel tightness of the levator scapulae on the top inner rim of the shoulder blade where the muscle is attached. The four thin muscle bellies and the vertebrae make the arrangement look like the rigging on a sailing clipper. If the shoulder is habitually lifted or slouched, this muscle and the descending trapezius are chronically shortened.

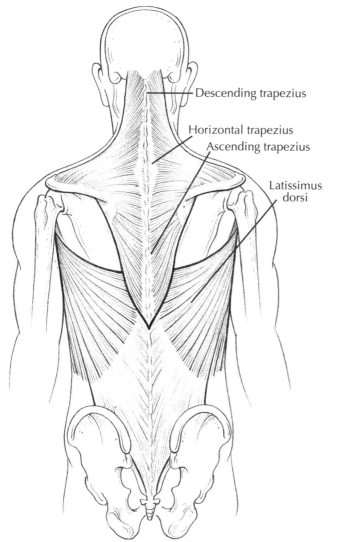

Descending trapezius

Horizontal trapezius
Ascending trapezius

Latissimus dorsi

1. Put the right hand on the left shoulder. Put the hand close to the neck so you are holding the trapezius muscle and the levator scapulae underneath.

2. Find a spot that feels tight, and press down on it with the middle three fingers. Imagine the fingers having the power to melt all tension in this area.

3. Lift the arm while still pressing down on this spot, and notice any changes in the muscle.

4. Lower the arm, and relax the fingers. Now find another spot on the muscle to press. Lift the arm again, and notice any changes in the muscles.

5. Repeat the action again with a third spot. This time, when you lift the arm, shake the hand and think of the wrist being very loose. The hand feels as if you are waving goodbye in a very limp fashion.

6. Slowly lower the arm, still shaking the hand.

7. Let go of the right shoulder, lower both arms, and shake out the hands. Rest the arms at the sides.

8. Stretch the arms out to the front to notice the difference in length. Do you just feel a difference, or is it also visible?

9. Lift both arms overhead. Which shoulder joint feels more flexible? Stretch the arms out to the sides (second position arms). Stretch the left arm out to match the right arm's length. Notice that creating length through tension does not feel comfortable.

10. With the arms still to the sides, swing the left, then the right leg to the front. Do you notice a difference in flexibility and ease of motion between the right and left hip joints?

From a muscular perspective, the shoulder blade is a very popular bone. No fewer than 17 muscles attach to it and allow it to move in three primary and two secondary directions. It anchors the movement of the arm in space and creates a base for movement for the torso when the hands are placed on the floor or holding on to a fixed object. The shoulder blade is shaped like a triangle with the inner border aligned with the spine. It is slightly concave toward the rib cage, so it is well adapted to the curvature of the upper rib cage. It has a ridge, called the spine of the scapula, and two further projections, the coracoid process to the front of the body and the acromion towering over the shoulder joint. The following exercise releases shoulder tension, creates more length in the spine, increases the mobility of the shoulder joint, and makes shoulder movements feel delicious.

1. Inhale while lifting the shoulders upward, and exhale while slowly lowering them. Visualize the filaments sliding in the trapezius muscle. As you lift the shoulders, the filaments slide together; as you lower them, they slide apart.

2. Repeat the lifting and lowering twice more, then move the shoulder blades in a variety of directions.

3. Imagine the shoulder blade sliding on the back, floating on a cushion of air. As you inhale, imagine the depth of this cushion increasing (figure a).

4. Now imagine the acromion to be soft and floppy like a bunny's ear. See the shoulder blade's inner structure—airy, spongy bone. Imagine the breath filling the spaces within this bone, making the shoulder blade light and fluffy like foam in a bubble bath.

5. Lift the shoulder blades as you inhale, and lower them as you exhale. Imagine them dropping all the way to the floor.

6. Lift the arms over the head, imagining the shoulder blades dropping downward. Release all tension down the back and out the tail (figure b).

7. Once your shoulder blades are released, you may notice that it is easier to feel the movement of the upper spine and that the spine feels lengthened.

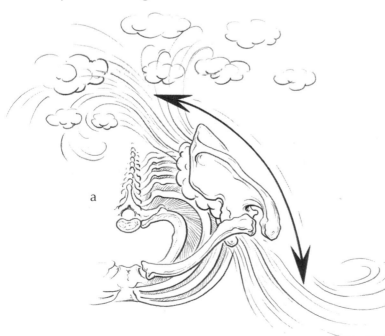

a

b

This exercise provides an effective way to release shoulder tension with a partner. The aim is to connect the sense of released shoulders to common dance movements. Perform this exercise before a class or conditioning routine to increase your freedom of movement in all limbs.

1. Have a partner perform a plié in second position. Watch how deep she can go and notice her ease of motion. Ask her how smooth the action feels.
2. Stand behind your partner, hold the upper arms, and lift the shoulders by pushing up against the arms (figure *a*).
3. Slowly lower the shoulders, keeping the action regular and smooth (figure *b*).
4. Repeat the lifting and lowering two more times. You may notice that your partner wants to do the movement on her own and can't really let go of her shoulders and entrust her weight into your hands. Let her know that it is all right to drop the shoulders.
5. Lift your partner's shoulders again and perform a plié together with her as you slowly lower her shoulders (figures *c* and *d*).

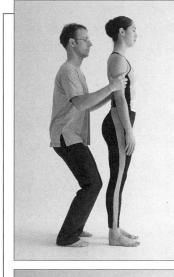

6. Move back up from the plié together with your partner, and repeat the action two more times.
7. Let your partner perform the action unassisted. Rather than actually lifting and lowering the shoulders, she images the dropping of the shoulders as she moves downward.
8. Notice the depth, ease, and feel of the plié:
   - Does your partner have more range? How do the hip joints feel? Has turn-out increased?
   - Does the action look smoother?
   - Ask your partner how the plié feels. Also, notice changes in the alignment of the back and pelvis.
9. Switch roles with your partner and repeat the exercise.

a

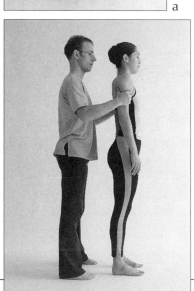

b

c

d

The following exercise stretches, strengthens, and releases tension in most of the shoulder muscles. You may want to wear a T-shirt while doing this exercise, because the band is wrapped around the shoulder. Once you have the basic setup, be creative and try your own movement variations.

1. Select a 3-yard loop of red or green Thera-Band. Place the right foot on the loose ends to firmly hold the band against the ground. Now loop the other end around the left shoulder. One length of band will be stretched along the front, and the other length will be stretched along the back of the body. You should feel a moderate amount of pull on the left shoulder.

2. Circle the left shoulder by lifting it up and moving it to the front, down, and back again (figure a). Repeat this motion four times, imagining a well-lubricated shoulder joint as you do it.

3. Circle the left shoulder to the back four times.

4. Lift the left shoulder up to the head, and move the head toward the shoulder (figure b).

5. Slowly lower the shoulder, and move the head away from the band. Image the sliding apart of the trapezius and levator filaments.

6. Repeat the lifting and lowering three times.

7. Now remove the band and notice the freedom in the left shoulder movement. Compare arm gestures, perform a port de bras, and notice the difference in the movement of the shoulder blade between the right and left sides.

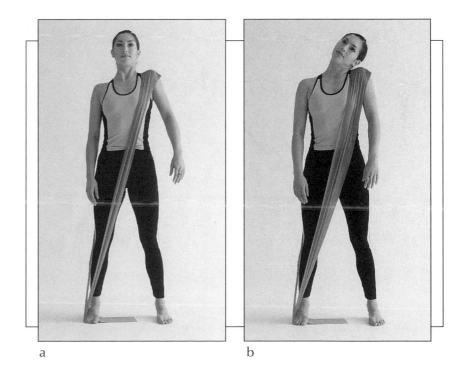

a   b

Flexible Bones, Flexible Joints

Joints are where two bones meet and are able to move relative to each other in a manner determined by the structure of the joint and the surrounding ligaments. A classic joint includes the bony surfaces covered by hyaline cartilage, a joint capsule, and various stabilizing ligaments. The cartilage, together with joint fluid called synovia, allows for a practically friction-free environment. Thinking of something slippery will help you image synovia. Through synovia you can feel gliding within all the body's joints.

An imbalance in muscles can often be corrected by balancing the bones. You can approach the experience of joints directly through movement, but if you lack a felt experience for the location and movement of a specific joint, it may be helpful to start with imagery or touch.

4.15   LUBRICATED JOINTS

By moving the hand and arm vigorously, you stimulate the thousands of sensory organs for tension, pressure, length, and vibration in the arm joints, muscles, and skin, providing the brain with a clear map of the movement potential in the arm and paving the way to more flexible and directed action.

1. Wiggle the fingers, then move the wrist and all the joints of one hand. Think of many small joints in the hand moving without effort, slippery surfaces gliding over each other in a frictionless world.

2. Extend the movement to the forearm and elbow. Feel wigglishly liberated, with endless movement possibilities as you start moving the upper arm and shoulder. Dwell on the notion of soap that is all lathered up and so slippery that it pops out of the hand at the slightest squeeze. Or imagine the sensation of massage oil being rubbed on the skin.

3. After a minute or two, rest both arms at the sides and see whether you notice a difference between them.

4. Move both arms and lift them up above the head to see whether one shoulder and arm feels more flexible and alive.

Bones encompass many different sensations, depending on where you focus. For one, they are varied in shape: flat and thin, long and short, round and square. In the following exercise you will dive into the inner world of the bone. What you discover can greatly enhance your freedom of movement.

Because bone is constantly being built and reabsorbed by bone cells (called osteoblasts and osteoclasts), it is held in a delicate balance between accumulation and resorption. Like a house that has one crew building it while another crew is taking it down, the bone is full of dynamic life. Neither team should gain the advantage, or the bone will slowly be destroyed, as is the case in osteoporosis and osteoarthrits.

1. To imagine the layers of a bone, find a partner and hold his lower arm or lower leg bone.

2. Feel the skin of the bone, the periosteum. It is the slippery stocking of the bone, continuous throughout the body. The joint capsule is really a denser continuation of the periosteum. Skate your fingertips over the periosteum. It may feel like an ice rink without the coldness.

3. We often think of bone as the compact part below the periosteum. Think of bone, and you may feel something hard and tubular on your inner kinesthetic screen. This layer below the periosteum is truly the hard stuff of the bone, the part that supports weight and levers the body through space. If you dive deeper into the bone, you enter the cathedralic realm of the trabeculae.

4. The trabeculae, literally "little beams of wood," are responsible for distributing the forces through the bone in a multitude of directions. Wherever forces travel through bone in the mind's eye, trabeculae accumulate to support that routing. The arrangement of the struts and beams of the Eiffel Tower in Paris provides a good picture of the arrangement of the trabeculae. The routing of the trabeculae is even continued across the joint space into the next bone. Imagine forces traveling as waves moving through the bone and the joints, and create a sense of communication and linkage among all the bones of the body.

5. Take a moment to kinesthetically delve into the spaces between the trabeculae to feel them around you, magnified to the size of a forest.

6. You might feel the trabeculae as hard and unchangeable rock, but through imagery and touch, you can give them a new identity as a rubbery, flexible underpinning for the cortical bone.

7. Discover not only the compression but also the tensile (pull) aspect of the trabeculae. Imagine flexibility residing in the cellular structure, within the struts and pulls and myriad interweavings of minute proteins.

8. Ask your partner to move both arms simultaneously, and notice the difference in flexibility and ease of motion.

9. Switch roles with your partner and repeat the exercise.

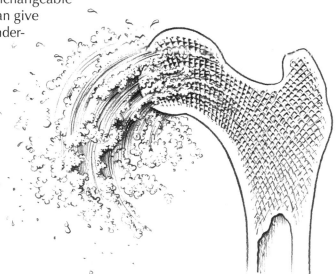

Because this book does not have enough space to cover the all the bones and joints in the human body, I have picked one facial bone for further exploration. Usually you would not pay attention to the way bones in this area pertain to dance technique. For further information on bones and joints, see *Dynamic Alignment Through Imagery* (Franklin 1996b).

1. The ethmoid bone is tucked inside the skull. Visualize it behind the nose and under the forehead. It weighs only 1.5 grams and has been likened to a miniature crystal palace.

2. When you breathe through the nose, air passes along the ethmoid. Tiny nerve endings tucked into the ethmoid pick up scents and relay them to the brain. Imagine the air caressing the ethmoid behind the nose.

3. Focus on the ethmoid to create a more erect spine, and to create more freedom in the neck by helping to center the head. It is a delicate and lightly built bone. Imagine it floating up like a kite in the wind. This floating improves the flexibility of the shoulder and hip joints by creating more space in the junction between the skull and the top of the spine. Focusing on the ethmoid will give you a sense of centeredness in the head and clarity about the movement you are about to perform.

It may seem odd that the ethmoid relates to a feeling of lift in the spine, but in animals the sense of smell is an alarm system that elevates the head so the eyes can have a larger overview of the surrounding area. Because the nerve endings relating to the sense of smell are located in the ethmoid, this elevation is closely related to this bone. In a dangerous situation, an animal also braces itself by lowering its center of gravity and ensuring that its balance allows it to move in any direction necessary. An elongated spine and a low center of gravity are also helpful in dance technique, allowing for quickened coordination and improved balance.

Creating Fluid Neck Mobility

Many dancers hold tension in the neck, tongue, and jaw. Once you release the neck, you find that the head is more mobile and aligned and that you have more power to move through the pelvis and legs. I have found that dancers who release tension in the neck can leap and turn better.

A dancer may be strong from the point of view of muscular power when measured in an individual joint, but when it comes to using this power within the whole body movement, power is lost from lack of coordination. For example, two cars may have the same power and therefore should achieve the same speed, but if one car's brakes are stuck, that car has to first overcome this resistance before it can transfer power to forward motion. Tension in the neck is especially deleterious to coordinated movement, because the neck is where the body (with the help of muscle spindles) measures the relationship between the head and the rest of the body. If the neck is tight, the body's overall coordination is disrupted.

Small muscles (suboccipitals) connect the base of the skull to the top of the spine. These muscles are important for fine-tuning the position of the head relative to the spine. If they are tight, they restrict the movement of the head, causing the whole spine to be less flexible. Many ballet dancers carry tension in this area, because they have been trained to look slightly upward for aesthetic reasons. If these muscles have the opportunity to lengthen in other ways, looking slightly upward is not a problem.

1. Perform a few movements, such as a plié, and if you are sufficiently warmed up, perform a leg extension, a few battements in any direction, and a pas de bourré. Pirouettes in parallel or turned out may also be interesting to compare. By performing these movements at the beginning of the exercise, you will be able to more distinctly appreciate its results.

2. Place the middle fingers of both hands on the back of the skull, and slide them downward until you feel the top of the neck. Place the fingers at the very top of the neck, just under the skull (figure a).

3. Move the fingers circularly, starting up and out to the side (figure b). After performing several circles, rest the fingers for a moment.

4. Tilt the head back slightly, and let the fingers sink deeper into the muscles at the back of the neck. Imagine sinking the fingers into a bowl of pudding. With the head slightly back and the fingers deeper than before, repeat the circling action. Keep breathing as you do this.

5. Finish by nodding the head front and back and thinking of the muscle filaments sliding apart and together. They slide apart as you nod forward and together as you nod back.

6. Shake the hands, drop them at the sides, and notice how the neck and shoulders feel.

7. Repeat the actions you practiced before you started the exercise, and notice any changes. If this exercise makes you feel dizzy, it may be because you have been holding a lot of tension in the area that is now released. Sit down for a moment, and take a few deep breaths to recuperate.

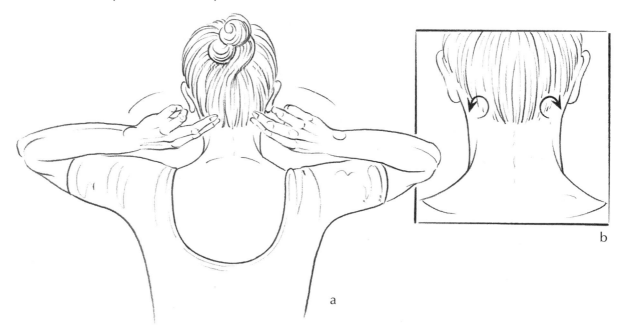

a

b

4.19 CURTAINS DROP

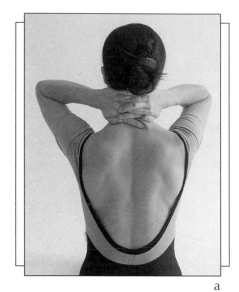

a

You have already used the neck touch for some earlier exercises. Now you will combine neck imagery with shoulder imagery for a superior tension release. As always, notice the effect on your alignment and state of mind. Releasing tension in the neck and shoulders is always helpful when you are nervous before a performance or audition.

1. Place the hands on the neck with the fingers interlaced (figure *a*).
2. Take a moment to send breath into the neck.
3. Think of the many layers of muscles in the neck relaxing one after another, like a series of curtains dropping. Feel each neck muscle melt as you imagine each curtain dropping, releasing.
4. When the mind's eye arrives at the bony spine, imagine the muscles letting go of any excess hold on the bones.
5. Send several deep breaths through all the layers, all the way to the cervical vertebrae. Move the head gently in various directions as you conjure this image.
6. Slowly remove the hands and place them in the armpits (figure *b*).
7. Again, start with breathing into the area. Send the breath deep into the armpits. Let the breath expand outward and create more space in the armpits (figure *c*).
8. Imagine that the breath can dig the tension out of the armpits, and feel that tension dropping out of them.
9. Slowly remove the hands.
10. Notice the new sense of alignment and relaxation.

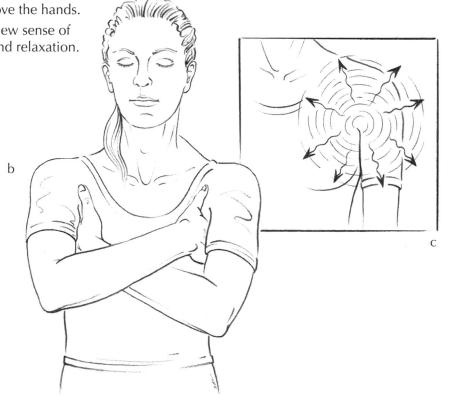

b

c

The large ligamentum nuchae (neck ligament) runs from the bottom of the back of the skull to the top vertebrae of the thoracic spine. It also attaches to the cervical spinous processes and looks like a flag placed at the back of the neck. Many muscles attach to this flag, which you will now try to release with the help of a towel and imagery.

1. Take a towel in both hands and place it across the back of the neck (figure *a*).
2. Move the towel back and forth, and imagine the muscles of the neck releasing all tension into it.
3. Image the ligamentum nuchae fluttering like a flag in the wind (figure *b*). As you move the towel it simulates the wind blowing the ligament.
4. Move the towel as long as it feels comfortable, and enjoy the newfound ease in the neck.

Tension in the hands translates to tension in the shoulders and neck, and vice versa. The following image frees up the hands through the bones in the wrist (the carpals).

1. Move the arms and hands through a variety of gestures. For example, lift the arms over the head, down to the side, and back to a resting position next to the torso. Swing them forward and backward or to the side, noticing the ease of motion in the shoulders.
2. Imagine the carpals are made of cork and floating in water (figure *a*). Move the hands and arms with this image.
3. Now move the hands with the image of the carpal bones within the wrist suspended from above by puppet strings (figure *b*).
4. Move the arms over the head again, to the side, forward, and backward using the cork or puppet string imagery.
5. Using this imagery, perform some familiar arm gestures from dance class.

Rolling Balls for Relaxation

Young Soon Kim, director of White Wave Dance Company in New York, never goes anywhere without rolling balls. She looks for them before she packs her dance clothes. Each ball is at least slightly larger than a tennis ball and is made of rubber (or plastic) filled with air to make it quite resilient. (See the references and resources list on page 234 for information where you can find these balls.) I first encountered the use of balls as a means to release tension and improve alignment at the studio of Elaine Summers in New York. Initially I did not recognize that using the balls necessarily had any relationship to enhancing dance technique. But after trying some of the exercises, I was astonished by their positive effect on my technique. The exercises improved my alignment and flexibility, and they freed me of tension spots that were inhibiting my technique. (See also chapter 3, pages 44-49.)

What follows is my personal approach, developed over the last 15 years, to using rolling balls to help dancers experience more freedom of movement. I sum up ball rolling in three phrases: *Search, Discover, and Let Go* (of tension). You may place the ball under various areas of the body to serve as a ball bearing between your body and the floor. This enables you to move very slowly compressing and releasing muscles and, depending on the size of the ball, discovering tension points and melting them with the balls themselves, imagery, and breathing.

One of the reasons ball rolling is so effective is that you move in a different pattern on them than you usually do when standing up, resulting in a kind of cross-training effect, where you relieve the muscles and joints of the usual stresses and activate them in fresh, innovative ways. The nervous system gets a chance to try out new pathways for movement control, and gravity tugs on the body at different angles. Again, to make the most of your ball rolling, be sure to apply to dance your newfound freedom in your muscles and joints without too much delay. This way the nervous system can record your improved range and ease of movement.

When using the rolling balls, follow these guidelines:

- Never roll the ball under an acute injury or an area of acute pain. It is, however, helpful to roll the balls under areas that have scar tissue from earlier injuries to create more flexibility and elasticity. If you feel a good pain that is merely the result of muscle tension, using balls is advisable.

- Move very slowly and smoothly. By moving the body too fast, you tend to simply jump over tension spots instead of smoothing them out.

- Keep breathing freely, especially if you discover a tension spot.

- Be creative about how you initiate movement.

- Do not use tennis balls for ball rolling. On many surfaces the tennis balls will slide rather than roll, making it difficult to move them to a new position without using the hands. Also, the tennis balls are harder and smaller and may cause too much pain when pressing into a tension spot, making it difficult for you to remain in a relaxed state for releasing tension.

- Once you have practiced sufficiently with a softer ball, you may then graduate to a harder, smaller ball.

- Do not use rolling balls if you have acute sciatica.

The gluteals are often full of tension points that you do not notice until you use rolling balls. If you are doing this exercise for the first time, go very slowly and spend a maximum of five minutes with the balls under the pelvis. The following exercise releases tension in the lower back and gluteals, leading to gains in hip flexibility.

1. Place two rolling balls under the buttocks. Space the balls wide enough so you feel comfortably supported. Figure a shows a variation of the exercise that improves balance and engages the hamstring by placing two balls under the feet.

2. The position of the balls is variable. You may place them under the lower portion of the gluteus maximus to the inside of the greater trochanters (figure b). Here you will be able to release tension in the deep rotators and the muscles related to the sciatic nerve, which can be seen as dotted lines in the illustration.

a

3. Move the pelvis very slowly. Try to move in all spatial directions.

4. Imagine the pelvis as a boat rocking on slow-motion waves. The balls are the waves, and the movement of the pelvis is the result of the movement of the waves.

5. When you encounter a tension spot, imagine it melting away. Think of a cube of sugar dissolving in tea, and transfer that idea of dissolving to the tension points.

6. You may also think of the breath as a powerful agent for dissolving tension. Breathe into the knots, and imagine the breath going to the center of the knot, dissolving it from inside out. Let the tension point dissolve outward from the center and all residue vanish into the floor, away from the body.

7. After five minutes remove the balls and notice the sensation in the lower back.

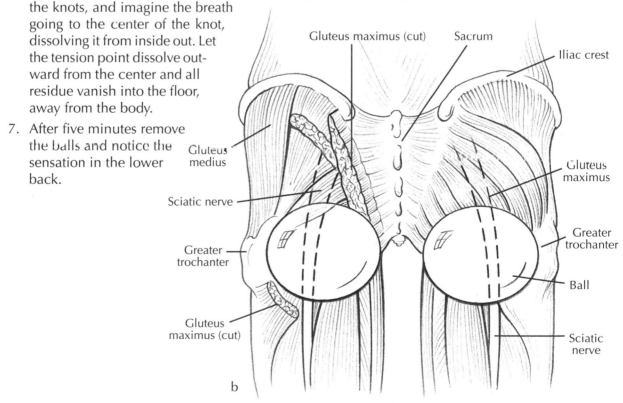

b

Rolling balls are effective for releasing shoulder tension. This exercise affects many muscles of the shoulder girdle and arm, such as the triceps and the muscles that attach to the shoulder blade. If performed creatively, it can be astonishingly effective in releasing shoulder and neck tension and increasing the range of movement in the arms.

1. Lie supine. Place one or two balls under an arm. You should be able to move the arm and shoulder blade in a variety of directions. Place a rolled towel or a ball under your head for comfort.

2. Stretch the arm away from the torso, and pull it back in. Now experiment with a variety of movements: Rotate the arm in and out, and move the shoulder blade up and down. Be creative and move slowly. You may also choose to move the head (figure a).

a

3. When you rotate the arm outward visualize the subscapularis and pectoralis major releasing into length (figure b).

4. Once you have explored this feeling for a few minutes, move the ball closer in and place it under the outer edge of the shoulder blade. Plenty of muscles here can benefit from being released (teres major and minor, infraspinatus), but if it feels too painful, move the ball back out to a position under the upper or lower arm.

4. After a few more minutes, remove the ball, and compare the feeling between the shoulders. You may feel that the shoulder blade on the side you practiced is much lower and melts into the floor.

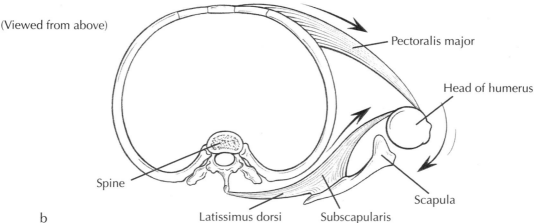

(Viewed from above)

Pectoralis major

Head of humerus

Scapula

Spine

Latissimus dorsi

Subscapularis

b

This exercise is excellent for releasing tension in the calf muscles. Do it after a strenuous rehearsal, class, or performance to reduce stiffness that may be experienced the following day.

1. Sit down and stretch the legs out in front of you. Place a rolling ball under each calf (see figure).

2. Move the feet in a variety of ways: Flex and extend the ankle, circle the ankle, wiggle the toes, and flex and extend the toes.

3. Rest for a moment, and imagine the calf muscles melting down over the balls.

4. Reposition the balls further up or further down on the calf, and repeat the foot movements in this position.

5. Bounce the calves gently on the balls, keeping the feet floppy and loose. Change the position of the balls several times until you have worked the whole length of the calves.

This exercise is recuperative. It relaxes the spine, the whole body, and the mind while creating better alignment. The effect is like a vacation at the beach. The spinal nerves are relieved of tension, benefiting the organs.

1. Place three medium-sized balls in a line.

2. Position the back on the balls so you can feel supported under the head, back, and pelvis.

3. Rest, or, if you choose, perform small, wiggly movements.

4. Remain on the balls for as long as it feels rewarding.

5. Roll off the balls sideways, and notice the ease of your alignment in the supine and standing positions.

Creating Flexibility Through the Organs

One of the last things we think about when we are trying to improve flexibility is our organs. But as you'll discover, they should be included in your repertoire of flexibility building methods. Consider this: If your organs were immobile, it would be impossible to move the spine. For example, the liver has to move forward, over, and down over the stomach if you flex the spine. Not only are the movement of the organs intrinsically connected to the movement of the joints and muscles, but often what we experience as a restriction in movement in the muscles or joints is organic in nature.

Organs have a variety of movement possibilities. They can move relative to each other or relative to adjacent bony, muscular, or connective tissue structures. Organs are surrounded by a fluid that makes these movements easier and smoother. The fluid can be compared in its function to the synovial fluid within the joints. The goal of the following exercises is to discover how much easier it is to improve your flexibility once you become aware of the organs.

4.26   FLEXIBLE SPINE WITH THE HEART AND LUNG

Organs form soft joints with each other. The left lung and heart, for example, form an organic ball-and-socket joint (figure a). The abilities of the heart to move within the lungs and to move within its own container, the pericardial sac, are important for its healthy functioning.

a

b

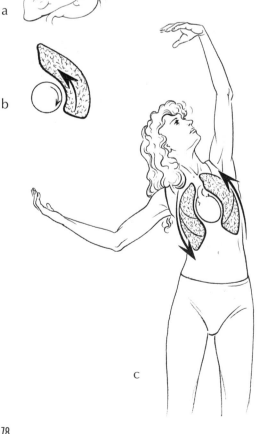

c

1. Visualize the left lung creating a jointlike socket around the heart. The heart is the ball of the joint (figure b).

2. Now lift the left arm over the head, and slowly bend the spine and arm to the right.

3. Visualize the left lung (the socket) sliding up over the heart (figure c). The right lung slides down the heart. Move back to the starting position, and imagine the left lung sliding down along the heart and the right lung sliding up along the heart.

4. Repeat the sidebend with the sliding imagery several times until you can clearly visualize the movement.

5. Lower the arm, and notice how the two sides of the body feel.

6. Stretch both arms to the front, and see whether you feel a difference in length. Bend the spine to the left and right, and notice any differences in flexibility and ease of motion in the spine.

7. Now visualize the heart moving counter to the lung. If the lung rotates to the right, the heart rotates to the left, relatively speaking. If the lung rotates to the left, visualize the heart rotating to the right.

The liver is the largest gland of the body and serves an important role in detoxifying the system. It is very heavy, weighing about 1.5 kg, and its movement has a considerable effect on alignment and flexibility. It lies under the diaphragm and is bordered by the rib cage on the right and the stomach on the left. The right kidney is located behind the liver, and the large intestine is below it. Most of the liver resides on the right side of the body, but the left lobe, a smaller section, overlays the stomach on the left side of the body.

The liver forms an organic ball-and-socket joint with both the diaphragm and the stomach. The diaphragm plays the role of the socket relative to the liver, and the stomach takes on the role of a ball relative to the liver. If you feel as if you are getting warm during this exercise, it may be because the temperature of the liver is a bit higher than the average temperature of the body. This exercise is particularly ideal for a winter warm-up.

1. Place the right hand on the lower ribs on the back right side of the body. Place the left hand on the lower front right ribs (figure a). You are now touching most of the liver, which is halfway covered by the rib cage.

2. In a comfortable standing position, bend the middle (thoracic) part of the spine, and visualize the lung and diaphragm sliding forward and down over the liver.

3. Lift up the spine again, and think of the diaphragm sliding up over the liver (figure b).

4. Repeat this action several times, then slide the diaphragm and lungs sideways to the right over the liver and up to the left over the liver.

5. After repeating this movement several times, visualize the joint between the liver and the stomach. Bend forward, and slide the liver over the stomach. Straighten the spine, and slide the liver back up.

6. Repeat the action several times, then move the liver in any way you like. It can move forward, backward, or sideways, or it can turn in any way. See the liver as a popular organ dancing within the many surrounding organs—lungs, diaphragm, stomach, kidneys, and intestine. The liver slides with ease within all these surrounding structures.

7. Now remove the hands, and perform the following tests:
   - Lift both arms overhead, and move them to the back. Which side feels more flexible?
   - Lift the right, then the left leg. Which hip joint feels more flexible and smoother in its action?
   - Balance on the right and left leg alternately.
   - Perform a side extension and an arabesque with the right, then your left leg, and compare the height and ease of elevation of the legs.

8. The organs that take up the space of the liver on the left side of the body are the spleen, pancreas, and stomach. Place the left hand on the back left side of the lower rib cage and the right hand on front left side of the lower rib cage.

9. Bend the spine forward, back, and to each side, and imagine the spleen moving up and the stomach down. Extend the spine, and imagine the stomach moving up and the spleen down.

10. Repeat this seesaw action several times while visualizing the organs.

11. Perform a little dance with the organs on the left side of the body.

12. Remove the hands, and notice your spinal alignment, flexibility, and release in shoulder tension.

a

The large intestine affects hip flexibility and the pelvic alignment. The large intestine is madup of several parts that form a kind of rectangular bridge. The ascending colon lies on the right side of the body, the descending colon on the left, and the horizontal colon spans the area between the lower ribs on the left and right rib cage. The cecum is the area where the small intestine enters the large intestine, and the sigmoid is the loop located in the left pelvic half. The rectum is the final segment of the large intestine (figure a). The large intestine responds to inhalation by being slightly stretched between the widening rib cage.

1. Touch the area between the right pelvic crest and the belly button. This is the general location of the sigmoid colon.

2. Flex the right leg at the hip joint, and imagine the sigmoid colon resting down into the pelvic bowl. Don't push the organ forward as you lift your thigh, but imagine the organ dropping down and back, assisted by the gentle push of the hands (figures a and b).

4. Repeat the flexion five times, continuously visualizing the sigmoid colon resting down.

5. Take a moment to compare the hip flexibility on the right and left sides of the body, then repeat steps 1 through 4 on the left side. Take special notice of the flatness of the belly. You may discover that the abdominal muscles feel more toned on the area you have been touching. Also, the pelvic half on the sigmoid colon side will feel more effortlessly lifted.

6. Now perform plié in second position, and visualize the large intestine resting down into the inner surfaces of thc iliac wings (figure c). Imagine the organs being carried by the smooth, broad surfaces of the iliac wings. Imagine the organs increasing flexibility by informing the hip about warmth and softness. You may find that your plié is deeper and easier. This result is also because of the relationship between the rectum and pelvic floor. Tension in the rectum transfers to the pelvic floor, which keeps the hip bones from making the necessary adjustments for a flexible plié.

7. Perform a leg extension to second position while maintaining a feeling of the sigmoid on the left and the cecum on the right dropping down into the pelvis as the leg extends. This movement helps create more flexion in the hip socket while maintaining pelvic alignment.

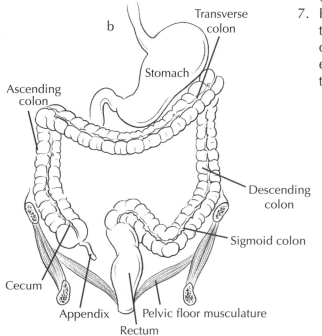

b

Transverse colon

Stomach

Ascending colon

Descending colon

Sigmoid colon

Cecum

Appendix

Pelvic floor musculature

Rectum

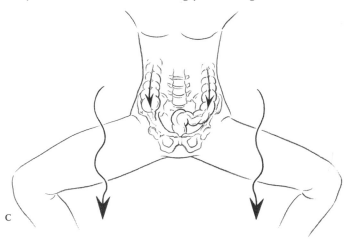

c

The kidneys are organs of blood filtration and fluid regulation located at the back of the body wall under the diaphragm. They are halfway covered by the ribs (see figure). Each kidney is connected to the bladder by a long tube called the ureter. Touching and moving the kidneys is helpful for releasing lower back tension and for increasing the flexibility of the spine, especially for rotations. Breathing and kidneys are related. When you inhale, the kidneys move down an inch or two with the diaphragm; when you exhale, they move up again. Being aware of the movement of the kidneys and their placement on the left and right sides of the spine can be helpful for turning. It may sound odd to feel your kidneys, but try it out and learn by experience. The following exercise improves balance and releases shoulder tension.

1. Rotate the upper body to the left and right.
2. Rub the hands together for a minute to create warmth, then hold the hands 3 to 4 inches apart, breathing into the space between the hands.
3. After a minute or two, place both hands on the back at the level of the kidneys.
4. Imagine the kidneys being bathed in the warmth of the hands. Send the breath into the kidneys, and imagine them expanding and contracting in rhythm with the breath.
5. As you inhale, feel the kidneys moving downward; and as you exhale, feel them moving upward.
6. Remove the hands, and notice your alignment. Bend the spine to the right and left, rotate the spine to the right and left, and note any increase in ease of motion.

Stretching for Flexibility

Stretching is the most common method for improving flexibility. At this point you have discovered other ways to improve flexibility: by releasing tension, moving the organs, using rolling balls, and imaging. But these methods do not make stretching obsolete; stretching can still be one part of your complete flexibility program. Because extensive literature on stretching is available, this section emphasizes only how to improve and retain the effects of stretching through awareness and imagery.

If performed correctly, stretching releases muscular tension, increases the temperature of the muscles to make them more fluid and flexible, releases toxins from the muscles, gives greater elasticity to the muscles and joints, and improves strength by increasing the mechanical advantage you can generate with the limbs. Stretching can prevent injury and assist in rehabilitation after an injury. Stretching may also just feel good and be an intuitive method to increase focus and concentration for dance. It can teach you a lot about joint and muscle function.

Stretching may also reinforce what you do not want—a sense of restriction. When you go into a deep stretch, you are traditionally instructed to go to the *edge* of the stretch (or even pain). Once you feel a stretch in the muscles, the sensory organs send instructions to the muscle fibers to contract to keep the muscle from overstretching.

This contraction is the opposite of what you want to achieve. Breathing and relaxation techniques may alleviate it, but not entirely. Because flexibility relates to the way you experience the body, you should avoid sensations that reinforce a sense of restriction and tightness, locking the pattern of tightness into the nervous system and confirming the fears that initially led you to stretch. In this instance it may be better to achieve flexibility through exercise strategies involving movement, touch, and imagery.

In most cases it is easier for the dancer to associate newfound flexibility with the movements he is actually doing. If the dancer wants to achieve a higher extension, he can learn to increase height by providing the muscles and joints with the necessary alignment, touch, and imagery information. The main question to ask yourself before stretching is: *Does it help me move better?* This depends on whether you are able to transfer the stretching's gains into a whole-body movement sensation.

Using imagery can help improve a stretch by increasing your concentration and by relaxing and deepening the breath. It can also help you clarify the location of the stretch and focus on specific muscles, organs, or joints while increasing whole-body involvement. The following list describes several types of images that are suitable for stretching practice.

- Feel the muscle as crystalized honey becoming fluid again after softening in warm water. This image is similar to what actually goes on in the muscle. Concentrate on the process of softening, not just on the muscle being fluid.

- Watch the area you are stretching melt like ice cream, butter, or wax that has been placed in the sunshine. Focus on the area where you feel the most tightness and see it melt, whether or not this is the target area for the stretch. This tight point may then shift to another spot. Keep following it with the mind's eye. Do not let it escape. Melt it down.

- Gently knead the muscle, like dough, making it more flexible and elastic.

- Imagine being able to breathe in and out through the muscle, as if the muscle cells were tiny lungs. Imagine the breath spreading between all tissues, creating more space within them.

- Direct the breath to the points that feel tightest. Imagine the breath loosening the areas like air bubbling up in a Jacuzzi bath.

- Breathe into the spaces between the small bones such as carpals and tarsals, and the joints between ribs and thoracic spine.

- If you notice a specific point of tension, imagine this point to be a ball of sand; push on the ball and watch it crumble.

- Imagine water (or your favorite liquid) flowing over the surface of the bones beneath the muscles, soothing and opening the muscles.

- Imagine a brush moving along the muscle's line of action from the origin to its insertion on the bone or from its insertion to the origin (depending on the location and purpose of the stretch). Watch the brush disentangle the fibers and loosen all knots. You may also watch two brushes start at the center of the muscle belly and move away from each other in opposite directions.

- Imagine that each individual fiber glitters like a silver strand in the sun. Bring the reflecting light between the fibers. Let the fibers reflect light off of each other.

- Visualize tight strands of muscle stretching like taffy or gum.

chapter 5

Aligned Movement for Improved Technique

I am watching a dance class at a Broadway studio in New York City. "Alignment and movement efficiency are intertwined," says Israeli-born ballet teacher and choreographer Zvi Gotheiner. "If your body is not aligned, your tension level increases." He goes on, "Tension makes technique difficult." His students listen, but changes come slowly, because many imbalances need correcting. "Align your head over your pelvis, shoulders neither forward nor back, pelvis balanced, and the feet and knees aligned with the hip joint."

Why are these changes so difficult to translate from words into action? One reason is that once the body has gotten used to holding the increased tension level, which is the hallmark of incorrect alignment, it feels normal to you. Changes, even if they are beneficial from a biomechanical standpoint, may feel uncomfortable in the beginning.

I continue watching the class and notice each dancer's body image as they move across the floor. This overall sense of each dancer's body has been formed by years of input by teachers, other dancers, as well as their own fears and aspirations dancing around in their heads.

Some dancers make the alignment corrections called for, others overcompensate, and others simply increase their tension level in an effort to change. Some are able to embody corrections and change their posture by noticing their imbalances and implementing a new sense of alignment, and others urgently need guidance. Their current body image gets in the way of technical progress. It is going to take some time for the bodies to try, accept, and implement new strategies of sensing, initiating, and experiencing movement.

But the students in this class may be the lucky few. Their teacher is experienced and knows how to help them achieve better alignment. He sees the potential of each student and provides the necessary kinesthetic information to help each make the changes to improve their dance performance.

Releasing Tension for Dynamic Alignment

Some dancers tense the muscles of their neck and shoulders with every movement, even a simple gesture of the leg. Since they are not well aligned, they increase the effort needed to achieve their movement initiation. They may think that they are developing power, when in reality they are developing what hinders their power—exerting extra effort in muscles where it is not needed for the movement they are doing. This inefficiency is not only deleterious to technique but can also predispose a dancer to injury and to early deterioration of joints, muscles, and soft tissues. Many dancers' strategy to create stability is based on fixing muscles and bones in set positions, which works reasonably well when movement is minimal but does not work for dance requiring stability during expansive movement gestures.

Biomechanically speaking, the aim of dance training is to transfer the body weight efficiently, with a minimum of distortion, tension, and energy use. This technical definition, however, should not make you forget that dance is an art form and not simply an exercise technique.

According to Roger Tully, a London teacher of classical dance who was taught in the Mariinsky tradition, a dancer needs to move with aplomb, a traditional ballet term denoting the imaginary plumb line that delineates the central axis of the body and guides us to our center of gravity. "The aplomb allows the dancer to establish himself in relationship to his center of gravity and to have not only a center but a circumference from where to move out into space and back in from space," he stated while discussing his teaching methodology with me. "Moving a well-aligned body (with aplomb) allows the legs, arms, and head to find good position in a natural way. Just focusing on the leg and arm action without having a sense of the whole will create mechanistic dancing without a sense of flow and line."

To better understand moving with dynamic alignment (aplomb), look at a common exercise in dance, such as a leg brush or a battement tendu. Ideally you can move the leg from the hip joint with minimal effort, creating a slight overall adjustment in the postural muscles but not a big increase in tension. The action in this case is focused on the hip joint, while the rest of the body remains fairly calm and stable. The leg action is part of a whole-body gesture, not just an isolated event. Stability is not achieved through restricting movement but by efficient balance of forces.

- Dynamic alignment is created by balancing forces with minimal effort, rather than compensating for postural distortion by increasing tension.
- In dynamic alignment the balanced interaction of the joints, muscles, and body systems ensure economical weight transfer through the desired cycle of movement.
- Balance is created by countering the forces at their place of origin, not by countering an imbalance with an increased level of tension.
- Alignment is a whole-body sensation, not the positional fixation of the parts of the body. Being centered is a physical state around which the body can move with great freedom without ever being forced into a position.

Many dancers tilt the pelvis and bend the spine to the side of the supporting leg in a brush to the side (second position). After a dancer has been doing this additional movement thousands of times, it becomes habitual. However, most dancers are flexible enough in the hip joint for this to be completely unnecessary. Often when you ask a dancer why he is making this movement, he is quite surprised to hear that his pelvis is not aligned. In the worst-case scenario, this kind of alignment distortion leads to pain and injury. While injuries may be credited to something you did wrong that day, in reality most injuries are set up by years of inefficient movement. Conditioning for alignment in dance helps you discover the most efficient and effortless solution for every movement.

If you are well aligned when not moving, this alignment does not necessarily carry over to your dancing merely by you pulling in the belly button and buttocks. A posture assumed for alignment while standing is not useful if it does not result in economy of movement. So movement, not rigidly assumed postures, is the defining criterion for dance alignment. As soon as you move, staying centered or regaining a center can be achieved through balancing forces throughout the body (see chapter 3). If you are taken off center by one of your movements and you tighten your abdominals, shoulders, and neck, you can stabilize yourself momentarily by reducing movement to regain your center. In dance, however, this approach is counterproductive. Dance alignment needs to allow for large movements in space, a feeling of freedom, and a trust in the body's ability to react to any force created by a balancing counterforce. Preemptive tightening is not the solution. Recent research supports this notion that movement skill is inversely proportional to the unnecessary muscle activity that occurs during its performance (Charman 1999). In other words, the more unnecessary muscle activity is, the less technical facility it provides.

The old school of alignment revolved around teaching how to hold or fix certain parts of the body into a better position while moving the limbs. Methods that emphasize holding or tightening create the feeling that good alignment is connected to a certain elevated tension level, so dancers may think that by performing abdominal strengthening exercises they are on the path to a strong center. This is a problematic road to tread. While working with the Swiss Olympic Gymnastics Team for many years, I learned that you can have incredibly powerful abdominal muscles and still be out of alignment and unstable when moving. The question is not, *Do dancers need to strengthen the abdominals;* in most cases they do. The key to stability lies in distinguishing and then balancing the various abdominal muscles among themselves (local muscle activation) and within the whole system of muscles (global muscle activation) to create better moving alignment.

For example, research has shown that the transversus abdominis muscle needs to be seen as separate from the other abdominal muscles in its function to create trunk stability (Richardson 1999). This kind of fine-tuned control requires a dancer to become aware of which muscle is being activated during exercise. A good image that supports the function of the transversus abdominis is that of a zipper moving up the front of the pelvis to activate the local muscles.

Dismiss the notion that there is one miracle muscle that you can hold on to create stability. If you think this way, you create a tension pattern in part of the body that causes another tension pattern and so forth. For example, tension in the diaphragm can trigger a tight neck, possibly causing you to hold the shoulders higher than necessary, elevating the center of gravity, and leading to a continuous degrading of movement efficiency. Also, holding the breath as a habitual response to effort during dance training or conditioning can lead to substantial rises in blood pressure.

I have watched dance classes where exciting steps and music create a dancer's high, but the dancers spend their time vigorously reinforcing unhelpful movement patterns because they do not receive any correction. The dancer often has intuitive knowledge of how to dance correctly, but it may have been overridden by contradictory information provided by a series of teachers and pressures. Usually the mind overrides the voice of the body to a point where it cannot be heard anymore. In the hundreds of seminars and classes I have taught, I often encounter dancers who need to be reconnected to the body's intuition. Once this reconnection occurs, their potential springs forward and they make great progress in their dance performance.

Now you will discover how to create alignment by balancing forces rather than through tension.

Balancing Forces for Better Alignment

If, while in the standing position, you want to lift a leg without disturbing your spinal alignment, you have two choices:

1. You can consciously hold in the abdominal muscles and tighten the back and all kinds of muscles in an effort not to move the back. If you hold in the abdominals, breathing will be difficult, because they are antagonists of the diaphragm. Also, according to McGill (2002) pulling in (hollowing) the abdominals is less effective than generally activating them for stabilizing the spine.

2. You can balance the forces in the hip joint by visualizing the countering movement of the hip socket around the rotating ball of the femur. In this approach, you focus on what needs to move to maintain alignment as opposed to focusing on what needs to be held to maintain alignment. The human nervous system is able to find an efficient solution when the focus is on movement. The idea is that rather than letting movement create a distortion in alignment and then keeping it at bay with tension, you should maintain alignment in the first place through balanced action of the joints and muscles.

The following alignment exercises are most useful to produce efficient and effortless movement. Keep in mind that your approach to alignment should mirror economy of movement. If you move with efficient alignment, minimal effort will produce a maximal range of movement.

In this experiment, feel the effects of balancing forces in the hip joint.

1. Note the feeling of your upright, standing posture. Does the pelvis feel tilted forward or backward? How does the position of the head feel relative to the spine and pelvis?

2. Bend to touch the floor, and note how far you can go and how easy it feels to do this in the muscles of the leg. How high can you comfortably lift the leg?

3. Now visualize the right hip joint. See the ball of the femur sitting in the socket. As you lift the leg, the ball rotates backward from your perspective. As you lower the leg, the ball rotates forward in its socket.

4. Visualize the forward and backward rotation of the ball in the socket several times, then compare the ease of movement in the hip socket between the two legs.

5. Repeat the visualization with the left leg.

6. Now bend the upper body forward in the hip joint. (Keep the spine relatively straight).

7. Visualize the hip socket moving over the ball of the femur. Imagine it sliding with ease like a well-oiled ball bearing.

8. Come back up, and visualize the socket sliding backward over the ball of the femur. Repeat this movement several times until you can visualize it clearly.

9. Repeat the same movement, only now visualize the ball rotating backward relative to the socket as you bend forward and the ball rolling forward relative to the socket as you come back up. Repeat this visualization several times.

10. As you come back to the standing position, notice whether the hip socket feels any different than before:

    - How easy is it to lift the leg?

    - Has the hip flexibility increased? Lift the leg, and notice whether it feels easier to perform this movement. Perform a brush or battement tendu, and notice the ease of movement.

    - Notice whether it is easier to touch the floor.

    - Notice your pelvic alignment, and go for a short walk to feel the efficiency of the leg moving in the hip socket.

11. Most likely you will have discovered an improvement in flexibility and ease of movement as well as a feeling of alignment in the pelvis. These benefits will not occur if you try to maintain your alignment by holding. Tighten the abdominal muscles, and lift the leg. Notice that you can't lift the leg as high, and you are probably also tensing the shoulders.

Sensing Your Alignment

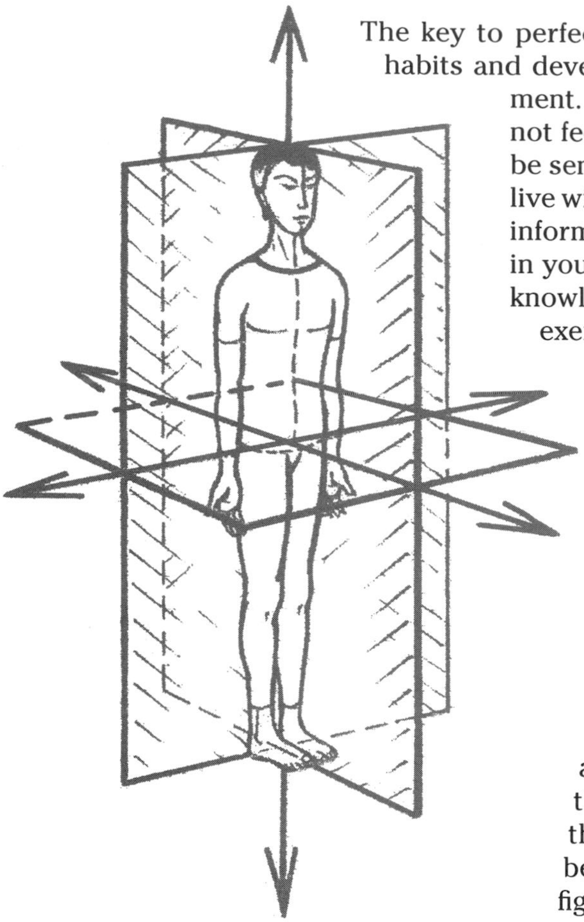

Figure 5.1 Planes through the body.

The key to perfecting your alignment is perceiving your own postural habits and developing a strategy that helps you create efficient alignment. As mentioned earlier, you may have poor alignment but not feel that anything is wrong. The nervous system may not be sending you information on the structural imbalances you live with day to day. So you have to get back into the stream of information between mind and body and sense the distortions in your posture, or nothing is going to change. Based on this knowledge you can use imagery, muscle and joint balancing exercises, and other methods to improve your alignment. The process of sensing misalignment and using corrective imagery or exercises is ongoing.

Alignment is a specific relationship of the bones of the body to geometric planes. In this case an imaginary median sagittal plane dissects the human body at the nose, the center of the chin, the breastbone and the pubic symphysis. An imaginary frontal plane dissects the human body at the atlanto-occipital joint, the tip of the shoulder, the greater trochanter, and just in front of the outer ankle bone. Distortion in posture can be found in the horizontal plane. The head may be turned to the right relative to the shoulder and the pelvis and rotated to the left relative to the feet. If you look at the body from above, both ears, the tips of the shoulder, the greater trochanters, and the ankles should ideally be located on approximately the same frontal plane (see figure 5.1). (For more information on this topic, see Franklin 1996b, pages 71–74).

Pelvic Floor Power

A strong, coordinated, and aligned pelvic floor significantly improves dance technique. If the pelvic floor is weak or tight, the spine and legs are not properly supported and tend to be misaligned. The benefits of pelvic floor training include a deeper, more elastic plié, higher jumps, better turn-out, more power for lifts, and, of course, improved alignment.

The pelvic floor consists of several layers of muscle stretched out at the bottom of the pelvis that are closely related to the deep pelvic organs. Their job is quite complex: On the one hand they need to support the organs, and on the other hand they need to be highly elastic for evacuation and childbirth. You achieve this pelvic floor support through increasing the elasticity, strength, and balance of all structures involved. The following exercises (adapted from my book, *Pelvic Power: Mind/Body Exercises for Strength, Flexibility, Posture, and Balance for Men and Women,* Franklin 2003, page 34-36) are designed to introduce pelvic floor awareness to your dance technique.

The pelvic floor is rimmed by the following bony structures: the tailbone and sacrum in back, the pubic symphysis and pubic bones in front, and the sit bones at the sides (see figure). If you draw imaginary lines between the sit bones, you divide the pelvic floor into a front and back half or two triangles on top of each other. If you draw a line between the pubic symphysis and the tailbone, you create two halves or two triangles positioned next to each other. If you imagine both lines crossing each other, you create four triangles. These triangular sections of the pelvic floor need to be balanced both in shape and strength for the pelvic floor to support your alignment.

1. From a standing position, touch the right sit bone and left pubic bone.
2. Visualize the area between your two points of touch. This is the front right triangle of the pelvic floor.
3. Keep touching the right sit bone, only now also touch the tailbone. Visualize the area between these two points; it is the right back triangle.
4. Remove your hands and notice the different sensation between the two halves of the pelvic floor.
5. Lift the right knee, then the left knee, and notice whether the right hip joint feels smoother and more flexible.
6. Stand on the right leg, then the left. You may notice that your balance has improved on the right side and that the pelvic right half feels lifted compared to the left. Imagery and touch do create alignment without increasing tension and interfering in movement.
7. Repeat the touch and imagery on the other side.

Leg and spinal alignment is closely related to pelvic floor alignment. The bridge between the spine and the pelvis is the sacrum, which forms the base of the spine and part of the pelvic rim. Once you discover how the pelvic bones and floor and the sacrum move, you can balance your alignment down through the feet and up to the head.

1. Stand with legs parallel and knees slightly bent. Tilt the pelvis forward and backward, and notice how this action affects the pelvic floor. Notice in which position the pelvic floor muscles lengthen and in which position they shorten.
2. Perform a plié with the feet placed in a wide, turned-out stance (second position), and notice how the pelvic floor is affected. Notice in which position the pelvic floor muscles lengthen and in which position they shorten.
3. With the knees slightly bent, turn the legs in and out, and notice how the pelvic floor is affected.
4. Alternately bend the right and left knees, and notice how the pelvic floor is affected.
5. Perform a passé retiré leg lift and leg extensions to the front, side, and back or a dance movement of your choice. Can you sense any movement of the sit bones, sacrum, or pubic bones? Do you feel any length changes in the pelvic floor musculature?

5.4 DEEPER PLIÉ WITH THE PELVIC FLOOR

The plié is a basic movement in most forms of dance training. I ask dance students why they practice pliés in their training, and they often have difficulty explaining why. The answers I have heard include *to strengthen the legs, to increase turn-out,* and *to help you feel your center.*

These answers are all correct. A fundamental role of the plié is to lower and lift the body's center with proper alignment. The plié acts as a spring to move the upper body vertically or to propel it through space. Pliés are performed at the beginning and the end of most dance steps. If your plié is not well aligned, your technique will suffer.

The plié is an excellent conditioning exercise for the muscles of the legs, pelvic floor, and lower spine. A coordinated pelvic floor produces a flexible and well-aligned plié. Awareness of this area can increase the movement range and ease of motion of a plié in minutes.

1. Focus on the action of the sit bones as you move down into a plié in second position (figure *a*). You may notice that they move apart slightly as the pelvic floor muscles act eccentrically (lengthen) and the tailbone moves back slightly.

2. During the upward movement, imagine the sit bones converging as the muscles act concentrically (shorten) and the tailbone moves forward slightly (figure *b*).

3. If you do the opposite movement, you will notice how the pelvic floor interferes with alignment: Try to move down in a plié while tightening the pelvic floor. This tightening results in a harmful shoving forward of the knees. The only solution now is to push the knees back into alignment, causing much tension or even pain in the hip joints. When a dancer tucks his pelvis by tightening the pelvic floor in an effort to align it, he is actually pushing his legs out of alignment. If you keep the sit bones spread apart and the tail back when you stretch the legs as you move up from a deep plié, the lower back arches.

4. Plié a few more times with the correct coordination—eccentric muscle action allowing the sit bones to spread as you go down, the tail swinging back; concentric muscle action with the sit bones moving together, and the tail swinging forward as you go up. Remember that these movements are an automatic part of your coordination. Just visualize the correct movement of the bones and muscles to support the action; do not exaggerate the movement.

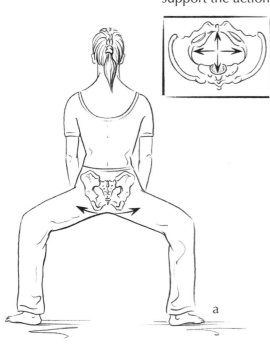

5. Imagine the pelvic floor as a flying carpet that lowers and lifts you in a plié.

6. When performing a plié with an accompanying port de bras, imagine the arm movements being initiated from the pelvic floor. Allow the pelvis to move a fraction earlier than the arms.

7. If you think of the pelvic floor and feet spreading as you plié, you will gain flexibility in the leg joints.

a

b

Tilting the pelvis affects the pelvic floor. Pelvic tilts are common in dance and when supported by pelvic floor awareness, they eliminate the chance of strain on the lower back or knees. When the pelvis tilts forward (anteriorly), the pelvic floor widens, and the tailbone moves away from the pubic symphisis (figure *a*). When the pelvis tilts backward (posteriorly), the pelvic floor tightens, and the tailbone moves toward the pubic symphisis (figure *b*).

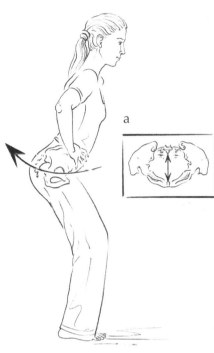

a

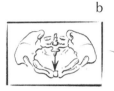

b

1. Initiate the tilting of the pelvis from the muscles of the pelvic floor. This sensation differs from creating the same movement from the hip flexors or extensors or the abdominal or lower back muscles. See whether you can be active in the pelvic floor throughout the range of movement with minimal involvement of other muscles.

2. Notice that contracting the abdominals contracts the pelvic floor musculature as well. For spinal flexion, these two groups of muscles act as synergists (they contract together).

3. Notice the relationship of the pelvic floor to breathing. On inhalation, both the abdominals and the pelvic floor muscles lengthen to accommodate the organs displaced by the downward movement of the diaphragm. On exhalation, they shorten to support the upward return of the organs.

4. Notice what happens to the pelvic floor when your rotate the legs in and out. When you turn the legs out, the musculature in the back half of the pelvic floor shortens while the musculature in the front lengthens. When you turn the legs in, the front half shortens and the back half lengthens (figure *c*).

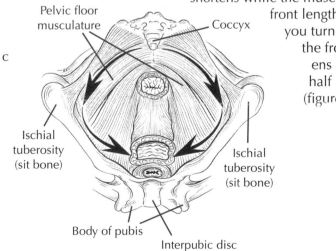

c

Pelvic floor musculature

Coccyx

Ischial tuberosity (sit bone)

Ischial tuberosity (sit bone)

Body of pubis

Interpubic disc

The sacrum is closer to the geometric center of the body than any other bone. In aligned standing, the center of gravity hovers in front of this bone. When you move the legs or spine, the sacrum reacts. The sacrum can support or impede these constant movements of dance. This exercise helps you understand the connection between the sacrum, pelvis, legs, and spine.

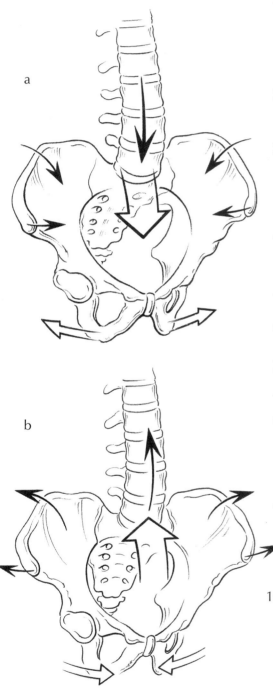

a

b

1. Place a hand on the sacrum, and detect the bumps on the back of the bone. These bumps are the spinous processes of its five fused vertebrae. To feel the movement of the sacrum, it is easier to touch the adjoining bones that are easy to feel under the skin, the tailbone and lumbar spine.

2. Place the middle finger of one hand on the tip of the tailbone, and place the middle finger of the other hand on the spinous process of the fourth or fifth lumbar vertebra.

3. Tilt the pelvis forward, and notice how the lumbar spinous processes move forward and the tail moves back. The sacrum is doing a forward rotation movement called nutation (deriving from the Latin for nodding.) At this point the sacrum is only doing the first half of a nod (figure a).

4. Tilt the pelvis backward, and notice how the sacrum moves back and up. This movement is called counternutation, the second half of the nod (figure b).

5. Tilt the pelvis forward again and notice that nutation is linked with the spreading of the sit bones.

6. Tilt the pelvis backward, and notice that counternutation is linked to the converging of the sit bones.

7. Notice that nutation causes the lumbar spine to extend (the feeling is hollowed spine), while counternutation causes the lumbar spine to flex (the feeling is rounded spine).

8. Notice that the tailbone moves in the opposite direction of the top of the sacrum. If you tuck the tailbone, you cannot nutate or extend (hollow) the lower spine. Try to arch the spine to the back with a tucked tail, and notice the impediment to moving this way.

9. If you move the tailbone backward, you cannot counternutate (flex) the lower spine—the lower back resists. This resistance is a built-in coordination of the body. If you respect the way the bones move naturally, your technique will improve. If you oppose them, you will cause strain.

10. Shake out the hand that was touching, and stand with a neutral pelvis: You may notice that the pelvis feels different, perhaps more aligned and free. Just becoming aware of how the bones move aligns the body.

The sacrum performs a slight nutation when you move downward in a plié and a slight counternutation when you move upward in a plié. If you can support these movements with imagery, you will have a well-aligned spine and legs as well as a deeper plié.

1. Perform a plié in second position. Imagine the sacrum nutating as you go down. The tailbone swings slightly to the back.

2. Imagine the sacrum counternutating as you come up. The tailbone swings slightly forward.

3. Notice what happens when you do the opposite movement: When you move down in plié, imagine the sacrum counternutating. Most likely your knees are pushed out of alignment as in step 3 of exercise 5.4. When you move up in plié imagining the sacrum nutating, the back arches.

4. Practice again with the correct coordination (steps 1 and 2).

5. If the back arches unless you actively tuck the tail forward when performing plié, the hip flexors may be tight. Stretch or align the hip flexors to provide more length for these muscles. The hip flexors are antagonists to the pelvic floor. When they shorten, the pelvic floor musculature lengthens. Practice the exercises outlined in this chapter for aligning the pelvic floor as well as the iliopsoas exercises in chapter 7 (exercises 7.11 to 7.15).

6. Imagine the spine as it relates to sacral nutation and plié. As you move down, think *allowing spinal curves,* or imagine a soft wave through the spine. As you move up, think *lengthening spinal curves,* or imagine a string attached to the top of the head pulling the head up and the spine into length. If you reverse the imagery for the downward and upward plié, the legs will feel stuck, because the imagery does not support the balanced movement of the bones and joints.

5.8 PELVIC FLOOR AS A FAN

The muscles of the pelvic floor are arranged in several layers in patterns that can be visualized as a fan originating from the tailbone (figure a). The outer rim of the fan is formed by the coccygeus muscle that connects the tailbone and bottom of the sacrum to the spine of the ischium. The levator ani muscle consists of the iliococcygeus and the pubococcygeus. The iliococcygeus connects the side of the tailbone to the inside of the pelvis opposite the hip joint. The pubococcygeus outer fibers connect the tailbone to the pubic bone, and the inner fibers form a loop around the anus.

The rectus abdominis is the muscular continuation of the pubococcygeus and usually acts in synergy with this pelvic floor muscle (figure b, female pelvis). I focus on the pubococcygeus, because this muscle, if felt and visualized, helps to create a well-aligned lower spine and pelvis. The pubococcygeus also helps to reduce excess tension in the gluteals.

1. Touch the right sit bone, and slide a finger up the back of the bone about one inch. If you keep the finger close to the bone, you will notice that a bulge keeps you from sliding further up. This obstacle is the inner obturator muscle as well as the spine of the ischium, and it is what you are looking for.

2. Place a finger on the spine, and touch the tailbone at the same time. This position is not the most comfortable one, but try to hold it for one minute.

3. Imagine the connection between the two points, tailbone and spine of the ischium, as active and alive. Imagine communication happening between these two points.

4. Imagine the two points coming closer together as if you could contract the pubococcygeus at will.

5. Imagine the two points moving farther apart, as if you could lengthen the muscle at will.

6. Repeat this one more time before you let go of your touch.

7. Compare the alignment of the right and left sides of the pelvis by standing on one leg. Lift the right and then the left leg, and extend each leg to compare flexibility between sides. You may notice that the pelvis on the side you touched and visualized feels more lifted while the hip joint feels smoother and more flexible.

8. Repeat the exercise on the other side.

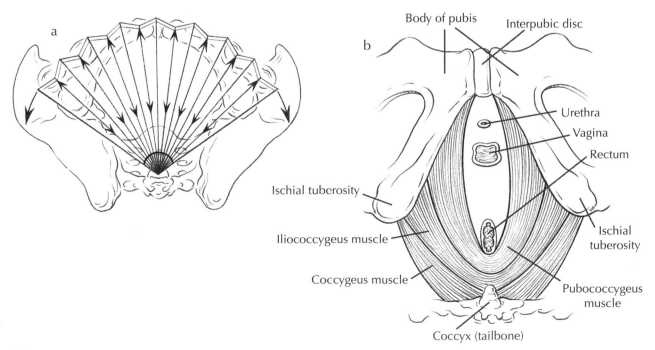

The levator ani leaves an opening in the front half of the pelvic floor. This triangular area is covered by an expansion of muscle and connective tissue called the perineum. It attaches to the sit and pubic bones (figure a). The perineum consists of a muscular sheath, called the transversus perinei, and connective tissue.

When you move downward in a plié, you stretch the perineum. When you move back upward, the perineum can support the action by contracting. The force of the muscle is relatively small, but its action is important for the coordinated action of the pelvis. The perineum increases the range of your turn-out and helps organize the power of your jumps. Because of connective tissue relationships among the muscles of the pelvic floor and the hamstrings and adductors, the flexibility of the leg muscles can be improved by creating more elasticity within the pelvic floor.

1. Perform a second position plié, and notice the depth of your movement and the amount of turn-out available.
2. Lie supine, and place two balls or a rolled towel under the pelvis.
3. Flex both legs at the hip joints and knees.
4. Place the hands on the inside of the knees.
5. Visualize the muscles in the perineal triangle.
6. Lift the legs by initiating a contraction in the perineal triangle. Image the triangle shrinking (figure b).
7. Lower the legs by initiating an eccentric contraction in the perineal triangle. Imagine the triangle widening (figure c).
8. Repeat the movement six times, focusing on the initiation from the perineal triangle.
9. Remove the balls, rest, and then stand up and perform a second position plié. Notice the changes in your flexibility and ease of movement.

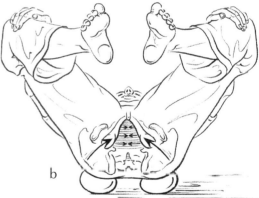

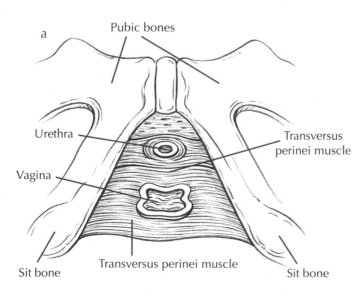

a

Pubic bones

Urethra

Vagina

Transversus perinei muscle

Sit bone

Transversus perinei muscle

Sit bone

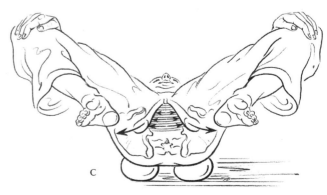

b

c

5.10 PELVIC HALF AS A WHEEL

Visualize the two pelvic halves as wheels that rotate slightly when you flex the leg in the hip joints. This rotation of the pelvic half is minimal, but needs to be balanced on both sides of the pelvis to create good alignment and prevent lower back pain. The image also improves stability when standing and helps to increase flexibility in the hip joints.

1. Perform a second position plié.
2. Lie supine, and hold the right leg. Imagine the right pelvic half as a wheel spinning toward you (see figure).

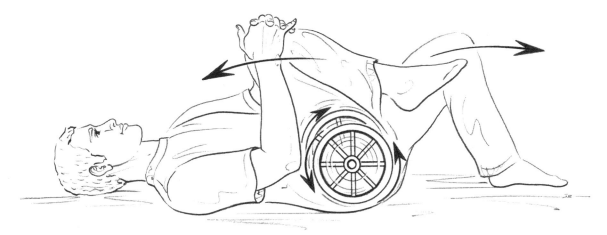

3. Release the leg, and as you lower the foot to the ground, imagine the right pelvic half as a wheel spinning away from you.
4. Repeat the action and imagery five times.
5. As you lift the right leg again, think of the other pelvic half as a wheel rotating in the opposite direction.
6. Repeat this action and imagery three times.
7. Stretch out both legs, and swing the right leg, then the left leg up from the hip joint. Notice the difference in your power for initiating the movement and flexibility between the legs.
8. Stand up and notice the difference in stability and alignment between the two pelvic halves by balancing first on the right and then on the left leg in a passé retiré position.
9. Repeat the exercise with the other leg.
10. Once you have practiced with both legs, stand up, perform a second position plié, and notice your pelvic alignment and ease of motion.

As you have seen in the previous section, the pelvic floor muscles act eccentrically during a downward moving plié. All muscles are balanced by another group of muscles; in this case the transversus abdominis and the lower back muscles (erector spinae) oppose the action of the pelvic floor muscles. The rectus addominis mirrors the length changes of the pelvic floor muscles as you plié. Balancing these opposing muscles with the pelvic floor creates superior strength and alignment while moving.

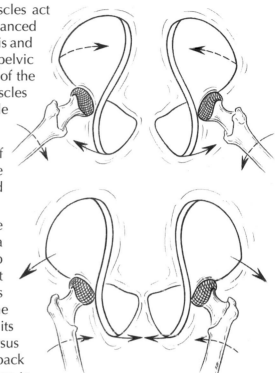

1. Plié, and notice the sit bones moving apart. The bones of the pelvis are twisted plates (figure a). As the sit bones move apart, the pelvic halves rotate inward, allowing the top and front pelvic half to move together.

2. The other end from the sit bones on the pelvic half is the anterior superior iliac spine (ASIS). You can feel it as a prominent bony bump under the skin at the front and top of the pelvis. Here and all along the rim of the inner part of the pelvic crest are the attachments of the transversus abdominis muscle, which runs horizontally toward the rectus abdominis, located in the center, and attaches to its connective tissue sheath. Above the pelvis the transversus abdominis attaches to the connective tissue of the lower back (lumbodorsal fascia) and creates connective tissue tension to support the lower back.

a

3. Although the movement of the bones is small, this muscle acts concentrically in opposition to the pelvic floor muscles in a downward plié movement (figure b). The rectus abdominis is working together with the pelvic floor. Place the hands on the front of the pelvis, and slide them toward the center as you plié downward to support the shortening feeling (sliding together of filaments) of the transversus abdominis.

4. In the upward plié movement, the transversus abdominis acts eccentrically, working together with the transversus abdominis. Place the hands on the front of the pelvis, and slide them outward toward the pelvic crests as you plié and upward to support the widening feeling (sliding apart of filaments) of the transversus abdominis.

5. Repeat the pliés, focusing on the lengthening and shortening relationship of the pelvic floor and transversus abdominis.

6. Sense the lower back musculature as it relates to the action of the pelvic floor. Place the fingertips of both hands on the lower back muscles—the bulges next to the lumbar spinous processes. As you plié down, visualize and feel the pelvic floor musculature widening and the lower back musculature shortening slightly. As you go up, visualize and feel the pelvic floor musculature shortening and the lower back musculature lengthening. These are subtle changes, so feel and visualize them, but do not exaggerate the action.

b

7. Notice the lifted feeling in the pelvis and also your range of movement and stability. The spine may feel lengthened, and the shoulders may feel relaxed. Once you get the feel for these relationships, you do not have to think about anything but your dancing. The coordination becomes automated.

If the pelvic floor and transversus abdominis muscles work in a balanced and antagonistic fashion, you have good pelvic alignment with plenty of freedom in the hip joint. Every plié constitutes a dynamic training of the pelvic floor and deep abdominal muscles.

If, on the other hand, your strategy to keep the pelvis aligned is to contract the abdominals, you block the swiveling action of the pelvic halves, because you hold the ASIS (anterior superior iliac spine) in a fixed position. This action stops the sacral movement and impedes the hip joints' movements. Overriding the natural movement of the bones with force causes pressure in the hip joints. This is one of the reasons dancers often report tight and sore hip joints and low extensions. It is not overwork, but a lack of information on how to create dynamic balance and strength in plié by activating and aligning the pelvic floor. If all the muscle and bone actions confuse you, use metaphorical imagery to get the feel of it as you move.

1. On the downward movement of plié, the back of the pelvis widens like a fan, and the front integrates (figure *a*). On the upward movement, the front of the pelvis widens like a fan, the back integrates (figure *b*).

2. Repeat the action several times focusing on only the front side of the pelvis, then on the back.

3. Finally, try to combine the front and back activity into one image.

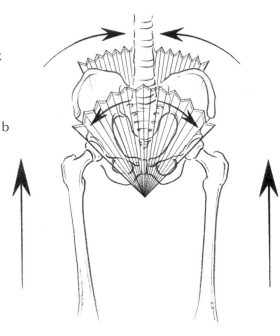

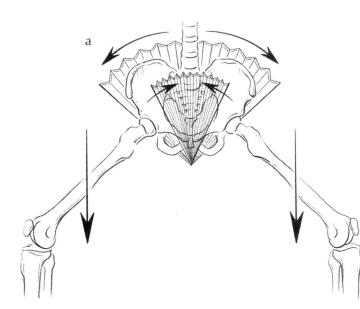

The pelvic floor is not the only floor in the body. Other significant somewhat horizontal partitions are formed by the first rib circle and by the diaphragm. All three of these floors of the body should coordinate to create alignment. In the following exercise, you will use breath and imagery to become aware of and strengthen the connections among these three floors.

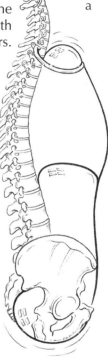

a

1. In a standing position, visualize floors from bottom to top: the pelvic floor, the diaphragm, and then the first rib circle.

2. Inhale, and notice the changes in the floors. The pelvic floor and the first rib circle expand, and the diaphragm moves down and shortens (filaments slide together) (figure a).

3. Exhale, and notice the changes in the floors. The pelvic floor and the first rib circles integrate, and the diaphragm moves up and lengthens (figure b).

4. Keep breathing and imaging until you can create a clear connection between the activity of all the floors.

5. If the floors are well aligned, your turns and jumps will improve. If you are sufficiently warmed up, try some turns and jumps while imagining the floors. Also notice the changing relationship of the floors in forward and sideward bending movements of the torso.

You can also practice aligning the floors in the constructive rest position. By imagining the floors as circles, align them with each other and perpendicular to the floor and imagine them sinking into the floor simultaneously. Once you stand up, move the arms over the head, to the front and side. Notice the changing relationship of the rib circle to the pelvic circle. Perform an arabesque and développé leg extensions to the front, side, and back, and notice the harmonious change in the relationships of the circles. Notice how much the circles tilt when you do this (figure c). Are the changes similar for both legs?

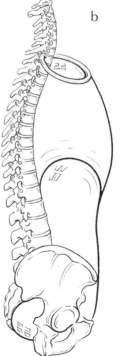

b

c

5.14 ALIGNING THE SHOULDERS AND FIRST RIB

Upper body alignment is important in dance. Round shoulders need to be corrected for technical as well as aesthetic reasons. If the shoulders are slouched forward, you reduce the mobility of the arms and neck. Balancing and turning are much more difficult with rounded shoulders. The problem is not solved by simply pulling the shoulders back.

To have naturally relaxed and aligned shoulders, the first rib level should approach the horizontal plane, the shoulder blades should be low on the back, and the spinous process may be perceived as hanging downward. (See also Franklin 1996b, pages 215–223). If the first rib is pushed down in front, it compresses the ribs and organs and increases muscular tension. By relaxing the shoulder muscles, especially the trapezius, you can feel the first rib.

1. Touch the back of the neck with the right hand, and massage the neck muscles. Think of the many layers of muscles that are responsible for maintaining the alignment of the neck as folds on folds of soft, velvety curtain.

2. Glide the fingers downward until you feel a bump at the bottom of the neck. This bump is the spinous process of the seventh cervical vertebra. Rub this process gently, then push it down softly and think of it melting. Visualize the breastbone floating upward.

3. If you can reach it comfortably, rub the spinous process just below.

4. Repeat the procedure using the other hand.

5. Shake both arms for a moment to release all tension, then feel your upper body alignment; you may feel more lifted in the breastbone than before.

6. Now lift the shoulder blades, and drop them slowly, thinking of the trapezius muscle melting and the scapula sliding down the back. Lift your shoulders again, and drop them slowly and think of the front of the first rib floating upward as if it were being lifted by a magic string.

7. Perform a port de bras movement, and visualize the first rib circle spreading out like water rings (see figure).

8. Now feel the position of the first rib as you move the arms into various positions. Does the first rib feel level? Do the arms feel like an extension of the first rib?

9. Try to visualize the first rib in pirouettes. (This image may be difficult in the beginning.) Does it move back? Does it tilt to one side?

Organic Alignment

Organs are not just dead weights that you carry around to regulate the body's functioning. They are in fact important for posture and the sound functioning of the joints. Tension in the organs puts additional strain on the musculoskeletal system. Often back pain and alignment problems can be relieved by discovering the organs in movement. This discovery includes having a sense of their size, weight, location, and spatial relationship. If an organ is contracted or tense, the skeletal muscles in the vicinity often tighten up as a result. Becoming aware of the organs makes movement easier and improves alignment, balance, and flexibility.

To access the organs through touch and imagery, it helps to focus on weight, space, expansiveness, and grounding, as well as a timeframe that is slow and free flowing. Another way to access organs is through their movements during breathing and through physiological rhythms.

Each organ has its own feel in movement and touch and its specific mind-state. According to Chinese medical tradition, the kidneys are the organs of basic energy. They are also a filtering and regulating organ, balancing the body's water content. The adrenal glands, which sit on top of the kidneys like little slanted hats, are the organs of rest in activity and active rest (not unconscious rest). The kidneys and adrenal glands are located just beneath the diaphragm and are constantly moving up and down with the breath. Between the kidneys we find the celiac or solar plexus, an accumulation of nerves (figure 5.2). Awareness of these organs, developed by experiencing them through touch, sound, and imagery can help your rotations in dance.

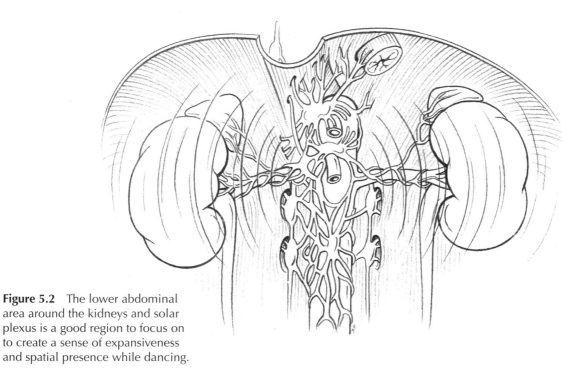

Figure 5.2 The lower abdominal area around the kidneys and solar plexus is a good region to focus on to create a sense of expansiveness and spatial presence while dancing.

Organs are suspended from ligaments and buoyed by other organs. They are provided with lift through the suction of the lungs and the diaphragm, which acts as an antigravity device to levitate and stack the organ column. The liver weighs one and a half kilograms but does not feel heavy because of the lift provided by the diaphragm.

5.15 THE KIDNEY-BLADDER-KIDNEY TRIANGLE

The kidneys are biological filters vital to your health. Every minute, one fifth of the body's blood travels through the kidneys, is purified, and is adapted to the specific needs of the cells. This amounts to a filtering capacity of 1,800 liters each day. The kidneys excrete urine that is collected in the bladder.

The two kidneys and one bladder form an imaginary triangle. The kidney-bladder-kidney triangle is an image that creates alignment, balance, and more power for movement. By focusing on the triangle, you gain a three-dimensional focus and a feeling of depth inside the abdomen.

1. From a standing position, place the right hand on the pubic bone. The bladder is located behind this bone at the front center of the pelvis.

2. Place the left hand on the left upper abdomen, just below the left ribs at the level of the kidney.

3. Focus on both organs, and see them as being related and connected. You may feel that they are coming closer together, or moving apart from each other. Both organs are actually always moving a bit as a result of breathing and other processes. Breathe into these organs. Start with the kidneys, then focus on the bladder.

4. Exhale with an audible *sss* while focusing on these organs. Imagine the *sss* causing the organs to make more space for themselves.

5. Remove the hands, and notice any differences between the sides of the body.

6. Stand on the left leg, and notice how it feels to plié. Stand on your right leg, and notice how it feels to plié.

7. Lift the left arm straight up, and notice how the shoulders feel. See the arm connected to the kidney-bladder-kidney triangle. Do the same with the other arm, and you may notice that the connection does not feel as clear.

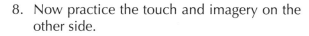

8. Now practice the touch and imagery on the other side.

9. Compare lifting the arms with your focus on the shoulders to lifting the arms with the focus on the inner triangle. The shoulders may feel less strained when lifting from the triangle.

The intestine can be likened to a strong, muscular tube. This muscle is not weak, because it works many hours each day. By imaging the intestine as an internal support, you may discover a new sense of alignment and strength.

1. Lie supine on the floor, and take a moment to notice the breath. Feel the body being supported by the floor.

2. Visualize the inside of the body, the organs that create your inner volume and weight. Do they feel as if they are in the front or in the back of the body? Do they feel pushed to the right or the left? Do you feel any one of them moving with the breath? Can you visualize any organ specifically?

3. Focus on the large intestine and how its ascending and descending parts lie on each side of the body. Notice their length from inside the pelvic bowl up to the kidneys. Now visualize the large intestine resting on the back body wall. Breathe into the large intestine, and feel it lengthen as you inhale and shorten as you exhale. Keep breathing into the intestine until you have a good feeling for its length and location.

4. Stretch the arms overhead, and visualize the large intestine on each side of the body lengthening between the pelvis and the diaphragm. Place the arms at the sides to feel the weight of the large intestine. Let it drop down as if it could sink through the body and rest on the floor itself.

5. Let the mind be free of any imagery for a minute or two. Then roll to the right side, and get up slowly. Notice whether you feel any change in your alignment.

6. Imagine the large intestine supporting you as you perform a développé extension or another dance movement (see figure).

Lungs and Heart

Many dancers are unaware of the tension they hold in the lungs; they simply think it is muscular tension. But the lungs contain a lot of smooth musculature located around the alveoli and bronchi. The alveoli are sacs where oxygen is absorbed into the blood. The walls of these sacs are extremely thin, only .002 of a millimeter, or three cells, thick. The alveoli remind me of foam surrounding the branchlike bronchi, the tubes that transport air.

If you release tension in the lungs, the upper chest will begin to feel open and light, and you will improve spinal and pelvic alignment. The upper chest will feel naturally lifted, and the arms will have more freedom to move in space. The contraction and expansion of the lungs relates to the first rib circle and pelvic floor. When you inhale, the lungs expand, and the first rib circle widens. The diaphragm contracts (filaments slide together) and moves down, causing the pelvic floor to widen. When you exhale, the lungs contract through the upward movement of the diaphragm. The first rib and pelvic floor narrow. Muscularly speaking, the diaphragm's action is in opposition to the movement of the pelvic floor, first rib circle, and lungs (figure 5.3).

The relationship between the rib cage and the lungs is strong. Freedom in the lungs increases the flexibility of the rib cage. Imagine the ribs as a container filled with the lungs (as well as the heart and parts of other organs). If the substance inside the container is rigid, the surface of the container is not free to move. If the content is mobile, the surface is more flexible. You can't move ice frozen inside a balloon, but once the ice turns to water, the surface of the balloon is movable. This is how it feels when the lungs start to let go of tension. The rib cage is elastic, floating on the supportive lungs.

The lungs are divided into separate parts called lobes. The right lung has three lobes, and the left has two (to make space for the heart). For simplicity I refer only to the upper and lower lobes. The upper lobes are mostly in the front of the body, and the lower lobes are mostly in the back.

In collapsed posture, the upper lobes are forced downward over the lower lobes of the lungs. If you use muscular force to lift the shoulders and upper torso into better alignment, you will feel a tendency to collapse once again.

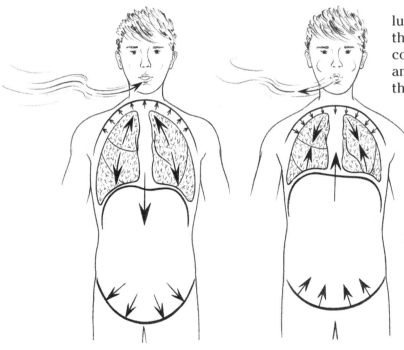

Figure 5.3 Notice the movement of the first rib circle and the pelvic floor as you inhale and exhale.

Because all tissue in the body is adaptive, the lungs and the surrounding connective tissue have changed to accommodate the collapsed position, even though this might be detrimental to the body. To change a downward collapse of the lung back to its original position, it is helpful to work with the lung directly, using touch and imaging a repositioning of the lobes.

This exercise improves upper body alignment, lifts the chest without muscular strain, and creates more space for deeper breathing. It also reduces pressure on the heart and diaphragm.

1. Visualize the lobes of the lungs as stacked wedges that slide on top of each other. If possible have a partner delineate the separation of the lungs with his hands on the front and back of the body using figure 5.3 as a guideline.

2. Move the chest up and down, and visualize the upper lobes sliding on the lower lobes (figure *a*).

3. Once you have gained a sense of the mobility of the two lobes, imagine the lower lobes sliding down and forward. Imagine the upper lobes sliding back and up (figure *b*). It may help to inhale as you slide the upper lobe upward. Think of the lower lobe resting, or even pushing on the diaphragm as you slide the upper lobe upward.

4. Notice that it feels easy to maintain upper body alignment. Feel the lower lobes resting on the diaphragm and the upper lobes floating up.

5. Try some dance movements with the feeling of the lungs supporting the spine.

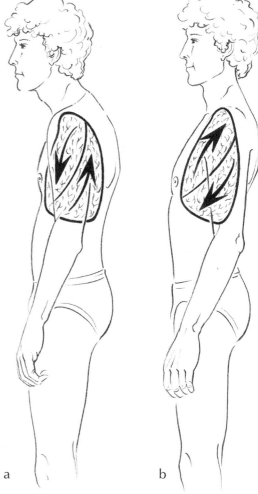

a   b

Imagining the heart is a fast and simple way to improve alignment. In a few minutes you can create a sense of lift in the upper chest, which also can lift your mood. The heart is in constant motion. It rests on the diaphragm and moves with the breath. On exhalation it rotates clockwise (from your point of view), and it is slightly compressed as the diaphragm ascends. On inhalation it rotates counterclockwise, and it is slightly stretched as the diaphragm descends. These actions constitute a constant inner massage for this vital organ and support the flow of blood to the heart muscle itself.

1. Allow yourself to slouch forward and notice whether this feels easy or uncomfortable.

2. Come back to an upright posture and place one hand over the heart, whichever feels more comfortable to you.

3. Visualize the heart behind the ribs and sternum, framed by the right and left lungs. It is slanted downward to the left and slightly to the back and is located more on the left than the right side of the body.

4. Now think of a space between the heart and the sternum and ribs in front. Breathe into this space.

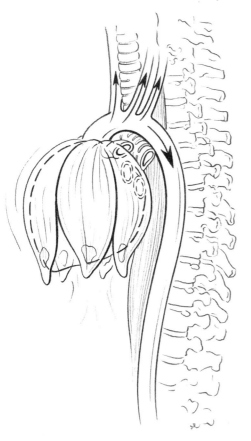

5. Then imagine a space between the heart and the blood vessels and spine in back, and breathe into this space.

6. Imagine a space between the heart and the right lung. Imagine a space between the heart and the left lung. Imagine sending your breath into these spaces. Feel the heart being buoyed by the space surrounding it.

7. Think of the heart being light and floating up. Imagine the heart being supported by the aorta behind it like a flower being lifted toward the sky by its stem (see figure).

8. Remove your hand and notice how your upper body posture feels. Do you still feel like slouching, or is there an actual resistance against lowering the upper chest?

9. Try some dance movements with this new sense of heart.

Slowly flexing the spine from top to bottom in the standing position is a common exercise in dance, especially modern dance. For a dancer this is an opportunity to look inward, to let go of tension, and to improve alignment.

The facet joints between vertebral processes are rather flat, and the two surfaces can slide on each other when you bend and rotate the spine. Think of this sliding to release tension and create length in the spine. The intervertebral discs make up 20 to 33 percent of the length of the spine and are between 3 mm (cervical) and 9 mm (lumbar) thick. At birth the fluid content of the central part of the disc (nucleus pulposus) is 88 percent, and at age 77 it is about 65 percent (Norkin and Levagie 1992). The daily fluid content of the disc depends on movement and alignment. Visualizing the discs during exercise and dance can greatly contribute to a sense of length and alignment of the spine.

a   b   c

1. Stand in a comfortable position with the feet parallel (figure a).

2. Slowly drop the head forward (figure b).

3. As you slowly roll down the spine, think of spinal facet joints sliding, joint surface on joint surface (figure c).

4. Experience this action as very slippery and equal on both sides of the spine.

5. Focus first on the cervical spine, then on the thoracic spine, then on the lumbar spine.

6. When you have rolled all the way down, place the hands on the floor, and bend the knees slightly, then rock some of your weight forward onto the hands. Feel the weight of the head, and imagine the ribs dropping toward the shoulders on both sides of the spine.

7. Image the space between the individual vertebrae widening and the discs expanding. You may also perform slight side-to-side rocking movements to open the joint spaces.

8. Then place your weight all the way back on the feet, and slowly roll up, imagining the facet joints sliding, first in the lumbar, then in the thoracic, and finally in the cervical spine.

9. Image plump, fluid-filled discs in the space between the individual vertebral bones (figure d). In the mind's eye, fill them with plenty of liquid so they can form strong, cushiony supports between the vertebrae.

10. Once you are erect, allow the lower ribs on the side of the body to drop and the first rib to float up. Feel the head resting centered on the top of the spine.

11. Repeat the rolling down and up two more times with the same imagery.

12. Notice any changes in your alignment, and perform a leg movement, such as an extension to the side, front, and back, and notice how it affects the spine. Perform small hops while imaging the resilience of the discs as if they were miniature waterbeds. This exercise will help you to gain a sense of lift and length in your core, and release tension in the shoulders.

d

Visualize the organs as they are stacked up in the torso: At the bottom and center is the bladder, on top of which the uterus or small intestine rests (see figure). On each side of the bladder are the lower parts of the large intestine. On the left is the sigmoid colon, and on the right is the cecum. The large intestine forms two pillars at the right and left of the abdomen, reaching up to the kidneys. Between these pillars is the small intestine. Above the transverse part of the colon are the stomach and pancreas on the left and the liver on the right. Above the diaphragm are the two lungs and to the center left, the heart. Above the heart rests the thymus gland. The head can also be considered to contain an organ, the brain. The brain has the consistency of gelatin (with a lot of intelligence mixed in). To simplify the image, focus on the brain, lungs, large intestine, and bladder in the following roll-down.

1. Sit comfortably in a chair, and initiate the movement starting from the brain. Let the brain drop forward and down, followed by the top part (top lobe) of the lung.

2. The lower lobes of the lungs follow, then the large intestine, down to the bladder.

3. As you come up, think of dropping the large intestine into the pelvic bowl; you can even think of pushing it downward to help lift the spine.

4. Then lift the upper part of the large intestine, the lower and upper lobes of the lungs, and then the brain.

5. When you are all the way up, let all the organs rest into the pelvis and move through the pelvis while you remain centered on the chair.

4. Repeat the roll-down and roll-up three times before you check out your new postural feeling.

You can also perform a roll-down while thinking of the nerves, spinal cord, and brain. This roll-down is especially helpful to create a sense of anxiety-free alignment.

Lungs

Kidneys

Intestine

Bladder

chapter 6

Strengthening the Center

The strength and coordination of the lower back, hip, and abdominal muscles are important in dance. But many dancers lack strength in precisely this area (Molnar and Esterson 1997). Conditioning these muscles in a balanced way is a complex task, but by focusing on the key players—the diaphragm, the iliopsoas, the lower back, and abdominal muscles—you can ensure strength in the center.

This chapter will teach you the steps necessary for strengthening the center. First, you learn what it means to be centered. You then explore the functioning of the diaphragm and why its strength and elasticity is important for central control and strength. The next step is to create balanced strength in the iliopsoas and deep lumbar back extensors to allow you to breathe freely while exercising. Finally, you coordinate the abdominal and spinal muscles with imagery, and you strengthen them using Thera-Bands.

In the last few years the concepts of central control and core strength have been introduced to the world of dance conditioning. The Pilates technique, for example, emphasizes strengthening the abdominal muscles in a specific fashion to gain better movement control and balance.

If the center of the body is defined as an area from which you can achieve the most effortless control and guidance for the whole body, then different exercise and somatic techniques have a variety of centers depending on the discipline. For example, in ideokinesis and the Hawkins Technique the pelvis is important for efficient movement; in Pilates the abdominal and deep spinal muscles are the center, and in the Alexander Technique the neck is of central importance. Other methods have designated the chest area, the top of the spine (atlas), or the feet as central. It is not a question of which method is right or wrong but of realizing that all these methods are useful, depending on the person and the situation. There may be days when awareness of the neck makes all the difference to help you feel centered, but on other days you may achieve optimal coordination by focusing on the pelvis or feet.

Stability is created through concerted action of the whole body in dialogue with a centered mind. It is a mental image as much as it is physical fact. If you have an off-balance day, a day where your balance doesn't work, you haven't suddenly lost all the strength you have gained through your conditioning routines. It is physically impossible to lose strength so suddenly. The change has happened in the mind directing the nervous system.

I want to dispel the notion that merely strengthening the right muscles is sufficient to center you. If it were that easy, then being centered would be simply a matter of strength, and there would be no need to reeducate the nervous system as a whole. For example, if the trapezius muscle is tight, it is difficult, if not impossible, to experience alignment and centeredness. Your control is dominated by the restrictions in the neck and shoulders. If you strengthen the abdominal muscles and the shoulders remain tense, you will then have stronger abdominal muscles as well as tight(er) shoulders. You may have more force, but you will still not be centered, and your balance and turns will not improve.

You can, however, strengthen the muscles that are *located* centrally in the body, and learn how to initiate movement from that center. Conditioning exercises cannot replace increased awareness of the whole body and its interrelated functions. Through conscious movement you may learn how to support your dance from the newfound muscles located in the center. To move with less effort and a sense of unity in the whole body, you have added your awareness to every exercise and dance step. The shoulders start letting go, because their tightness has lost its usefulness as a compensation for other weaknesses. Being centered is ultimately an emotional-mental-physical state, so I suggest practicing calm and collected concentration to benefit most from every exercise you do. The diaphragm and iliopsoas muscles serve as good starting points for centering exercises, because training these muscles has a calming and a strengthening effect.

Core Strength for Efficient Breathing

Efficient breathing is important in any peak performance activity and needs to be considered part of any conditioning routine for dance. The most important muscle for breathing is the diaphragm, which consists of a large muscular dome with a flat central tendon (figure 6.1). It is attached to the lower end of the sternum, to the lowest six ribs, and to the spine via two muscular extensions called crura. The crura are arranged vertically on the front of the spine and help to pull down the diaphragm on inhalation. The diaphragm weaves into the fibers of the transverse abdominal muscles and has various connections to thoracic and abdominal organs such as the liver. The diaphragm has three major openings: one for the esophagus, one for the aorta, and one for the vena cava. (For further reading on this subject, see also Franklin 1996b, pages 261–263.)

Although we can experience the diaphragm as the most important muscle for breathing, in a sense every muscle in the body supports our inhalations and exhalations. In deep breathing during exercise, the body functions as a giant bellows involving a myriad of muscles in the breathing process. Likewise, every tense muscle, even if it is located in the foot, jaw, or hand, reduces breathing capacity.

A popular method to improve alignment and to create strength in the abdominal muscles is to pull them inward and upward toward the spine. This strategy may make you look thinner for the time you are pulling in, but it also makes breathing more difficult and reduces joint flexibility by increasing the body's general tension level. It also reduces the stability of the lumbar spine (see chapter 5). To better understand why pulling in the abdominal muscles is not beneficial to breathing, take a brief look at the evolution of the diaphragm.

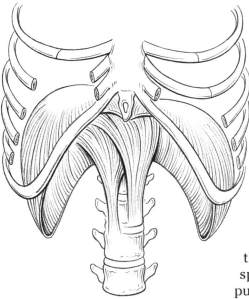

Figure 6.1 The diaphragm is the most important muscle for breathing; it separates the thoracic cavity from the abdominal cavity.

Fish don't have a diaphragm. They breathe by letting water pass through the gills and extracting oxygen, which transfers directly into the bloodstream. Land animals cannot function with gills, because air would not pass through the gills with enough pressure to be extracted. A land animal with gills would have to be running at 150 miles per hour all the time to be able to breathe! So the first land-dwelling animals evolved a system to suck air into the newly evolved lungs by expanding the ribs. This system, however, had a drawback: As the ribs expanded, the air was pulled into the space created by the widening ribs, but so were the abdominal organs. So, a connective tissue sheath was developed at the bottom of the lungs. This sheath acted as a barrier to keep the organs out of the space destined for the incoming air.

As animals became more complex, this sheath became a muscle that could push the organs down during inhalation, expanding the lungs to a greater degree. For this pushing to happen efficiently, one problem had to be solved: where to put the displaced organs. In a fish, ribs are all along the spine from head to tail, so there is no place for displaced organs to go. In mammals, the ribs reach down only to the twelfth thoracic vertebrae. The lower ribs were replaced by the abdominal muscles that function as elastic rib replacements in conjunction with diaphragmatic breathing. The vestiges of the actual ribs are the transverse processes of the lumbar and cervical vertebrae, which now serve as important attachments for spinal muscles.

The abdominal muscles owe their existence to breathing, not to pelvic positioning or alignment. They carry much of the weight of the organs in four-legged animals (and crawling babies). If you pull the abdominals inward, you will push the organs against the diaphragm, which is then not able to properly move downward during inhalation. The diaphragm and abdominal muscles are antagonists—when the one lengthens, the other shortens. You may want to sacrifice some breathing for a leaner look and the illusion of strength, but by doing so you create other problems.

The crura of the diaphragm have fibrous connections to the most important hip flexor muscles, the psoas major and the iliacus, known collectively as the iliopsoas (figure 6.2). If you pull the abdominal wall inward, you not only have trouble breathing, but you also lose some of the power and flexibility in the hip joint, spine, and shoulder girdle. If you think you need to correct your pelvic alignment by pulling in the abdominal wall, it may be time to instead look at improving organ tone, balancing the joint movement in the pelvis, spine, and legs, and conditioning the iliopsoas and deep lumbar spinal musculature.

On exhalation the abdominals help push the organs back up into the diaphragm, helping the lungs to expel air. The shallow breathing resulting from holding the abdominals reduces their natural conditioning; the deeper you breathe, the more the abdominal muscles condition, 24 hours a day. This superior abdominal exercise also provides you with more energy than a holding strategy. Also, when you hold in the belly, you compensate by breathing with the upper chest, raising your center of gravity and making you less stable for turns and balances. Upper chest breathing tends to make you feel anxious and tense, hence the need to concentrate on abdominal breathing.

The abdominal organs actually aid inspiration by using their weight to pull the diaphragm down. Expiration is aided by the lungs, which retract elastically on exhalation and help to pull the diaphragm upward. Therefore, organ-assisted breathing is impeded by habitually pulling in the belly (Schiebler, Schmidt, and Zilles 1997).

Once you have gained deep pelvic strength and balance, you will have more flexibility and better pelvic alignment, feel less high-strung, and even have flatter-looking abdominal muscles.

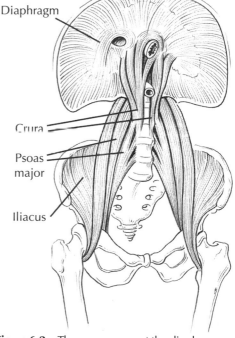

Figure 6.2 The crura connect the diaphragm to the iliopsoas (hip flexor) muscles.

6.1 LIBERATED BREATHING

The following explorations help you become aware of how tension influences breathing and flexibility. Once you notice that breathing freely helps flexibility, do not be overly concerned about your abdominal muscles popping out. Once you have conditioned the deep lumbar muscles, the abdominals will fall back (to describe the feeling) toward the spine naturally without impeding the breath.

1. Perform a high leg kick, and notice how smooth the action feels in the hip joint.
2. Pull in the belly, perform a grand battement, and notice the elevation of the leg and the smoothness of the hip joint.
3. Repeat the action with relaxed breathing. How high does the leg go?
4. Arch the spine sideways (lateral flexion) to the left and right.
5. Then pull in the belly, and do the same movement. You may notice that you have lost flexibility in the spine.
6. Lift and lower the arms over the head.
7. Pull in the belly, and repeat the movement: You may have less range or feel resistance in the shoulders as you perform the movement.

You can always force the movements just described using more strength, but you will be exerting additional pressure on the joints and accelerating their wear and tear, which is not a good strategy for someone who wants a long and healthy career in dance.

8. Now push the tongue upward against the hard palate, and clench the jaw. If you kick the leg or perform a passé retiré, you may notice that you have less ease of motion in the hip joint.
9. Relax the jaw and tongue, grand battement or passé again. The movement may feel easier.
10. While focusing on the breath, push the hands against both sides of the skull. Notice how this pressure affects breathing.
11. Let go of the head, and notice that you can now breathe more deeply. You may even feel the diaphragm releasing. In a sense the skull bones and the connective tissue beneath the brain are a sort of diaphragm.
12. To let go of residual tension in the diaphragm, visualize the diaphragm as a set of sails billowing in the wind.

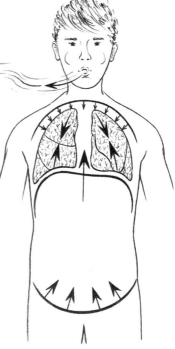

Although breathing is central to our existence, few exercises focus on conditioning the different body parts involved in the process. The first part of this exercise increases your breath awareness, while the second part focuses on lengthening the crura and the diaphragm. The exercise reduces strain on the spine, improves alignment, and helps create a sense of length in the front of the spine. It also strengthens the diaphragm and abdominal muscles, relieves stress, and deepens the breath.

1. Lie supine with the knees bent at right angles and the feet on the floor.
2. Let yourself breathe for a minute or two. Do not try to influence your breath; just witness it as if you were watching a performance.
3. Visualize the movement of the diaphragm. Watch it move down on inhalation and up on exhalation.
4. Visualize the lengthening and shortening of the muscle fibers of the diaphragm: filaments sliding together on inhalation, apart on exhalation. Pay attention to the lengthening phase, feeling the muscle fibers melting into length on exhalation.
5. Focus on the antagonistic action of the diaphragm and abdominal muscles. As you inhale, the diaphragm shortens and the abdominal muscles lengthen. As you exhale, the diaphragm lengthens and the abdominal muscles shorten. Let the abdominal muscles drop down toward the spine on exhalation as if they were a large leaf falling to the ground.
6. Now focus on the sliding filaments: As you inhale, the filaments of the diaphragm slide together and the filaments of the abdominal muscles slide apart. As you exhale, the filaments of the diaphragm slide apart and the filaments of the abdominal muscles slide together.
7. Notice how the organs are rocked between the diaphragm and the abdominal wall and pelvic floor. Your breathing is organ massage, toning the organs and helping to flatten the abdominal wall.
8. Watch the dome of the diaphragm move toward the head, and the edges of the diaphragm drop downward and inward with the ribs on exhalation. Watch it move downward toward the pelvis and the ribs move to the side and up on inhalation.
9. Stand up and walk around while watching the breath. Notice how watching the breath influences your movement. Perform a dance movement while watching the breath.

The crura are an important but neglected part of the diaphragm. They anchor the diaphragm to the spine, aid in deep breathing, and help support the lumbar spine. Through their relationship to the psoas major, they support flexibility in the hip joint.

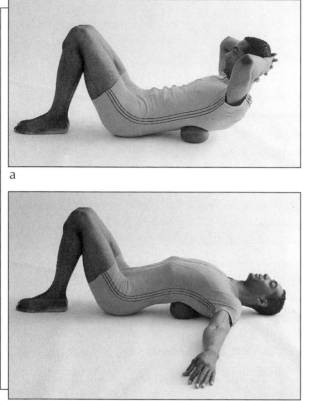

1. Focus on the crura. Imagine the dome of the diaphragm connected to the lumbar spine. Visualize the crura shortening on inhalation and lengthening on exhalation.

2. Place two balls next to each other under the upper back. You may also use a rolled towel.

3. Put the hands behind the head to create neck support (figure a).

4. Exhale, and slowly lower the head and upper back to the floor. Visualize the abdominal muscles lengthening.

5. Return to the starting position, and think of the abdominal muscles shortening.

6. Lower the head to the floor, and visualize the crura lengthening. Rest the arms for a moment (figure b).

7. Inhale as you return to your starting position. Imagine you can support the movement with the help of the shortening crura of the diaphragm (figure c).

8. Repeat the exercise four times, visualizing the lengthening of the crura and abdominal muscles.

9. Remove the balls, and notice changes in your breathing and the length and width of the back.

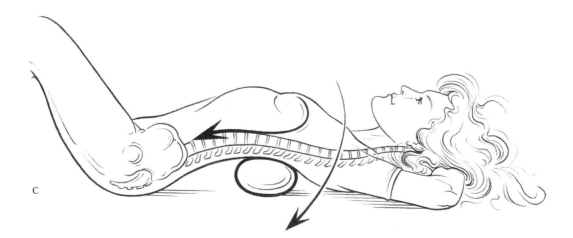

One of the most common movements in dance—found in all genres—is the plié. Doing a plié, you learn how to align and coordinate lowering and elevating the body's center of gravity. This skill is key to many dance steps. Breathing greatly influences the plié and can support or hinder its action. The following exercise explores this connection.

1. Perform several pliés, and notice smoothness and depth of the movement. Notice your style of breathing. Do you inhale or exhale as you descend? Do you inhale or exhale as you ascend? Which action do you prefer?

2. Rest for a moment, then place your hands on the back part of your lower ribs. Notice the breath. Imagine the incoming breath billowing the diaphragm like sails in the wind, causing the ribs to move sideways and back. Notice several breaths with this image. Notice that the diaphragm lifts its edge to follow the ribs sideways and up on inhalation, while the muscle itself shortens (figure a).

3. Place the hands at the top of the chest, and notice the spreading of the first rib circle and pelvic floor as you inhale (figure b).

4. Place the hands in front of the pelvic floor, and notice the narrowing of the pelvic floor and the first rib circle as you exhale. Repeat the image during several breaths (figure c).

5. Perform a descending plié, and visualize the diaphragm and pelvic floor spreading, opening like the shutter of a camera.

6. As you ascend, feel the pelvic floor narrowing like the shutter of a camera.

7. As you plié, feel the diaphragm resting on the organs like a silken cloth. Allow all tension to flow out of the diaphragm.

8. Ascend without losing the feeling of ease in the diaphragm.

9. Repeat the pliés with imagery until you notice changes in the range and fluidity of your movement.

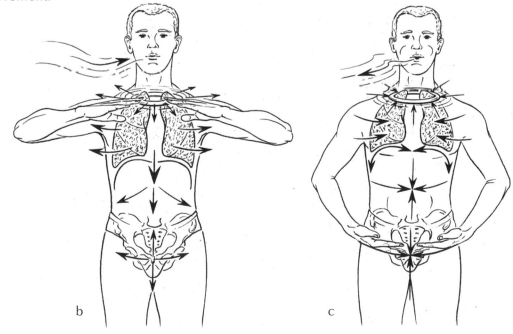

Miracle Muscles—The Iliopsoas

The iliopsoas is the primary hip flexor and the only one that can flex the hip joint sufficiently to lift the leg over 90 degrees. It consists of three muscles—the psoas major, the psoas minor, and the iliacus. The common element of the psoas major and the iliacus is their joint tendon, which inserts into the top of the thigh bone (femur at the minor trochanter. Conditioning the iliopsoas helps dancers improve lumbar stability, balance, and extension. Besides being the primary hip flexor, it may flex or extend the lumbar spine, depending on various factors (Norkin and Levangie 1992). Becoming aware of the iliopsoas may work miracles for the lower back and for the technique in general. In their study on conditioning and extension, Grossman and Wilmerding (2000) write, "Dancers are not considered competitive in the world of professional dance if they cannot maximize their extension in à la seconde. Hip flexor conditioning within the realm of technique class is generally inadequate for specific strength gain" (page 121). The psoas major has the advantage of originating on the spine and not the pelvis as is the case with the other hip flexors and has not spent all of its shortening power when the leg is lifted into extension. But it is not only strength that helps flexibility; it is also a resilient, flexible, and fluid iliopsoas that can shorten without tension to increase ROM.

Because the iliopsoas connects the pelvis and spine to the legs, it greatly influences pelvic alignment. Dancers frequently experience release from lower back tension and pain after regular performance of the iliopsoas exercises described next. Imbalance in the iliopsoas and lower back muscles may be an important cause of lower back pain. Teaching for the Swiss Arthritis Foundation, I have seen countless cases of people who have benefited from iliopsoas conditioning. The benefits range from improved alignment and reduced back pain, to the correction of organic abdominal disorders. It is hard to believe that a single muscle group can make such a difference to your alignment, coordination, and strength until you have felt it in your own body. Ruth Solomon at the University of California at Santa Cruz has developed a series of exercises to condition the iliopsoas and avoid the snapping hip syndrome. (For information on Ruth Solomon's videotape on iliopsoas conditioning, contact UC Santa Cruz, 2647 Old San Jose Road, Soquel, CA 95073, U.S.A.) But specific iliopsoas conditioning has not been a common part of dance training, perhaps because it requires increased awareness of the dancer and an anatomically versed teacher.

Good iliopsoas action is achieved by balancing the muscles of the pelvis using simultaneous lengthening and strengthening techniques combined with visualization. It is worth the effort—the hip joint gains flexibility, turn-out increases, the spine feels lengthened, the pelvis feels lifted, and the belly magically drops toward the spine without having to hold the breath.

The superficial layer of the psoas major originates on the sides of the twelfth thoracic and first to fourth lumbar vertebrae. It also attaches to the intervertebral discs of the lumbar spine. The deep layer inserts on the transverse processes of the lumbar spine. The iliacus originates on the inside of the iliac bone, the iliac fossa, and the lateral edge of the sacrum over the sacroiliac joint. Because it crosses the hip joint and has expansive attachments, it is a powerful hip flexor. Because it is located above the iliosacral joint, a tight iliacus pulls the sacrum down; a lengthened iliacus imparts the sense of lift to the sacrum. At least two things can happen if this muscle shortens: The leg moves toward the pelvis (hip flexion), or the pelvis moves toward the leg (anterior pelvic tilt). If the upper body remains upright this arches (hollows) the back. The reason the iliacus is joined by a common tendon to the psoas is to protect the back. The psoas reaches up the lumbar spine and prevents the iliacus from causing the back to arch when flexing the hip.

The psoas is a powerful stabilizer of the lumbar spine during hip flexion. Because it is able to flex the spine, especially across the lower lumbar vertebrae and sacrum, it counteracts the tendency of the iliacus to arch the back. It also is able to compress the lumbar spine to achieve more stability. The only reason to consider them as one muscle is because of their joint contribution to hip flexion. In most dancers, the psoas major needs more strength, and the iliacus needs more length. The abdominal muscles may also engage to keep the pelvis from tilting forward and arching the back in hip flexion. But if the abdominals are used exclusively to lift the front of the pelvis, the psoas major is not sufficiently trained to stabilize the lumbar spine, breathing is inhibited, and the sacrum counternutates (tucks the pelvis). All these factors contribute to reduced hip flexion and to a loss of leg alignment. Also, a nutated sacrum is more stable than one that is counternutated. Ideally, a dancer learns to engage the psoas major before the muscle's weakness is masked by abdominal exercises.

The iliopsoas tendon is a source of many problems for dancers. If the iliopsoas is not stretched and strengthened to create balanced movement patterns, the dancer compensates by using the superficial hip flexors, which eventually begin to feel sore and in the way of proper leg elevation. A common problem is the snapping hip syndrome, which is often experienced when moving in and out of an extension à la seconde. The underlying cause may be the snapping of the iliopsoas tendon over the minor trochanter or hip joint capsule. Snapping while moving into extension to the front may also be caused by the iliotibial band or gluteus maximus tendon snapping over the greater trochanter (Southwick, Michelina, and Ploski 2002). In many cases these problems can be resolved through modification of technique.

The iliopsoas and transversus abdominis musculature is also linked to the kidneys and the organs of the lower abdomen. The kidneys are located just in front of the psoas and quadratus lumborum muscles. Visualizing the flow of blood through the kidneys can help the underlying muscles contract and release in a more fluid fashion.

The third muscle in the group is the psoas minor. The psoas minor is reported to be absent in 40 percent of humans. Interestingly, anatomy texts I have researched from the early 1900s do not report this absence, although extensive cadaver studies were performed. It appears that an increasingly sedentary lifestyle does not require a psoas minor, which is an important muscle for the subtle adjustment of pelvic alignment. This muscle is interesting; it may be the deepest abdominal muscle. The psoas minor originates on the sides of the twelfth thoracic and first lumbar vertebrae. It inserts on the front of the pelvis (pubic rami) and on the inguinal ligament next to the rectus abdominis. If the psoas minor contracts, the front rim of the pelvis is pulled upward toward the twelfth thoracic vertebrae (figure 6.3). This lifting feeling is much appreciated by dancers. Many dancers lift by engaging the superficial abdominal muscles, reducing the flexibility of the joints of the leg previously mentioned. Once the psoas major and minor are strengthened, the dancers experience a revelation. The feeling of lift now originates deep in the pelvis. Sagging abdominal muscles caused by a forward tilted pelvis shorten naturally as the front rim of the pelvis lifts, making the abdominal muscles appear flatter. The abdominal muscles, especially the rectus abdominis, then aid in lifting the front of the pelvis without excessive tension because of their balanced tone–length relationship.

Contracting the gluteals is an equally unsuitable alignment strategy for the pelvis, because they extend the hip joint, and the movement

Figure 6.3 When the psoas minor contracts, it lifts the front of the pelvis.

in a plié involves flexing this joint. Likewise, if you try a battement with contracted gluteals, notice that the leg does not go very high. The gluteals are hip extensors, and they oppose the movement of hip flexion required for leg lifts. Often this fact comes as a surprise to the dancer who has been instructed to engage the gluteals to create a lifted pelvis. In the final tally, a dancer ends up with a weak psoas major, shortened iliacus and gluteals, and inhibited breathing, which in turn lead to a shallow plié, stiffness in the groin, lower back pain, and lack of extension and turn-out. Also, if the dancer forgets to hold in the abdominals and gluteals, the arched back reinstates itself in an instant.

The iliopsoas is also a weak internal rotator of the femur below 90 degrees of leg elevation. The ability of the iliopsoas muscle to both anteriorly tilt the pelvis and turn in the femur contributes to a lack of turn-out in dancers with an imbalance in the strength and length of the iliopsoas muscle. Dancers may try to prevent arching the back and rolling the feet and knees inward by contracting the abdominal muscles and tightening the gluteals, but they lose flexibility in the process.

Although stretching the iliopsoas does provide temporary relief, it does not rectify faulty movement patterns. Performing the following muscle balancing exercises accompanied by the appropriate imagery reeducates the nervous system to create more efficient movement. First, you will create awareness of the psoas major and condition its lumbar stabilization capabilities. Then, you will activate the psoas minor to help posteriorly tilt the pelvis (lift the front of the pelvis) and create length in the iliacus. Iliopsoas stretching may be part of the strategy if you are simultaneously increasing the balanced strength of the iliopsoas muscle. Conditioning the abdominal muscles and erector spinae is the next step.

The iliopsoas and transversus abdominis musculature is also linked to the kidneys and the organs of the lower abdomen. The kidneys are located just in front of the psoas and quadratus lumborum muscles. Remember that approximately 1,800 liters of blood flow through the kidneys daily. Awareness of this flow can help the underlying muscles contract and release in a more fluid fashion.

6.5 DISCOVERING THE ILIOPSOAS

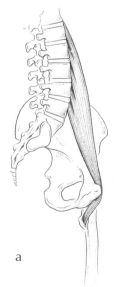

a

In this exercise you will visualize the iliopsoas and begin to develop a sense of location and direction in these muscles. This awareness is initially not so easy, because the muscles lie deep inside the pelvis and next to the spine.

1. Sit comfortably with the knees bent at 90 degrees and the feet flat on the floor.
2. Think of the iliacus, which connects the insides of the pelvis to the top inside of the leg. Think of the psoas major, which connects the sides of the spine to the top inside of the leg. The psoas is somewhat vertical as it travels next to the spine, but once it passes the pubic bone, it becomes more horizontal, front to back, as it finds its insertion on the top inside of the femur (figure a).
3. If you stand up and this muscle is tight, then the pelvis tilts forward, the lumbar spine is pulled toward the legs, arching the back (figure b). To avoid this problem, imagine the muscle filaments sliding apart as you stand up, and sliding together as you sit down.
4. Lie down supine in a comfortable position with the feet on the floor and the knees bent at a 90-degree angle.

5. Visualize the iliacus originating expansively on the inside of the iliac fossa and connecting with the psoas major to form a joint tendon attaching to the femur. Imagine the widely spread attachment of the iliacus on the inside of the ilium and iliac crest, and glide the fingers along the iliac crest to reinforce this sensation.

6. As it cascades over the pubic bone, imagine the psoas major as a miniature waterfall (figure c).

7. Once you realize that the top of the thigh is connected to the sides of the lumbar spine and the inside of the pelvis, you can imagine the distance between these two places increasing.

8. Visualize the line connecting the center of the knee with the center of the hip joint. Try to visualize the insertion of the iliopsoas on the femur (upper leg bone) being lateral (on the outside) on this line. The line connecting the center of the knee with the center of the hip joint is the rotational axis of femur. If the muscle shortens it flexes the hip joint and can also turn the femur inward around this axis. The action should remind you of the turning of a crank (figure d). A tight iliopsoas therefore limits your turn-out in a plié.

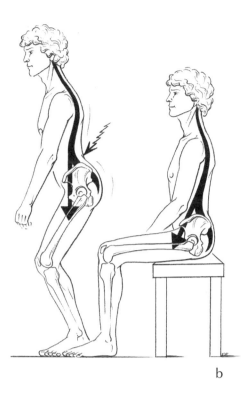

b

9. Flex the right leg over 90 degrees. Now the line of pull of the muscle moves to the inside of the rotational axis. Now the iliopsoas is an external rotator, and it will strengthen your turn-out in extensions. Standing, perform a passé retiré movement, and imagine the psoas major lengthening to aid your turn-out (figure e).

10. Lower the right leg, and perform the exercise with the left leg.

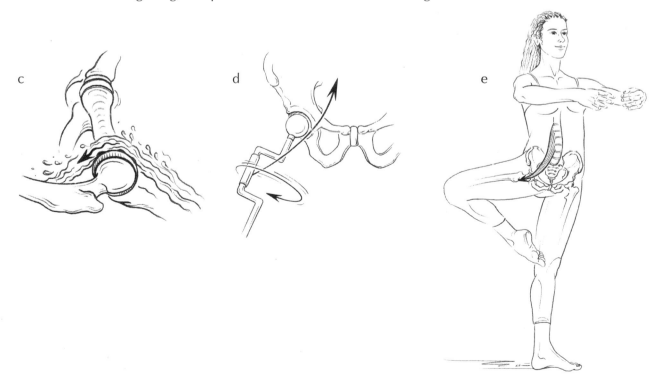

c

d

e

This exercise, adapted from André Bernard, the late master teacher of ideokinesis, gives us a sense of how the iliopsoas relates to the abdominal muscles and lower back. Focusing on these relationships is the first step to balancing these muscle groups.

1. Lie supine in a comfortable position, with the feet flat on the floor and the knees bent at right angles.

2. Lift the right foot off the floor, and notice whether this movement causes your abdominal muscles or lower back muscles to tighten, even minimally. Also, does your pelvis tilt forward or to one side as you do this? Are you pushing the left foot into the floor in an effort to lift the right foot? Are the shoulders and neck tightening? Notice the body's reaction to the leg lift without actively intervening.

3. Lower the right foot, and perform the same action with the left foot. Is the situation similar on this side, or does it feel different? Does the belly tighten more, less? Are you arching the back? Are you pushing the right foot into the floor to help lift the left leg?

4. Lift the right foot again, and imagine the psoas major flowing down next to the spine like a river. Lower the right foot, and lift the left foot while imaging the psoas as a river flowing next to the spine toward the femur (see figure).

5. Imagine the lower back muscles melting, dripping down like warm wax.

6. Repeat the movement five times on the right and left sides of the body.

7. Notice any changes in the lower back and abdominals. The back may feel more spread out after this exercise.

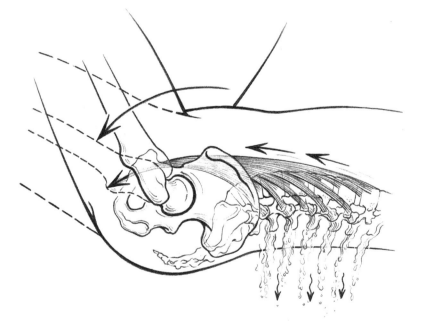

The following exercise creates a sense of the relationship between the hip joint and the ilio-psoas. Discovering the hip joint and activating the ideokinetic line of movement between the knee and hip socket creates a balanced length–tension relationship in the psoas.

1. Lie comfortably supine with the knees bent at right angles.

2. Notice how the back rests on the floor. Is the lumbar spine arched? Does the neck feel lengthened, tight, lifted? Are the shoulder blades resting comfortably on the floor?

3. Take a few minutes to monitor your breath and your posture as you rest on the floor.

4. Bend the right leg in the hip joint, and place the left hand on the top of the knee.

5. Imagine the head of the femur resting, even sinking into the hip socket. Imagine resting back into a comfortable armchair after a long day of work, and transfer this feeling to the femur head–hip socket relationship. It may be helpful to think of the jawbone resting into its socket as well. From a muscle balance perspective, the fates of the hip and jaw are often linked.

6. Slowly rotate the femur with the left hand. Try to be completely passive in the leg, initiating the rotation with the hand only. Keep thinking of the femur head dropping deeper into the socket.

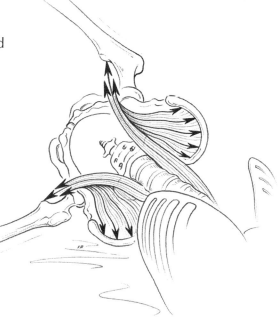

7. Add the image of the psoas flowing down next to the spine and over the hip joint. Imagine the psoas flowing deep in the gulley next to the spine. Imagine the iliacus spread out on the inside of the ilium like water gushing up onto a flat, sandy beach (see figure; see also figure on page 120).

8. Allow the movement in the hip joint, not in the lower back. Perform small circles with the knee, eight times to the right and eight times to the left, then stretch the right leg up vertically and shake it out. As you move, keep thinking of the femur dropping deep into the hip socket.

9. Before you repeat the movement on the other side, perform a gentle leg lift with the right, then the left leg to compare ease of movement between the exercised and the nonexercised leg. You may notice that the side on which you practiced feels more centered.

6.8 RELEASING THE LOWER BACK

By strengthening and lengthening the iliopsoas muscle, this exercise promotes a feeling of spreading and relaxation in the muscles of the lower back. It releases tension in the back and the hip joints after rehearsal or dance class.

1. Place two balls under the pelvis, and bend the knees so that the feet are flat on the floor. Lift the left leg up to the chest. Breathe freely, relaxing the abdominal muscles. It may feel comfortable to have some sort of support under the head.

2. Lower the left leg until the left foot is on the floor.

3. Slowly lift the left leg again as in step 1. Melt the lower back into the floor. Allow the shoulders and neck to stay relaxed.

4. Imagine that each knee is supported from underneath by a silk scarf, each end suspended from the beaks of two birds (see figure). The scarf lowers and raises the leg for you so you can stay relaxed and keep breathing.

5. Repeat the action seven times.

6. Remove the balls, and notice changes in the lower back and pelvis. You may feel lopsided, because the left pelvic half and lower back has relaxed and dropped.

7. Practice hip flexion, and compare the relative ease of motion of the left and right hip joints.

8. Repeat the exercise with the other leg.

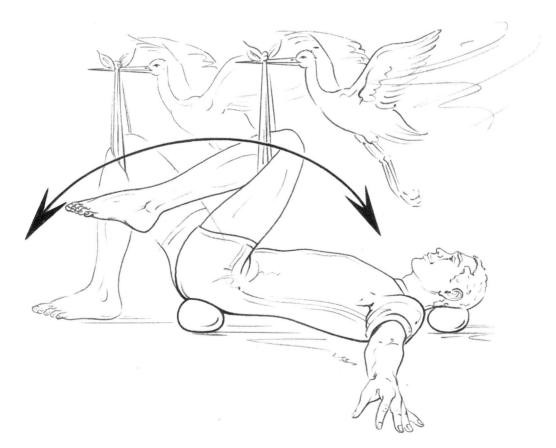

The following exercise emphasizes the eccentric strengthening of the psoas and iliacus muscles. I first encountered this type of iliopsoas training with Bonnie Bainbridge Cohen, the founder of Body-Mind Centering. The advantage of the approach is to create length while building strength. Also, the exercise allows for ample time to visualize the iliopsoas muscle in action. In the supine position, you can use the weight of the leg to load the iliopsoas while paying attention to the stability of the pelvis. The leg usually weighs about one sixth of one's body weight. As the leg is lowered in the following exercise, leverage is increased significantly. It is important not to lower the leg beyond a position that feels comfortable, especially if you feel a clicking sensation in the hip joint (often called snapping hip syndrome). If the clicking is painful, you should consult a licensed health care practitioner.

a

1. Lie supine, and place two balls under the pelvis.
2. Slowly move the pelvis on the balls in various planes, like a boat rocking on the ocean waves.
3. Hold the left knee against the chest.
4. Lift the right foot off the floor, and stretch the leg vertically into the air. Don't stretch the leg taught. The knee and ankle joints should feel relaxed (figure a).
5. Slowly lower the right leg while imagining the iliopsoas muscle lengthening. You do not need to lower the leg all the way to the floor. As soon as you feel any pressure in the lower back, an inclination to tilt the pelvis forward, or a snapping in the hip joint, bend your right knee and hip joints (figure b) and bring the leg back to the starting position.

b

6. As you lower the leg, image the muscles of the lower back melting into the floor and the psoas flowing downward like a river next to the spine. Visualize the iliacus spreading out inside the pelvis.
7. Repeat the movement seven times.
8. Remove the balls, stretch out the legs, and notice the differences between the left and right legs. Does the leg you exercised feel longer? More turned out?
9. Try a battement with the practiced leg, then the other. Do you notice any differences in ease of movement or hip flexibility? When standing and supporting your weight on the practiced leg, assess the position of the pelvis and the abdominals by placing one hand on the front and one hand on the back of the pelvis. You may feel more lifted in the pelvis and the belly may drop back on the practiced side.
10. Repeat the exercise seven times with the other leg.

You can also perform this exercise with one foot on the floor (figure c). This variation may be helpful if you have sore or tight hip joints, or if you are experiencing snapping hip syndrome. Also practice with different amounts of inward and outward rotation as you lower the leg.

c

RUBBER BAND LIFTS PELVIS

The following exercise combines ideokinetic practices with ideas derived from Body-Mind Centering. The psoas minor deteriorates rapidly if you are not moving actively on a daily basis. Most people, however, have at least a tendinous strap along the path of the psoas minor.

Both the psoas minor and rectus abdominis can pull the front of the pelvis upward, but the psoas minor has an advantage over the rectus abdominis. It is situated beneath the abdominal organs, so shortening the psoas minor does not trouble inhalation as does a tensed rectus abdomnis. If you can discover the psoas minor, you will experience a way to lift in the front of the pelvis without impeding the breath. By viewing the twin psoas minor muscles as force vectors and combining them, you will create the ideokinetic line of movement from the pubic symphisis to the twelfth thoracic vertebrae (see figure 6.3). Visualizing this line of movement helps to enliven the psoas minor and support the functioning of the psoas major.

In this exercise, you will attempt to lower both legs to the ground without actively engaging the abdominal muscles beyond regular breathing. This action may raise a few eyebrows. You may think of the abdominals as stabilizers of the pelvis, but voluntarily engaging these muscles would defeat our purpose of strengthening the psoas major and increasing its stabilizing power for the lumbar spine. I suggest letting the intellect rest until after you have experienced the exercise. Let the body teach you a lesson.

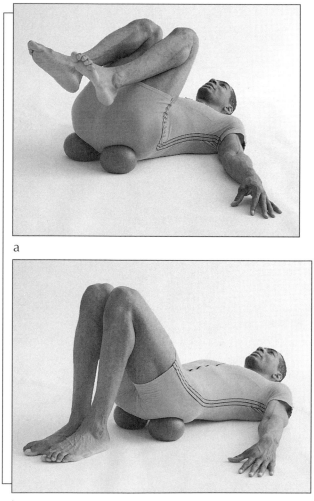

a

b

1. Lie supine with knees bent and feet on the floor, and place two balls under the pelvis.

2. Lift both feet off the floor, and allow the legs to drop back toward the torso. Feel relaxed in the hip joints, knees, and feet. Breathe easily, and relax the abdominal muscles (figure a).

3. Slowly lower the legs to the floor, allowing the shoulders and neck to stay relaxed.

4. Lower the feet to the floor (figure b).

5. Breathe freely. The abdominal muscles should not bunch up or push out. Notice whether you can keep the pelvis from tilting forward by allowing the abdominal muscles to drop toward the spine without using tension. This action is not easy and may feel impossible to begin with.

6. One at a time, lift the legs back up, and repeat the lowering of the legs using imagery.

7. Start by visualizing the psoas major muscle flowing down next to the spine (see exercise 6.7) while imaging the lower back melting into the floor.

8. Now visualize the psoas minor muscle connecting the front of the pelvis with the lumbar and thoracic spine.

9. Imagine the activity in this muscle increasing as the psoas major flows downward next to the spine (figure *c*). This movement allows the abdominal wall to effortlessly drop downward toward the spine.

10. Imagine the psoas minor flowing upward and the psoas major flowing downward. You can visualize the origin of the upward flow at the center of the pelvic floor (figure *d*).

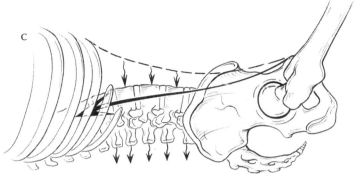

11. See the psoas minor as a strong rubber band pulling the front of the pelvis up toward the part of the spine behind the lower end of the breastbone.

12. Imagine a string connecting the pubic symphisis with the front of the twelfth thoracic vertebrae. Imagine two beads at each end of this string. Visualize the beads sliding toward each other until they touch. You can also think of the beads as being magnetically attracted to each other (figure *e*).

13. Repeat the leg-lowering action five to seven times, even if you are unable to keep the abdominals completely relaxed. This exercise takes a lot of patience and perseverance.

14. Remove the balls, and notice the spreading feeling in the lower back. Also, notice the fluidity and ease of your hip flexion. Notice how easy it feels to sit upright, and check your pelvic alignment in a standing position and in pliés. You may notice the back of the pelvis feels as if it is dropping downward.

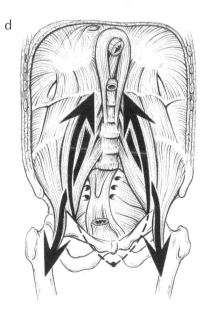

This exercise offers the chance to stretch out the legs and lengthen the iliopsoas muscle without it having to carry the weight of the legs. Ideally the floor you are exercising on is a bit slippery, so you can easily slide the feet downward (or wear socks to help slide).

1. Place the soles of the feet on the floor, and bend the knees at a 90-degree angle (as in figure b of exercise 6.10).

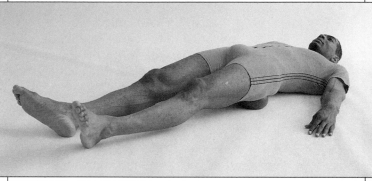

a

2. Slowly slide the feet along the floor until the legs are stretched out (figure a).

3. Rest, and imagine the lower back dropping to the floor.

4. Slide the legs back up, allowing the lower back to drop down toward the floor. Keep the shoulders, neck, and breathing relaxed.

5. Repeat these movements three times using imagery.

6. As you slide the legs in and out, think of the psoas lengthening and the lower back dropping to the floor. Imagine yourself standing with this lengthened sensation in the lower back.

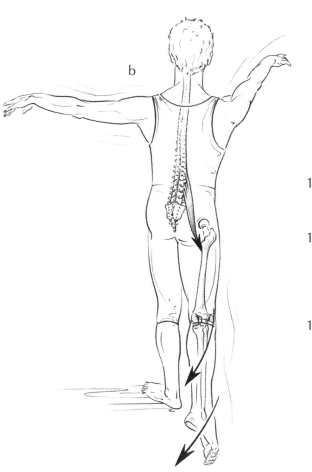

b

7. Stand upright, and imagine the weight of the pelvis resting on the femur heads.

8. Bend and stretch the knees, and think of bouncing the pelvis on the femur heads. Visualize the tailbone dropping to the floor. Think of the sit bones suspended below the femur heads.

9. Brush the hands down the sides of the leg and down the back of the pelvis. Imagine the sides of the legs releasing tension while the support of the femur heads increases.

10. Transfer weight from one leg to the other, and feel the weight being transferred from one femur head to the other. Keep imagining the tail dropping downward.

11. As you walk, think of each swing of a leg as a chance to lengthen the psoas major, to increase the distance between spine and leg. As you perform a battement tendu to the back, think of the leg being released into movement by a lengthening psoas major (figure b).

12. Imagine the front of the pelvis being levitated by the force of the psoas minor while the psoas major flows down next to the spine. If you use this image diligently while walking, you will turn this common movement into an instrument for better dance technique.

It is important to relax the iliopsoas regularly, after dance class and whenever the hips or back feel tight. This exercise releases tension in the whole leg and lower back and requires the help of a ballet barre, or even better, a partner.

1. Attach a Thera-Band securely to the barre, and fasten the looped ends around one of your feet. Lie supine with the legs stretched out. If you are working with a partner, she will cradle one of the legs in a loop of extra-resistant (gray) Thera-Band (see figure). If none are available, a large towel will do.

2. As you are lying on the floor, place one hand just inside the pelvic rim, and visualize the iliopsoas muscle beneath your hand. Imagine the iliopsoas resting fluidly next to the spine.

3. Rotate the leg inward and outward, and visualize the sliding action of the ilioposas filaments: together as you rotate inward and slightly flex the hip joint, and apart as you rotate outward and slightly extend the hip joint.

4. Remove the band, and compare the feeling on both sides of the pelvis and lower back.

5. Perform a low leg kick for comparative purposes.

6. Repeat the exercise on the other side.

7. Walk, and enjoy the feeling of psoas and hip joint freedom.

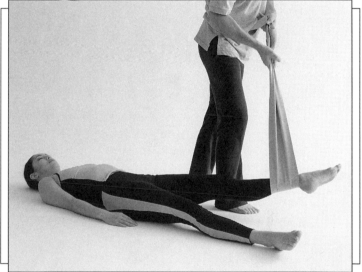

6.13   MELT INTO YOUR PLIÉ

The purpose of this exercise is to discover the iliopsoas as an important factor in a well-aligned and coordinated plié, which releases strain on the knees and keeps the torso and pelvis aligned by creating lift without tension. Iliopsoas awareness helps avoid dropping the weight into the knees.

The imagery promotes equal action of both legs and allows you to engage the adductors; a muscle group key to the specific strength needed in dance. The adductors can be engaged and felt when the iliopsoas muscle group has found balanced length and strength. The adductor–iliopsoas relationship is also described in Pamela Matt's book on the work of Barbara Clark called *A Kinesthetic Legacy, The Life and Works of Barbara Clark* (Matt 1993).

1. Perform a series of pliés in first, then second position, then in first position again. Visualize the sliding action of the iliopsoas muscle filaments, sliding together when you go down, apart when you go up.

2. Imagine the psoas major and the lower back muscles as fluid filled, which is very much the truth, because muscles, like most tissues in the body, are mostly water (see figure).

3. Keep this fluid sensation in the lower back and psoas major muscles as you move up and down in plié.

4. Think of sand particles floating in the fluid. Allow these sand particles to settle downward toward the pelvis.

5. Notice the points that tense up, if any, and think of them becoming fluid or settling downward as sand particles.

6. Feel how you direct the push of the foot on the floor, especially when moving upward into the inner thigh muscles (adductors) and psoas major. Feel these muscles creating a central core of support, allowing the periphery of the body to release excess tension.

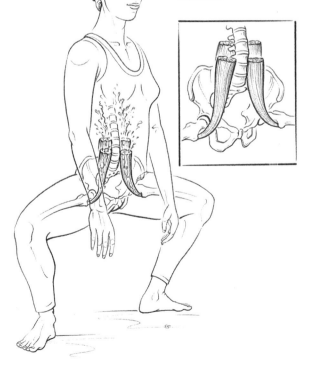

A common problem in dance technique is raising the pelvic half on the side of the extending leg, even in low leg positions, resulting in a sideward bending of the lumbar spine to the side of the supporting leg. This action distorts the supporting leg and may lead to pain in the lower back as the spine contorts to accommodate the pelvic imbalance.

When you first try to perform a développé without raising the pelvic half, you may find it difficult and not know where to get the strength to lift the leg. Many dancers overuse the superficial hip flexors to raise the leg, such as the rectus femoris or tensor fasciae latae. Also, if a dancer is in the habit of tucking the pelvis, she may overuse the abductors to raise the leg. Both of these strategies cause a feeling of tightness and strain above the hip joint, because these muscles are not suited to create high leg elevation. These habits reestablish themselves unless you inhibit them and focus on the desired initiation and supportive imagery.

1. Perform a développé to the front and side, and notice how high and easily your leg moves.

2. Place a hand on the pelvic rim on the side of the extending leg. Notice whether you initiate the développé by lifting the pelvic crest on the side of the leg raise.

3. Remove the hand and try to développé without the pelvic crest lifting up, even if the leg feels frustratingly low. Visualize the insertion of the iliopsoas on the top inside of the femur. Imagine this insertion floating up.

4. Visualize puppet strings attached to the minor trochanter pulling the leg into action. (You may also improvise a dance with this image to really appreciate it; see figure a.)

5. Visualize a downward flow within the psoas major muscle. The flow may feel like a vortex of water spiraling clockwise on the left and counterclockwise on the right. The more you can feel the fluidity of the psoas major, even when it is contracting, the higher the leg can go.

6. Perform a grand battement (high leg kick) while trying to initiate the movement from the contraction of the psoas major (figure b).

7. Before practicing with the other leg, développé the right and left legs and notice any changes in movement sensation.

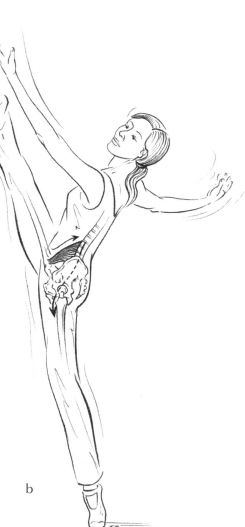

a

b

Well-coordinated iliacus and iliopsoas muscles are important for centered jumps. If your preparation for a jump involves tensing this hip flexor, the back will arch forward when you jump up or land, causing the shoulders and head to move back to compensate (figure *a*). When you land, the pelvis tilts forward, and you have to use a lot of muscle power to stabilize the body (figure *b*). Needless to say, this action hurts the lower back as well as your technique.

The usual correction for this problem is to tighten the abdominal muscles. This solution reduces the bounce and elasticity of the whole body that is key in jumping. It also counternutates the sacrum, creating a less stable iliosacral joint, which is not healthy when you consider the amount of force passing through this joint when you land. Stretching the iliopsoas alone does not solve the problem; you need to become aware of the lengthening action between the top of the thigh and the lower spine when you jump.

1. Practice a few jumps, and notice the feeling and movement of the lower back. If you breathe freely, does the belly pop out? This is a sign that the iliopsoas is not working effectively.

2. Go back to exercises 6.6 though 6.8, and perform a few jumps again. You may notice that the pelvis remains in a more lifted position, without you having to hold the belly as much, if at all. This position frees the breath and increases the body's ability to jump high.

3. Visualize what is happening in the iliopsoas as you prepare to jump and push off into the air. In the preparatory plié before jumping, the iliopsoas shortens, and the filaments slide together. Then as you jump, the iliopsoas rapidly lengthens, and the filaments slide apart. This immediate releasing of the iliopsoas into full length is the key to fluid movement.

a

b

Elastic Length—the Spinal Muscles

The next six imagery exercises prepare the back muscles to benefit more from the conditioning exercises that follow later, by releasing tension and promoting balanced muscle action. You will start with some general imagery for the muscles of the back and then dive down through the muscular layers, using imagery to increase awareness. Visualize the back muscles as a pattern rather than trying to memorize origins and insertions, which wouold be nearly impossible.

MULTIFIDI FOR STABILITY   6.16

As seen from the back (posterior view) the multifidi are part of a deep diagonal series of muscles running up the whole spine (see figure). Seen from the side (lateral view), the angle of pull of the multifidi runs vertically upward from the sacrum to the spinous processes. Aside from being strong extensors, this angle allows the multifidi to stabilize the lumbar spine through compression. It is like keeping a stack of letters from fluttering about by surrounding them with a rubber band running down the sides of the stack.

Do the following exercise for a sense of support in the lower back and pelvis with a focus on the the multifidi.

1. Imagine the multifidi coming alive with new strength to pull the spinous processes down and back.
2. Add the transversus abdominis, integrating the front of the pelvic crests toward the midline of the body.
3. Feel the psoas major lengthening downward and the minor pulling the front of the pelvis upward.

6.17   TOUCHING THE ERECTOR SPINAE

The following exercise increases your awareness of the back muscles and helps you to discover imbalances. You will stay general, not yet focusing on specific muscle groups.

1. Stand comfortably on both legs, and put the fingers on the muscles of the back on both sides of the spine. They can be felt prominently in the lumbar area.
2. Shift the weight to the right leg, and lift the left foot off the floor.
3. With the fingertips, feel the contraction of the back muscles.
4. Shift back to the left leg, and lift the right foot, noticing the reaction in the back muscles.
5. Go back and forth a few more times. Does the bulging of the back muscles feel similar when you are balancing on the right and left legs?
6. For a moment, let the arms rest on both sides of the body, and notice changes in your spinal alignment resulting from your touch.
7. Lean forward, and flex the lumbar spine with fingers on the lower back muscles. Notice whether the muscles on both sides are working equally. In this position bend the spine slightly to the right and then to the left. Does this action feel the same on both sides? Does one side feel more difficult?
8. Come back to an upright position. Standing on the right leg, perform a low arabesque extension. Place the fingers on the back muscles. Does one side feel significantly shorter than the other?
9. Standing on the left leg, perform a low arabesque. Does the situation feel similar to the right side, or is it quite different? What adjustments do you need to make for your arabesque to feel similar on the left and right sides?
10. Rest in an upright standing position, and notice that even merely checking out the back muscles has changed the feeling in the lower back.

6.18   FLOW IN THE SPINAL MUSCLES

Let's now go into action with imagery and movement to discover more detail about the back muscles. This helps fine-tune the engagement of the muscles when you start conditioning with the added resistance of a Thera-Band. You shouldn't just build strength; you should build technique.

1. In a comfortable standing or sitting position, imagine the muscles on both sides of the spine melting downward. Can you feel the muscles melting within their connective tissue sheaths, like honey sliding down the inside of a plastic container?
2. Take a moment to focus on breathing. As you exhale, feel the breath traveling down both sides of the back equally. Imagine the breath as an active force that can remove tension points. It may help to imagine the breath as warm wind on a hot summer day (unless it is a hot summer day and you would prefer a cool breeze).
3. Imagine the back muscles to be soft beeswax. Visualize two droplets of wax melting down on each side of the spine, starting from the back of the head. Do they arrive at the sacrum simultaneously?
4. Imagine the sacrum suspended from the back of the head by the muscles of the back. Imagine this suspension to be elastic like a rubber band.

The following imagery creates a sense of width and support in the back, helps to align the spine, improves balance, and supports a feeling of length and lightness in the arms.

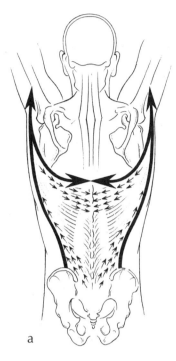

1. Place the arms in second position or horizontally to the side, or stretch them overhead.

2. Visualize the attachments of the latissimus dorsi muscle to the pelvis, sacrum, and lower back. Imagine how this broad muscle condenses into a narrow slip that connects to the top and front of the upper arm bone (see also figure *b* on page 64).

3. Imagine an upward flow through the latissimus dorsi from its attachments to the pelvis, sacrum, and lower back all the way to the front of the arm bones (figure *a*).

4. Imagine a downward flow from the arms to the middle of the back (sixth thoracic vertebrae). See these two rivers creating a wide-based support for arm movement. Imagine this flow supporting the arms from underneath, creating a sense of width and breadth all the way to the fingertips.

5. Imagine the lengthening latissimus dorsi creating the force for powerful arm gestures (figure *b*). Counter the action with a downward lengthening of the gluteus maximus.

a

b

As seen from the rear (posteriorly), there are two basic patterns to the muscles of the back: a somewhat vertical pattern and an upward and inward diagonal pattern. The vertical muscles are mostly superficial, and the diagonals generally deeper.

The muscle closest to the spine in the vertical pattern is the spinalis which connects spinous processes with each other. Lateral to the spinalis is the longissimus and furthest out the iliocostalis. These divisions are not strict; they overlap quite a bit. Viewed from the side there are also patterns of vertically and diagonally arranged muscles. Together with the various connective tissue sheaths these muscles create a complex interweaving network (figure a).

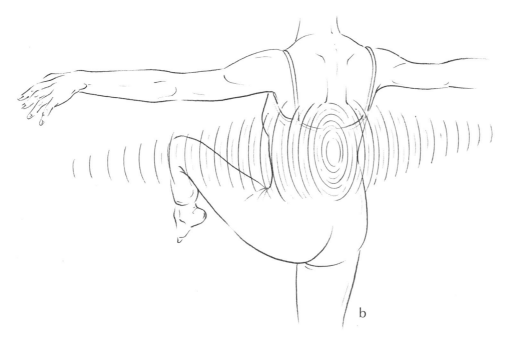

1. Imagine the spinalis widening outward like the rings created in a pool of water, but imagine that this pool is in the frontal plane (figure *b*). The widening may be easier to visualize on inhalation.

2. Imagine the pattern of the longissimus muscle in a slight outward direction as the muscle travels from the sacrum to the ribs. When lengthened, the longissimus will help to create a sense of support in the lower ribs.

3. Image the longissimus as a fountain that originates on the sacrum. Imagine this fountain spurting refreshing liquid up the back to support the back of the head (see figure 8.4).

4. The iliocostalis thoracis connects the transverse processes of the upper spine and ribs with the back of the lower ribs. Imagine the back segment of the lower ribs dangling from both sides of the base of the neck through this muscle. Let this image help you to create a sense of lift within the rib cage.

a

b

The deep erector spinae and the psoas major may also combine to stabilize the lower back like a guyline system (figure a). If the psoas is thought of as a rope that connects the transverse processes of the lumbar spine with the legs, then shortening this rope causes the lumbar spine to be pulled forward and down, hollowing the back and tilting the pelvis forward (figure b). This idea goes hand in hand with shortening the deep erectors. When dancers encounter this situation, they usually contract the abdominal muscles, resulting in tight backs. When the iliopsoas and the deep erector spinae lengthen, the lumbar spine flexes and the front of the pelvis lifts (posterior pelvic tilt; figure c). To reach a more subtle level of spinal muscle balance, consider that the lowest part of the psoas major runs in front of the axis for flexion and extension of the lumbar spine and lumbo-sacral joint. The contraction of this segment of the psoas flexes this part of the spine, especially if supported by a lengthening of the deep erectors (figure d).

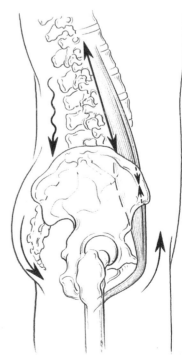

a

1. Image the psoas major and deep erector spinae keeping the lumbar spine in centered balance. The system is like a pyramid, the most stable structure conceived by humans.

2. If the back is too arched, visualize elongation in the deep psoas and the deep erector spinae muscle fibers (filaments sliding apart).

3. Visualize the lower superficial psoas major fibers shortening (filaments sliding together) to support flexion in the lumbar spine, helping to lift the front of the pelvis.

4. If the back tends to be too flat, visualize the opposite.

5. Touch the bony knobs, the posterior superior iliac spines (PSIS) at the back of the pelvis next to the sacrum. Below and to the outside of these knobs, find the origins of the deep erectors.

6. Massage these points. It may feel painful if these muscles are overstrained from compensating for a tight iliopsoas. After the massage you may notice relief in the lower back and a more lengthened lumbar spine.

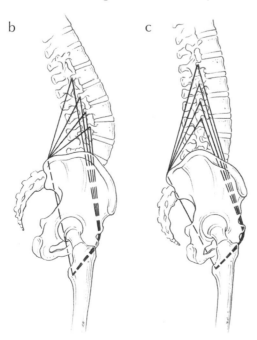

b   c

d

6.22 LENGTHENING HAMSTRINGS AND ERECTOR SPINAE

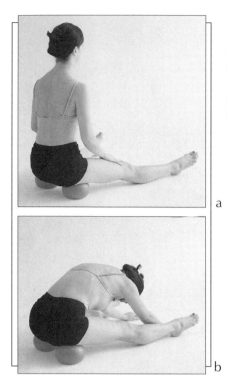

a

b

The multifidi and other lower back muscles have connective tissue connections to the gluteals and hamstrings. This connection causes their action to be somewhat linked, and makes their tension levels interrelated. If the gluteals and hamstrings are tight, so are the lower back muscles and vice versa. For this reason, it is helpful to visualize both muscle groups lengthening at the same time.

1. Sit on a rolled towel or two balls, with the legs stretched to the front (figure a).
2. Slowly flex the spine, allowing the weight of the upper body to do most of the work.
3. Roll down as far as you feel comfortable, visualizing the hamstrings, gluteals, and back muscles sliding apart (figure b).
4. Roll the spine back up, visualizing the hamstrings, gluteals, and back muscle filaments sliding together.
5. Place the hands under the thigh and on the hamstrings muscles. Sense the filaments sliding under the hands. As this happens, allow the muscles to melt into the hands.
6. Repeat the exercise three to five times, then remove the balls and check the ease of your sitting position.

6.23 GLUTEAL TENSION RELEASE

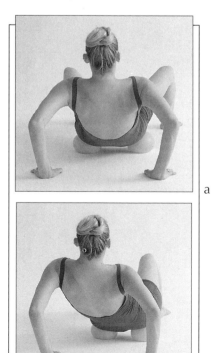

a

b

This is a simple exercise to release tension in the gluteals, hamstrings, and lower back muscles. Again, the reason so many muscles are affected is because of the mechanical linkage of these muscles through the connective tissue.

1. Place two balls under the gluteals, and use the arms to support the body's weight on the balls (figure a).
2. Rotate the pelvis to the left and then the right (figure b), and release any tension spots in the right and left gluteals, respectively. Feel all tension pour out of the muscle and into the floor.
3. Remove the balls, and notice the feeling of release in the lower back. Notice that the back of the pelvis is dropping downward while the front lifts up. The shoulders will feel more relaxed and it will take less effort to perform leg extensions.

The following exercise feels like swimming the breaststroke, only you are holding a Thera-Band. It strengthens the erector spinae, latissimus dorsi, trapezius, and arm extensors.

1. Attach a Thera-Band to a fixed object so the line of pull is parallel to the floor.

2. Lie supine, and hold one end of the band in each hand. Stretch the arms out in front of the body (figure *a*).

3. Pull the band toward you, and lift the chest (figure *b*), bringing the hands under the chest while turning them inward (lower arm supination). Feel the lifting power coming from all the layers of the back musculature, starting with the deepest layer.

4. Stretch the arms out to the sides while turning the hands out again (lower arm pronation; figure *c*).

5. Stretch the arms forward again, and return to the starting position.

6. Inhale as you bring the hands toward the chest. Exhale as you stretch the arms to the side and forward.

7. As you initiate the movement, imagine the tailbone reaching down and forward toward the pubic bone. Keep the abdominal muscles alive by thinking up from the pubic bone to the ribs and breastbone (figure *d*).

8. Feel the deep part of the psoas major, closest to the spine, lengthening. The filaments slide apart as you arch the torso upward. To fine-tune the psoas major, imagine the front part of the muscle knitting together. These ideas keep a lengthened feeling in the lower back, even though you are arching the spine.

a

b

c

9. Notice the changes in back alignment, and balance in a standing position. If you have used imagery, the changes will be much greater than if you had simply gone through the moves.

10. Repeat the exercise six times. Reverse the direction of arm movement, and repeat six more times. Increase to 24 in increments of 2 per week over a four-week period.

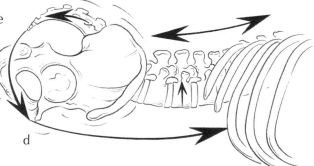

d

HOMOLATERAL CRAWL

This exercise resembles the homolateral movement of a lizard—that is, the arm and leg on the same side of the body move together. It is also an early developmental pattern that the child uses for locomotion before he or she is one year of age. You will use this pattern to create three-dimensional training for the muscles of the torso and back, and to elicit reflexes that help balance and coordinate the muscles of the torso and limbs.

The exercise is best done wearing pants, and on a wood floor. A carpeted floor offers too much resistance to the sliding motions required in the legs.

a

b

1. Attach a Thera-Band to a fixed object so its line of pull is parallel to the floor.

2. Hold one end of the band in each hand (figure a).

3. Move the right knee toward the right elbow, and move the elbow toward the knee, bending the spine to the right (figure b). Look toward the right knee as you do this action.

4. Return to the original position, and repeat the action on the left side, moving the left knee and elbow toward each other, bending the spine to the left, and looking toward your left knee.

5. Balance the sides of the back by imagining you are moving like a crocodile or a lizard (figure c). The movement is a combination of spinal extension and lateral flexion and rotation. Notice these actions happening in your spine simultaneously.

6. Feel the bending of the spine to be equal on both sides. Notice the activation of the muscles that connect the ribs to the pelvic crest, the quadratus lumborum, and the oblique abdominals.

7. Use the eyes to direct the movement. Keep the movement of the eyes smooth, and smoothness will be reflected in the way you use the muscles.

8. Keep the pelvis close to the floor. If you lift it, the back will arch, possibly causing tightness in the lower back muscles.

9. Repeat the exercise 12 times, and increase to 20 times in increments of 2 each week over a four-week period.

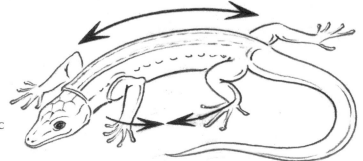

c

The following exercise strengthens the muscles of the back, the abdominal muscles, and the arm and hip musculature. It creates more flexibility in the shoulder, and increases the sense of length in the spine.

1. Attach a loop of Thera-Band to a fixed object at shoulder level. Move forward and backward from the point of attachment to adjust tension in the band.
2. Hold the loop of band overhead while flexing the spine (figure *a*). (Make a dance contraction.) As you flex, exhale and feel the abdominal muscles dropping toward the spine.
3. While flexing the spine and bringing the arms forward, focus on following muscles that are in the process of lengthening—the serratus anterior connecting the inner edge of the shoulder blades with the ribs, or the descending trapezius connecting the back of the head with the scapula.
4. Arch (extend) the spine while moving the arms to the back (figure *b*).
5. While extending the spine and bringing the arms back and over the head, imagine the latissimus dorsi and levator scapulae lengthening. Feel the deep knitting action of the transverse abdominal muscles to support the lower back.
6. While extending, feel the erector spinae muscle filaments sliding apart while flexing and sliding together.
7. Slowly return the arms and spine to the starting position.
8. Repeat 8 times, and increase to 15 times in increments of 2 each week over a four-week period.

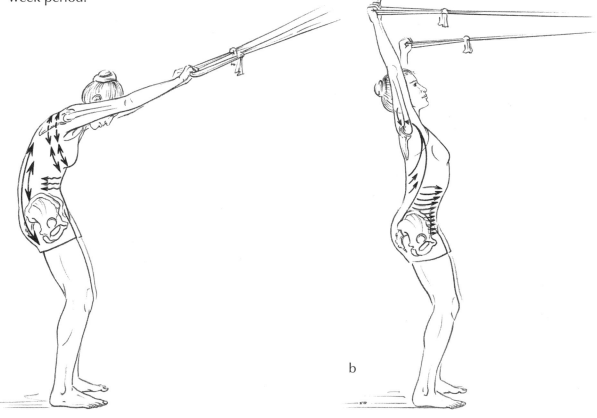

a   b

The rectus series muscles link the tailbone to the tip of the jaw. They used to be one long muscle in our primitive animal ancestors, but in our case the chain is interrupted by bony links. The muscles in this series are: the pubococcygeus connecting the tailbone to the pubic bone, the rectus abdominis connecting the pubic bone to the breastbone, the sternohyoid connecting the breastbone to the hyoid bone, and the geniohyoid connecting the hyoid to the jaw. All of these muscles help to flex the spine. They are opposed by the erector spinae, which runs along the length of the back. The erector spinae also consists of different muscles, albeit not interrupted by bony links. In this exercise, you will strengthen and balance these two muscle chains, benefiting the alignment and strength of the back.

a

1. Attach a Thera-Band to a fixed object at chest level. Move forward and backward from the point of attachment to adjust the tension level of the band. There should be sufficient resistance throughout the exercise.

2. Imagine the rectus series connecting the tailbone to the tip of the jaw. Touch the tail and the tip of the jaw before you start the exercise to get a sense of the length of this muscle chain.

3. Stand in parallel with the arms stretched forward with the end of the band in each hand.

4. Flex the spine along its whole length from head (atlas) to tail (figure a). Imagine the back of the spine lengthening.

5. Bring the arms forward while flexing the spine.

6. When you flex the spine, initiate simultaneously at the tailbone and at the tip of the jaw. Make sure the jaw stays relaxed, but don't jut it forward. Imagine the tip of the jaw and the tail coming closer to each other and the whole muscle chain working equally. Visualize the muscle filaments sliding together at the front midline of the body.

7. Pull the band down toward you, and extend the spine, starting from the tail and top of the head simultaneously (figure b). Keep the arms straight, and imagine the front of the spine lengthening. Also think of the tip of the jaw and the tail moving away from each other.

8. Create a harmonious curve through the whole spine, including the neck. Because the upper spine is so mobile in extension, we tend to move the head back too far.

9. Exhale as you flex the spine, and inhale as you extend the spine.

10. Focus on the rectus series of muscles several times until you get a sense of smooth and continuous action. Then do the same for the muscles in back. Focus only on the lengthening and shortening of the erector spinae filaments.

11. Finally, as you extend the spine, try to combine visualizing the lengthening of the rectus muscles in front with a shortening of the erectors in back. Visualize the shortening of the rectus series in front and the lengthening of the erectors in back as you flex the spine.

12. Repeat the exercise 12 times. Increase to 20 times in increments of 2 each week over a four-week period.

b

In-Depth Power—The Abdominal Muscles

I have discussed the rectus abdominis in connection with the tail–jaw series of muscles, and now I continue with the oblique abdominals and the deepest layer, the transverse abdominal muscles. I have also included some exercises that train the muscles forming the back of the lower body wall, the quadratus lumborum.

The oblique abdominal muscles (obliques) are part of a larger system of muscles that envelops the body in a double spiral arrangement. They are important for rotating the torso relative to the pelvis, which is a key component of powerful limb movement. They aid in lateral flexion of the spine and assist the rectus abdominis in flexing the spine.

There are two obliques, a more superficial outer layer and a deeper inner layer. The outer obliques (obliquus externus) run from the ribs toward the centerline of the body and connect to the aponeurosis (connective tissue covering) of the rectus abdominis. Imagine sliding the hands in your pants pockets, and you have the approximate fiber direction of the external obliques. The inner obliques are located in an opposing diagonal running from the midline toward the pelvic crest on the outside. The inner obliques each have the look of a fan spreading from its attachment to the pelvic crests.

Repeat each of the following exercises 12 times, and increase to 20 times in increments of 2 times a week over a four-week period.

HIP FLEXION WITH TWIST   6.28

This exercise strengthens the hip flexors and the rectus and oblique abdominal muscles. It also improves coordination by balancing the diagonal forces through the body from right shoulder to left hip and from left shoulder to right hip. It is an advanced exercise and should not be performed by someone with back problems. For a reduced level of effort, perform the exercise without a Thera-Band. In a healthy exerciser the exercise provides a sense of lower back ease and length through the training of the iliopsoas.

a

b

1. Tie a loop of Thera-Band around a fixed attachment 10 inches above the floor.

2. Lie supine, facing away from the attachment, and put one end of the loop around both knees.

3. Support the head with both hands, and lift your shoulders and feet off the floor (figure a).

4. Flex the right hip joint, twist the upper body to the right, and move the left elbow to the right knee (figure b).

5. Move back to center while the right hip joint extends.

6. Repeat steps 4 and 5 for the left side.

7. Focus on the oblique muscles that are lengthening during the exercise. When you twist the upper body to the right, think of the muscles between the right side of the rib cage and the left side of the pelvis lengthening. When you twist to the left, think of the muscles between the left side of the rib cage and the right pelvic half lengthening. Do both sides lengthen equally?

6.29 SWINGING LUNGS

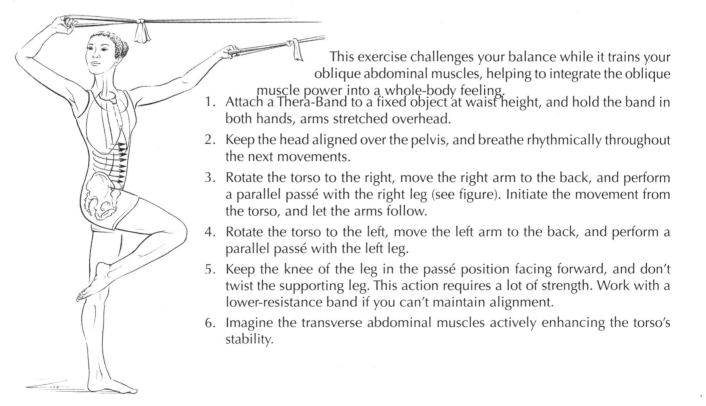

The aim of this exercise is to train the oblique abdominal muscles as rotators of the trunk in conjunction with the deep rotators of the spine. Because we are also using the whole body, the exercise also improves balance and coordination.

1. Attach a loop of Thera-Band to a fixed object at waist level.

2. Hold each end of the band or make loops to hold on to. (Special grips that you can attach to a loop of Thera-Band are also available; see the references and resources section list on page 234.)

3. Rotate the torso to the right, pull the band to the rear with the right arm, and step forward with the right foot (see figure).

4. Rotate the torso to the left, pull the band to the rear with the left arm, and step forward with the left foot.

5. If you flex the spine just slightly while you are rotating to the side, you will increase the activity of the oblique abdominal muscles.

6. The more you can relax the shoulder muscles, especially the trapezius, the greater your range of rotation.

7. Imagine the lungs swinging around the spine to create ease and lightness in the movement. Think of the lungs initiating the movement and the torso following.

6.30 OBLIQUE STRENGTH, RHYTHM, AND BREATH WITH PASSÉ

This exercise challenges your balance while it trains your oblique abdominal muscles, helping to integrate the oblique muscle power into a whole-body feeling.

1. Attach a Thera-Band to a fixed object at waist height, and hold the band in both hands, arms stretched overhead.

2. Keep the head aligned over the pelvis, and breathe rhythmically throughout the next movements.

3. Rotate the torso to the right, move the right arm to the back, and perform a parallel passé with the right leg (see figure). Initiate the movement from the torso, and let the arms follow.

4. Rotate the torso to the left, move the left arm to the back, and perform a parallel passé with the left leg.

5. Keep the knee of the leg in the passé position facing forward, and don't twist the supporting leg. This action requires a lot of strength. Work with a lower-resistance band if you can't maintain alignment.

6. Imagine the transverse abdominal muscles actively enhancing the torso's stability.

The upper abdominal twist emphasizes the strengthening of the rectus abdominis and the obliques. It also activates the intercostals (muscles between the ribs) that are actually the continuation into the rib cage of the line of pull of the obliques. This exercise may make traditional crunches seem effortless. It is another example of advanced conditioning for the abdominal muscles and should not be performed by someone suffering from a back problem. For a reduced level of effort, perform the exercise without the resistance of the Thera-Band.

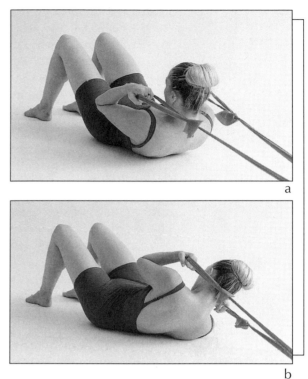

1. Attach a Thera-Band to a fixed object about 10 inches off the ground. Lie supine, facing away from the attachment of the band.

2. Hold a loop of band around each hand and place the hands next to the head. Alternately you can position the hands behind the head to create a cradling support. The knees form a 90-degree angle.

3. Lift the head, one vertebrae after another off the floor, keeping the hands next to the head. The back rim of the pelvis remains on the ground (figure a).

4. Twist the upper body to the right and then to the left (figure b). Return to center.

5. Visualize the sliding of the rectus and oblique abdominal filaments. The image created by the term *crunch* is not favorable for a good abdominal action, because the spine is overly compressed.

6. Focus on lengthening the spinal muscles as you roll up. Imagine that they could provide the power to lift you.

7. Roll back down to the floor, vertebrae after vertebrae, and repeat the movement as soon as the head touches the floor.

8. Think of being supported by water as if you were made of cork. Imagine the water pushing you up and back and forth as you twist (figure c).

9. To increase the effect on the obliques, drop the legs to the opposite side the torso is moving.

Activating the Transversus Abdominis

Often abdominal conditioning emphasizes the rectus abdominis with some consideration for the obliques and little mention of the transversus abdominis. The rectus abdominis is certainly important support for the abdominal organs, and it balances the action of the diaphragm. But a conditioned transversus abdominis is a major support for the lower spine and, together with a balanced iliopsoas, creates the slim and trim waistline so esteemed by dancers. It originates from the lumbar spine by a broad expanse of connective tissue, the thoracolumbar fascia. The lower part originates from the front of the pelvic crest. In its upper part, the transversus abdominis blends with the fibers of the diaphragm. Breathing is therefore a key element in the next exercise. As visualized in the standing position, the rectus abdominis runs vertically, and the transversus runs horizontally. It is advisable to spend some time exercising the iliopsoas and multifidi muscle groups before conditioning the transverses abdominis. The transversus abdominis is easier to experience and activate once the iliopsoas has contributed its share to pelvic balance.

One of the ideokinetic lines of movement focuses on activating the transversus abdominis as a key to aligned and centered movement. This line of movement narrows the front of the pelvis and can be supported by the image of a zipper moving up the front of imaginary pants, making them tighter in front (see Franklin 1996b, page 6). Nutation is linked to a concentric action of the transversus abdominis; counternutation (sacrum back and up) to the eccentric action of the transversus. Counternutation loosens the joint between the ilium and sacrum; nutation locks it into a tighter hold. Because many dancers tuck the pelvis in an effort to lift it and create a flatter contour for the buttocks, they actually make the pelvic girdle less stable and compensate by increased tension in their gluteals and quadriceps. These muscles then overdevelop, and the act of trying to make the buttocks vanish by tucking creates the opposite of what has been desired.

The concentric contraction of the abdominals—the rectus and obliques and the upper part of the transversus—pushes the organs to the rear and flexes the spine. What makes the lower transversus so valuable is its ability to counterbalance this action. When you nutate the sacrum, which tilts the pelvis forward, the rectus abdominis lengthens (concentric action) while the tranversus abdominis shortens (eccentric action). This change in the length of the transversus is not large, but it is enough to significantly stabilize the pelvis (figure 6.4).

This does not mean you should dance with a forward-tilted pelvis, but that conditioning the abdominals should involve an active concentric and eccentric component of the transversus abdominis muscle. Also, sacral nutation and anterior tilt of the pelvis link concentric action of the psoas with that of the transversus abdominis. Sacral counternutation and posterior tilt of the pelvis couple eccentric action of the psoas with eccentric action of the transversus.

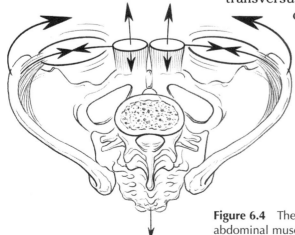

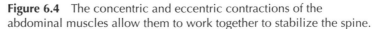

Figure 6.4 The concentric and eccentric contractions of the abdominal muscles allow them to work together to stabilize the spine.

Visualizing and initiating the pelvic tilting with a focus on the transversus greatly enhances your sense of pelvis control and centering, even though it takes a bit of practice. Most of us are not used to feeling the deep layers of abdominal muscles, and tilting the pelvis forward feels as if the belly is being pushed out without any abdominal support. The body does not let this dangerous lack of support happen; the transversus acts to create support in this position.

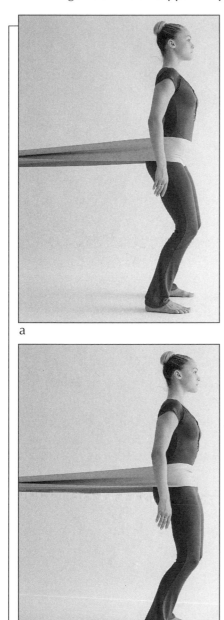

a

b

1. Loop a high-resistance Thera-Band (gray) around the pelvis, and attach it to a fixed object at hip level.

2. Standing, face away from the attachment, and push the pelvis into the band until you feel the abdominal muscles coming alive.

3. Tilt the pelvis forward, and sense the sit bones moving apart while the ASIS moves together.

4. Tilt the pelvis backward, and sense the sit bones moving together while the ASIS moves apart.

5. Tilt the pelvis forward by thinking of a concentric action in the lower transversus. Imagine this muscle as active and alive just at the inside and deep to the left and right pelvic crest. You may not be able to do this at the outset. Keep thinking this until it wakes up (figure a).

6. As you tilt the pelvis to the front, bring the rectus abdominis into focus. It is lengthening while the transversus shortens.

7. Tilt the pelvis to the rear, and think *eccentric* (lengthening) in the transversus. Think *spread* in the muscle at the inside, and *deep* to the left and right pelvic crest (figure b).

8. Tilt the pelvis to the back, and visualize the antagonistic action of the lower transversus and rectus abdominis: The rectus acts concentrically and the transversus eccentrically as the pelvic bones widen in front because of the posterior tilting of the pelvis.

9. Imagine the abdominals as a stretchy sweater (obliques and rectus) reaching down to the pubic symphysis and a pair of pants beneath (transversus) with a zipper starting at the level of the pubic symphysis. When you tilt the pelvis forward, the zipper of the pants moves up and pulls the pants together in front. The sweater stretches (figure c). As you tilt the pelvis to the back, think of the zipper moving down, slackening the pants to the side. The sweater shrinks elastically.

10. Repeat five times.

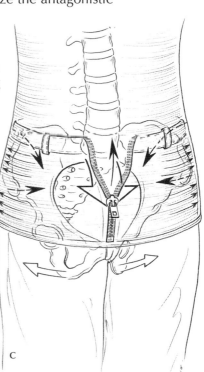

c

This exercise combines a traditional abdominal curl with awareness of the transversus abdominis. You use the transversus to stabilize the pelvis as you lower the torso out of the curl. Developing this awareness is valuable for reverse arching movements (spinal extension).

1. Attach a Thera-Band to a fixed object 10 inches off the ground. Lie supine with the torso facing away from the attachment, and place a loop of the band around each knee (figure a).

2. Place the hands behind the head for support, and let the band pull the knees slightly away from the torso.

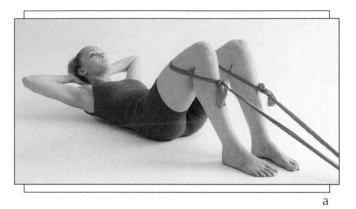

a

4. Feel length in the spine and openness in the hip joints.

5. Exhale as you lift the head, upper spine, and right leg, as in a traditional abdominal curl.

6. Inhale as you lower the head and upper torso slowly, drawing the waistline inward.

7. Repeat the movement (steps 5 and 6) lifting the left leg.

8. Experience the rectus abdominis and the transversus abdominis as separate muscles. As you lift the head and upper spine, feel the rectus abdominis filaments sliding together. As you lower the head and upper spine, feel the filaments of the transversus abdominis sliding together, slimming the waistline (figure b).

9. Image the transversus abdominis as a cylindrical shape-changing muscle cone deep within the other abdominal muscles. The cone narrows as you lower the back and head to the floor.

10. As you lower the back to the floor, employ the hands that are placed behind the head to gently pull backward, and lengthen the spine.

11. Repeat the exercise 12 times, and increase to 20 in increments of 2 each week over a four-week period.

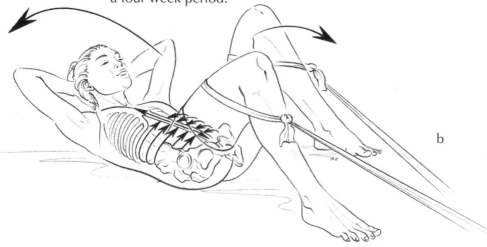

b

Quadratus Lumborum

The quadratus lumborum is squarish and flat in shape. It extends between the upper rim of the pelvis and the lowest rib with connections to the transverse processes of the spine. This muscle is important for alignment, because it controls the connection between the back of the rib cage and the back of the pelvis. It is intimately connected with the state of the iliopsoas group and the abdominal muscles. Once you condition the quadratus lumborum, your alignment and freedom of movement in the pelvis and hip joint will improve.

The fibers of the quadratus lumborum display a woven pattern. They run straight up and down from the pelvic rim to the twelfth rib, as well as diagonally from the pelvic crest and ribs to the transverse processes of the spine (figure 6.5).

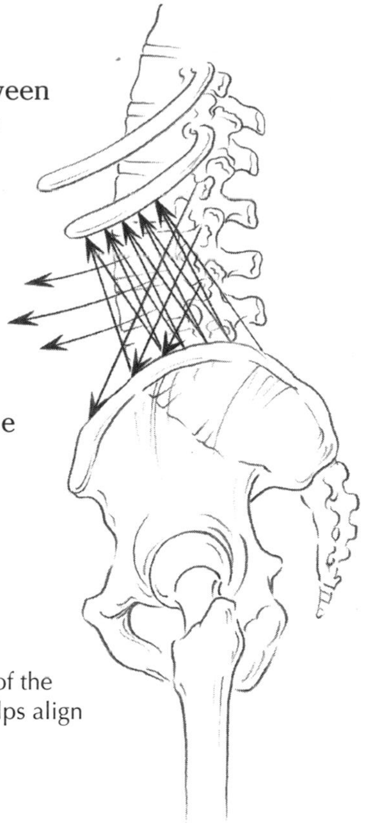

Figure 6.5 The woven pattern of the quadratus lumborum muscle helps align the pelvis and the spine.

EXPERIENCING THE QUADRATUS 6.34

Once you have conditioned the quadratus and iliopsoas, you will have a strong connection between the pelvis and rib cage. You may feel as if these muscles have sufficient force to create lumbo-pelvic alignment without excess tension in the abdominal muscles. You will have a sense of great power in the back body wall, a helpful notion for dancers who also sing. A natural hollowing of the abdominal muscles ensues, as if they were dropping back effortlessly. Magic does happen, but it takes a lot of practice.

1. Move the thumb along the upper rim of the pelvis, from front to back all the way to the PSIS.
2. Try to touch the lowest rib. This task is not as easy as palpitating the crest of the pelvis, but even a general touch in the area of the lowest ribs in back will suffice.
3. Once you remove the fingers, you may notice that your touch has already changed the alignment of the lower back.
4. Visualize a muscle connecting the two areas you have touched.
5. Place the hands roughly on the area covered by the quadratus lumborum. As you inhale, feel the muscle expanding and anchoring the lowest rib to the pelvis.
6. As you exhale, think of the quadratus lumborum as a continuation of the diaphragm all the way down to the pelvis.
7. Visualize the woven pattern of the muscle. Allow this weave to stretch elastically as you inhale.

The combined action of the diagonal fibers can pull the lumbar spine forward into extension and can assist in side bending. By anchoring the rib cage to the pelvis, the quadratus lumborum is important for keeping the hip level when you are lifting one leg. This anchoring is also important for stabilizing the diaphragm in breathing. Were the first rib not anchored by the quadratus lumborum, the diaphragm might move up when it contracts, making breathing impossible. Because the muscle adjoins the psoas major, these muscles influence each other. It helps to have a good sense of the psoas major before you begin to embody the quadratus lumborum.

a

1. Lie supine with two balls under the pelvis, and stretch the legs straight up (figure *a*).

2. Rock the pelvis back and forth 12 times by increasing the distance between ribs and pelvis on one side while shortening this distance on the other. Resist using the hip joints instead of the spine to initiate the action.

3. Stretch the left leg to the side, and hold the bent right knee with your hand (figure *b*).

4. Repeat the rocking action 12 times in this position. Let the pelvis move the stretched leg.

5. Increase to 20 repetitions in increments of 2 per week over a 4-week period.

6. Repeat steps 3 through 5 with the right leg.

7. Visualize the alternate lengthening and shortening of the quadratus.

8. Imagine the ribs trying to touch the pelvic crest and the pelvic crest trying to touch the ribs.

9. After completing the exercise, stand up and notice the position of the pelvis and the feeling in your lower back. Try a développé extension or a step of your choice with the newfound support of the quadratus lumborum muscle.

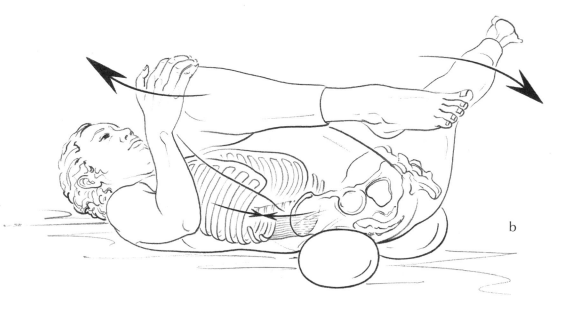

b

chapter 7

Building Power in the Legs and Feet

Most dancers are constantly concerned with the strength, flexibility, and aesthetics of the legs and feet. Surprisingly, many dancers have a negative image of their feet. I once was coaching a dancer with her plié when she announced, as if to warn me of impending doom, "I have awful feet." "You have awful feet?" I responded as I looked at her feet and could see nothing obviously wrong with them. I asked, "You mean you would like to improve your feet?" Nervously, she agreed.

This and similar experiences have convinced me how deleterious self-judgment can be when it comes to the dancer's body. A dancer imbuing a part of the body with a strong negative image blocks her road to improving that part of the body. Ask a group of dancers, *Do you like your feet?* and many will have reservations. Then ask them how they treat someone they do not particularly appreciate, and they begin to get the message. Sometimes the result of this foot fear is excessive foot training practices where the feet are forced to adapt to desired aesthetics. The key is to integrate increased strength in the feet and legs into a whole-body feeling. The position and movement of the feet reverberate throughout the body; a change in position in the spine and pelvis influences the feet. Therefore, improving coordinated action and muscle balance as you strengthen the legs and feet is the key to successful foot and leg conditioning.

I have seen performers who looked as if they had great feet on stage, but when their motion was analyzed, they were found to have less than average range and arch. These dancers used their feet in an advantageous way and strengthened their action with imagery (see also Franklin 1996a, pages 100–103). Even if the feet are not perfect from the prevailing aesthetic standard, this does not mean they are not suitable for dance. Often feet that have a very high arch from inherent flexibility are prone to injury from incorrect alignment and lack of strength in the supporting musculature. For the longevity of the dancer, foot strength and alignment are the primary concerns, and aesthetics should be secondary. What use are the beautiful feet if the dancer is sidelined because of injury? Besides, most foot imperfections can be resolved by conditioning that is based on sound understanding of the interrelationship of the joints of the feet, legs, and pelvis.

Let me describe an example of such an interrelationship: If a dancer turns out the feet more than the hip joint can accommodate, the feet tend to pronate, lowering the inner borders of the feet and dropping the front of the pelvis. As a response, the dancer may try to lift the inner border of his feet with extra muscular effort and supinate the foot. This action reverberates along the whole joint chain up the leg to the pelvic bones. The sit bones are pushed together, the sacrum counternutates, and ease of motion is lost in the hip joints. The knees are pushed forward in plié, and the dancer pulls them backward in an effort to keep them aligned. Pressure builds in the joints of the leg, feet, and lower back. Also, the muscle that supinates the foot is a powerful plantar flexor (foot pointer) as well (see following text for a note on terminology). A plié, however, requires the foot to flex dorsally (flex, in dancer terms). Obviously the movement of pointing the feet does not go well with the action of a plié. If the dancer trains in this set of circumstances, he will develop tense, hard muscles predisposing him to pain and injury.

Conditioning in and of itself only strengthens the deleterious pattern. Unless the movement is corrected through the dancer's personal experience of a preferable movement pattern, the problem will not be resolved. This resolution should proceed through using the correct amount of turn-out based on the dancer's anatomical potential and creating coordinated joint and muscle action through the legs and feet, which will in itself increase turn-out by releasing tension.

A note about terminology: Dancers often use the word *flex* to denote anatomical dorsiflexion of the ankle—a pulling up of the back of the foot toward the shin bone. In a pointed foot the ankle is *plantarflexed,* and the foot as a whole is in a flexed position. This terminology may be confusing because the term *flexion* appears to describe opposing positions of the foot. You may be able to remember what direction the foot is supposed to be going by thinking of dorsal fin (on a dolphin's back) for dorsiflexion and plants (plants are usually underneath your feet) for plantarflexion. For the action of the toes, I use the anatomical terminology flexion when bending them down and extension for lifting them up.

Strong, Coordinated Feet

Strong and well-coordinated feet are a cornerstone of a dancer's technique. In most styles of dance (except perhaps for contact improvisation and modern dance styles that use the hands and arms for balancing), the feet and legs are used proportionally more for support than the upper body. As a result, the feet need to withstand much of the body's weight in an infinite variety of constellations and speeds. Because of time constraints, most dance classes can offer only a limited amount of preparation for the feet. Inadequately conditioning the feet causes overuse syndromes and rapid wear and tear of the joints, muscles, and connective tissue. Knowledge of the coordinated action of the front and back part of the foot enables a dancer to gain her full ROM for the whole body. Many traditional ideas about how to correct the feet actually impede natural foot action, because they do not take a holistic approach. The foot does not have a life of its own. Rather, its movement is related to the movement of the hip, pelvis, and spine.

Before you exercise the foot with a Thera-Band, look at key extrinsic muscles that control the action of the ankle and foot and greatly influence your stability and power to move—the tibialis posterior, the peroneus longus, and the flexor hallucis longus. The extrinsic muscles of the foot, as opposed to the intrinsic ones located wholly in the foot, originate outside of and insert in the foot.

Having explored the complex movements of the pelvis and legs, we now address awareness of the feet. This exercise creates more flexibility and better alignment, from which strength is gained. I have seen dancers improve their balance and jumps just from doing this foot exploration.

1. Stand comfortably with the legs in parallel or in a turned-out position. Imagine the feet are on a flat unchangeable surface, such as hardwood or cement. Perform a plié and notice the flexibility and ease of movement of your ankle, knee, and hip joints.

2. Now image the floor as clay that adapts and supports changes in the foot as you plié. Notice the flexibility and ease of movement in the ankle, knee, and hip joints.

3. Lift the inner border of your feet (supinate) as you bend the legs and notice how this adversely affects the flexibility of the ankle, knee, and hip joints. Clearly, forceful lifting is not the solution.

4. Sit down, and with one hand firmly hold the right forefoot; with the other, hold the heel.

5. Twist the foot along its length as if it you were trying to wring water out of a wet cloth or sponge. Move your hands back and forth, slowly at first, then with increasing speed. Repeat this twisting several times.

6. Stand up and compare the feeling of the legs and pelvic halves in a plié. You may notice a significant difference in ease of motion and flexibility gains. Also, your balance will improve on the side that you touched, and jumps will be easier to perform.

7. Perform the same touch procedure with the other foot.

MOVING THE BONES OF THE FOOT   7.2

It is helpful to visualize the bones and muscles in action. If you do this while conditioning, your exercises will be more precise and coordinated, resulting in better dance technique. Build a positive image of the feet, recognizing problems but focusing on the solutions.

1. Hold one foot in both hands, and flex and extend the big toe (figure a).

2. Use the hands to increase the range of movement and allow flexion at the tarsometatarsal joints, where the small bones of the tarsus meet the long bones of the middle foot.

3. Repeat this action with each toe of the foot, one after the other.

4. Move the hands further back; push the sides of the foot down and pull them to the side. Imagine spreading the bones of the foot, creating space between them (figure b).

5. Imagine the foot as a fan you can widen out to the side. Try to move the big and little toes to the side (abduction).

a   b

Now that you have experienced the feeling of allowing the feet to change their configuration as you move the legs, you can appreciate its anatomical basis. Key joints in the foot are the subtalar, transverse tarsal, and tarsometatarsal joints (see Franklin 1996b, pages 173–186). These joints do not move independently of each other when bearing weight. As you move downward and back up in a plié, the front of the foot subtly twists, first supinating and then pronating. This movement is important for optimally supported leg action in the closed chain. The twisting action often occurs as a reaction to an uneven surface.

Twisting gives the feet an added dimension by which they can generate force and deal with the shifting load of the body as the center of gravity moves down and up. It also helps the foot to change easily between its dual roles of base of support and propulsion lever. By wringing the feet in exercise 7.1, you tuned the feet to this action. Now you can support the action by imaging anatomical changes as well.

1. Begin this exercise in a comfortable first position, or choose parallel or second position. Imagine each foot as two barrels on the floor. One barrel represents the back of the foot, and the other the front. The barrels touch in the tarsal area of each foot.

2. As you bend the legs, imagine the back barrels of both feet spinning toward the front of the body, while the front barrels spin toward the back. Spinning simply means that they stay in place and rotate. With imagery, exaggeration is permitted. The movement is just a small twist; the spinning barrels are intended to help you become aware of the feedback from the nervous system.

3. As you stretch the legs, the back barrels spin to the back of the body, and the front barrels spin to the front.

4. Repeat the action several times until you get a feel for it.

5. Appreciate what happens when you use the opposite image: As you bend the legs, let the back barrels spin to the back, lifting the inner border of the heel bone. As you stretch the legs, imagine the front barrels spinning out, lifting the inner borders of the front of the feet. Both of these images impede the flexibility of your legs. This image is complicated, but think of it as a game of body organization that need not be won instantly. As you plié, think of the pelvic halves turning in, the femurs rotating out, the lower leg turning in, the heel turning in, and the front of the foot turning out (see figure).

6. As you stretch the legs, reverse the actions: The pelvic halves turn out, the femurs in, the lower legs out, the heel in, and the front of the foot out.

7. Practice by selectively focusing on different relationships. You may also add the widening of the sit bones as you go down, which correlates to widening at the base of the skull.

Similar to efficient iliopsoas action with respect to the pelvis, the tibialis posterior helps the foot feel lifted. The tibialis posterior originates from the tibia, fibula, and the membrane between these two bones (interosseous membrane). It passes under the inner ankle bone and attaches to the tarsal bones (except the talus). It is a powerful inverter of the foot and can plantar flex the foot and ankle. It is important for maintaining a strong arch. Inversion may be simply described as a lifting of the inner border and a lowering of the outer border of the foot. Together with the peroneus longus and anterior tibialis, the tibialis posterior forms a sling similar to a powerful net grasping the tarsal bones and lifting them toward the lower leg. If the tibialis posterior is weak, the dancer's foot rolls onto the inner border, making it difficult to raise the heel and balance on the ball of the foot.

The ability of the tibialis posterior to lift the foot is important in actions requiring a smooth lowering of the body's weight. If the tibialis posterior is weak, the body is not sufficiently cushioned when landing from a jump. The resulting dropping down of the inner ankle bone strains the ligaments inside the foot.

1. Touch the inside of the shin bone, and feel its sharp edge. At the back of this edge you can feel the tibialis posterior when you invert and plantar flex the foot. This action involves the whole foot, and is also known as supination.

2. When you practice supination do not avoid a sickle-shaped foot action which, from the point of view of ballet aesthetics, is displeasing. It is important to strengthen the tibialis posterior. If you invert with a somewhat dorsiflexed foot, you engage the tibialis anterior.

3. When you lower the weight from a relevé position, imagine the tibialis posterior lengthening gradually.

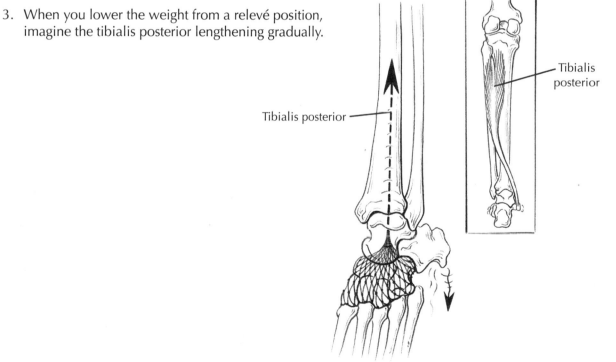

Tibialis posterior

Tibialis posterior

STRENGTHENING THE PERONEUS LONGUS

The peroneus longus arises from the head of the fibula and from the lateral surface of the fibular shaft. It runs vertically downward and behind the lateral malleolus (ankle bone). It passes through a groove in the cuboid bone that acts as a guiding channel much like a canal that directs water. It passes diagonally across the sole of the foot and inserts into the base of the first metatarsal (of the big toe). It opposes the tibialis posterior. The peroneus longus muscle helps to maintain weight over the central axis of the foot in the relevé action, and it supports the lateral arch of the foot (see figure). It also assists the large calf muscles, the gastrocnemius and soleus, in plantarflexing the foot.

The peroneus longus everts the foot, raising its outer border and lowering its inner border. You can feel the belly of the peroneus longus muscle on the outside of the lower leg when you evert. Its function in an ape is to aid the foot's grip when climbing trees. It still retains a bit of its grasping ability in humans, helping to stabilize the foot on the floor. Without enough strength in the peroneus longus, the ankle is in danger of falling to the outside when the heel is raised off the floor (relevé).

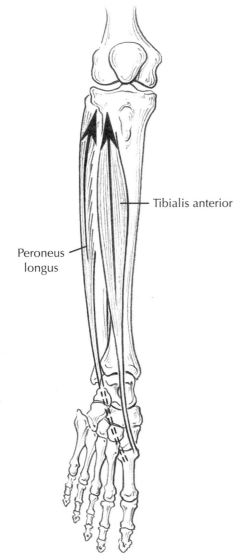

Tibialis anterior

Peroneus
longus

1. Standing with your weight equally distributed on both feet and with the legs parallel, raise the heel, and lift your weight up onto the ball of the toes. Visualize the peroneus longus supporting the outside of the foot and bringing your weight over the center of the foot, the second toe.

2. When raised on the ball of the foot, move the ankles to the outside, only to move the feet back to center again while feeling the activity of the peroneus longus.

3. Repeat this action several times before you slowly lower the feet down again.

Babies are not born with arches. The arch develops in response to stimulation through movement and weight bearing. The arch is therefore highly dynamic and is created by the shaping of the bones, ligaments, connective tissue, and by the activity of the muscles. The foot is well adapted to its functions of propulsion, weight bearing, sensing uneven ground, and shock absorption. As a sensory organ the foot is in constant dialogue with the dancing surface. The two relatively new developments in the nearly seven million years of human foot history are flat surfaces and shoes. Shoes limit the training of the foot just as they may help to support it. Flat floors eliminate much of the twisting and bending that keep the joints and muscles of the foot well conditioned. Faulty shoes and lack of variety in the training of the foot to compensate for flat floors are reasons why dancers have foot problems.

The flexor hallucis longus, the long toe flexor, is an example of a muscle important for maintaining the arch of the foot. This muscle originates at the back of the fibula and crosses diagonally down the back of the lower leg to cross under the inner ankle and down the inside of the foot to the big toe (see figure). The back of the talus and the underbelly of the sustentaculum tali provide grooves to channel the tendon of the flexor hallucis longus. The sustentaculum tali is a small bony balcony jutting out from the inside of the heel bone. Its name means the supporter of the talus. If the flexor hallucis longus is weak, the balcony is not supported, and the inner border of the ankle sags downward.

1. Visualize the flexor hallucis longus to help guide the big toe in the right direction in rapid moves across the floor.

2. Visualize the diagonal line at the back of the lower leg from the fibula to the inner ankle and to the big toe. It helps integrate the whole foot action when training.

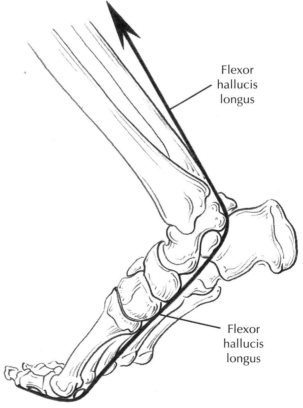

Flexor hallucis longus

Flexor hallucis longus

This exercise increases foot and ankle strength, improving jumps and leaps and all actions of the foot. It improves the flexibility of the hamstrings and, because of the sensory stimulation it provides to the toes, it also improves balance. What looks like a foot workout is beneficial for the whole lower limb, because the whole leg is learning to coordinate. The increased dynamic action of the foot helps release the lower back of the same side.

1. Use a medium-strength Thera-Band (red or green).
2. Before you start this exercise, check the flexibility of the hamstrings and back by leaning forward in a straddled sitting position and reaching for the toes. (Don't stretch; just check your range of movement).
3. Bend the knee, dorsiflex the foot, and loop the band around the large toe.
4. Flex the large toe against light resistance of the band (figure *a*). Then slowly extend the large toe, gently pulling backward with the band. Move the hand forward and back with the movement of the toe to keep the pull on the toe equal during flexion and extension phases. The other toes may flex and extend along with the large toe, but keep the ankle dorsiflexed.
5. Loop the band around the second and third toes, and flex and extend these toes (figure *b*). Emphasize the extension phase by making it a longer than the flexion phase.
6. Loop the band around the fourth and fifth toes. Gently flex and extend these toes.
7. Place the band lengthwise under the foot and across your heels and toes. Flex and extend all the toes against the resistance of the band (figure *c*).

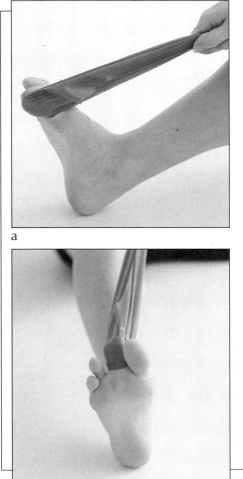

a

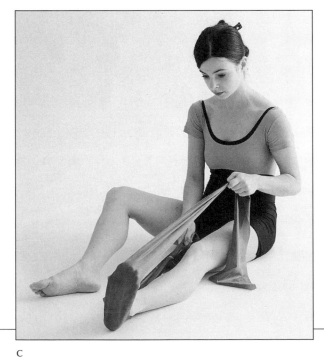

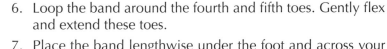

b

c

8. Now flex and extend the ankle, rolling the heel on the floor. Imagine the heel lengthening away from you as you dorsiflex the foot. Feel the toes stretching out as the foot plantarflexes. Extend the toes slowly as the foot moves back. Image the toes carving the space in an overcurve action, or think of digging through clay with your toes. Emphasize the eccentric phase of the movement. Do not let the toes snap back from the flexed position, even though the band is pulling to the rear. Slowly move your toes back.

9. Stretch out your leg on the floor.

10. Rock your pelvis forward as you point the foot. Notice the relationship between the pelvis and foot. Synchronize the movement of your foot, pelvis and spine: they all rock forward with the forward movement of the foot. Imagine the foot pulling you forward (figure d). Do not let the heel slide backward. Think of the sit bones and the heels as wheels.

11. Repeat the rocking motion 15 times if you are warming up, 30 times for conditioning purposes.

12. Remove the band and point both feet, placing them next to each other to compare their flexibility. Check the flexibility of your hamstrings by leaning forward over the respective leg on the left and right sides. You may notice an increase in flexibility on the conditioned side. Stand up and perform battement tendu with the trained and nontrained leg. Compare your foot action for jumping by doing small sautés first with one, then the other leg.

13. Sit back down and place both hands, one next to the other, under the hamstrings.

14. Keep the same action of the foot and pelvis forward and back and visualize the sliding filaments in the hamstrings musculature: As you move forward, they slide apart, as you move back they slide together (see figure).

15. Keep one hand under the hamstring and place the other hand in the crease formed above your right hip joint. Think of the pelvic organs around the hip joint relaxing and dropping in the process.

16. Loop the band around the foot as in the previous exercise and perform 15 rocking movements using sliding filament and organ imagery.

17. Gradually increase the range of movement of the spine, pelvis, and foot.

18. Compare flexibility in the hamstrings from left to right.

19. Repeat the exercise with the other leg.

d

a

b

c

d

To complete a foot workout you need to include inversion, eversion, supination, and pronation of the foot. In the latter part of this exercise you condition the toe extensors and the ankle dorsiflexors. If these muscles are not frequently and sufficiently strengthened in dance classes the dancer is predisposed to injury.

1. Lean to the outside of the leg and hold on to the Thera-Band looped around your foot. Use your weight to hold the band to the ground (figure a).

2. Invert the heel and sweep the foot inward. Think of grabbing the band with your foot. Feel the outside of the leg lengthening. Make sure your large inward sweep includes a plantarflexed phase to train the tibialis posterior and a dorsiflexed phase to train the tibialis anterior (figure b). Do not perform the action with the whole leg initiating from the hip joint. Keep the movement smooth in both directions.

3. Lean to the other side and loop the band under the leg that has no band attached to it (figure c).

4. Pronate the foot by pushing outward and up against the band. Make sure you initiate the action from the foot and not in the hip joint. Check your thighs, they should be relaxed. Feel the inside of the leg lengthening.

5. Repeat steps 1 through 4 six times if you are warming up, twelve times for conditioning.

6. Bend the knee of the foot you have been exercising. Loop the band around the top of your foot and sling the remaining segment around your back. Feel a stretch on the top of the foot by increasing the pull of the band.

7. Extend and flex the toes six times. You may feel the muscles on the top of the foot working hard. These short toe extensors are often understrengthened in dancers, causing a muscular imbalance between the toe flexors and extensors.

8. Dorsiflex the ankles (on a two-count) and plantar flex them (on a three-count). Repeat six times.

9. Hold the final dorsiflexion for an eight-count, then pull the foot into plantarflexion by shortening the band around the back. This action increases the stretch of the top of the foot (figure d). You are performing a contract-release stretch of the top of the foot (see chapter 4).

10. Remove the band, and check your flexibility by reaching for the toes on the side you have finished. Then reach for the toes on the side on which you haven't applied the band.

11. Stand, and notice the difference in your ability to balance be-tween the trained and nontrained side by balancing on one leg.

12. If you perform some hops on the trained leg and then on the other, you may notice a significant difference in elasticity of the leg and the ability of the foot to push off the floor.

13. Repeat the exercise with the other leg.

Once you have learned the sequences in exercises 7.7 and 7.8, you can perform them in a short amount of time. If you are warming up, even doing a few repetitions can be valuable. After a while you will notice that the muscles seem to remember the exercise benefits and respond more rapidly. If you are pressed for time, you can condition both feet at the same time with this exercise.

1. Loop a Thera-Band around both feet.
2. Point and flex the feet, rocking the heel and pelvis forward and backward.
3. Repeat the exercise 15 times.
4. Perform a circling action of the whole foot. Start from a supinated position, and sweep outward to a pronated position (figure *a*).
5. Move back to the supinated position (figure *b*).
6. Repeat the exercise 8 times.

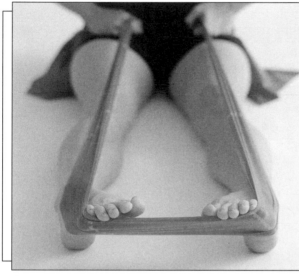 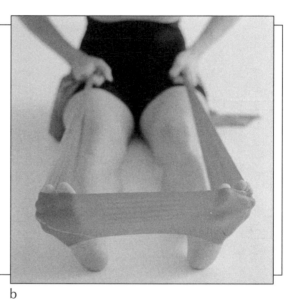

a   b

Dynamic Strengthening for the Hips

We now proceed to conditioning the muscles of the hip joint as well as those of the knee for stabilizing strength. Perform exercises 7.11 and 7.12 lying supine, using the floor as a teacher while working on specific muscle group strengthening. The remaining exercises in this section are performed standing. The advantage of conditioning in the upright position is the ability to build strength into movement shapes and patterns that you actually use when you dance. The nervous system learns to deal with increased resistance in a realistic setting for dance (see also chapters 8 and 10), resulting in an immediate sense of improved range and strength for these movements. If you return to performing somewhat more traditional conditioning exercises that are not related specifically to dance movement, you may perform them with greater skill as well.

The floor can show you whether you are initiating the movement correctly or whether you are jeopardizing the alignment of the pelvis and back to move the leg. The floor helps you to become aware of what muscles you tense unnecessarily.

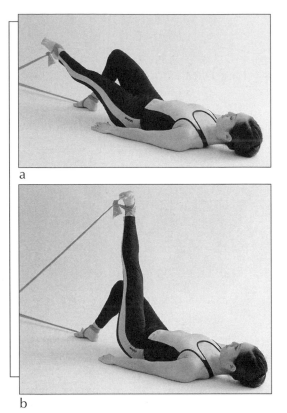

a

b

1. Use a medium-strength Thera-Band (red or green) to create a loop around the foot. Attach the other end close to the floor. Make sure the loop is not so tight that it impedes blood flow.

2. Lie supine on the floor, and lift the extended leg in a parallel position until you feel the resistance of the band (figure *a*). Initiate the movement in the hip joint; avoid tilting the pelvis forward and back. If you visualize the iliopsoas muscle as the main initiator of the movement, initiating from the hip joint will be easy.

3. Lift the extended leg further up in a parallel position against the band (figure *b*).

4. Lower the extended leg in parallel position. Throughout the movement keep the shoulder blades on the floor. Imagine the back spreading out and melting.

5. Visualize the pelvic half as a wheel. Feel the wheel rotating back as you lift the leg and rotating forward as you lower it.

6. Throughout the movement, create dynamic stabilization from the abdominal muscles. To support the transversus abdominis activation, visualize the ASIS moving toward the rectus abdominis muscle (figure *c*). Imagine this concentric action in the transversus abdominis as you lower the leg. Because you are practicing in the open-chain position, the action of the transversus abdominis is reversed from when you are standing.

7. Repeat the exercise 12 times for each hip, increasing to 20 times in increments of 2 each week over a 4-week period.

8. Perform the identical movement with the leg turned out and the foot dorsiflexed.

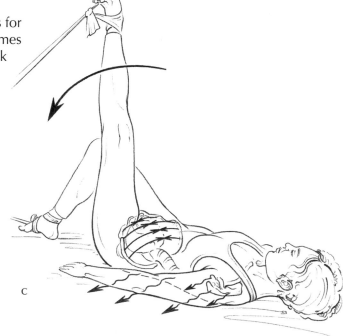

c

The muscles that extend the hip are the gluteus maximus and the hamstrings. The gluteus maximus arises from the iliac wing and crest and from the sacrum and sacrotuberous ligament. The gluteus is a hip extensor, abductor, and external rotator. It is assisted in external rotation and hip extension by the outer (lateral) hamstring, the biceps femoris. The inner hamstrings, important for extending the hip joint in the turned-in position, are the semitendinosus and semimembranosus (semis). Because many dancers train primarily in a turned-out position the gluteus-biceps group tends to have more power than the two semis. Through its connective tissue connections, the gluteus maximus can also help stabilize the knee and the lower back. But if its great strength is not balanced, it can also contribute to lower back and knee pain.

At the knee joint, the lower leg can turn out relative to the upper leg only if the knee is flexed to 90 degrees. The biceps femoris turns the lower leg out; the semis turn it in. If the semis are significantly weaker than the biceps femoris, the dancer may be predisposed to knee problems, because the knee will tend to remain in a somewhat turned-out position at all times. It is therefore important to balance the strength of the inner hamstrings during conditioning.

1. Fasten a short length of a Thera-Band to both feet, or place one end of the band under your knee while the other is attached to the ankle.

2. On all fours, lift the right leg to the back. Feel the tension of the band when the leg is stretched out horizontally to the back in an arabesque position.

3. Move the leg up and down against the resistance of the band in a turned-out position four times.

4. Move the leg up and down against the resistance in the turned-in position four times. The turned-in position may feel difficult because of the relative weakness of the inner hamstrings and a somewhat decreased ability of the gluteus maximus to extend the leg when turned in. The piriformis, the most important deep rotator of the hip, may also not be sufficiently stretched to achieve the turned-in position comfortably (see chapter 4).

5. Imagine the psoas major muscle filaments on the side of the gesturing leg sliding apart as you lift the leg, and sliding together as you lower the leg. This image prevents you from overly arching the back during the lift phase of the movement (see figure).

6. Imagine that you are bouncing a ball up and down with the sole of the foot. This image helps you to emphasize an initiation from the end of the leg (distal initiation), which increases your ROM. Feel the toes pushing the ball to create length in the leg.

7. Imagine energy flowing from the heart down the arms to the floor, and maintain a sense of elasticity in the upper spine.

8. Repeat steps 3 and 4, choosing any of the images provided in steps, 5, 6, or 7.

9. Increase the repetitions to eight times per position in increments of one each week over four weeks.

10. Before you repeat the movement with the other leg, compare your extension to the back on the left and right sides. The increased flexibility on the exercised side is from the powerful reciprocal inhibition effect on the hip flexors.

Strength in the Supporting Leg, Power in the Gesture Leg

The following Thera-Band exercises condition the muscles of the leg and pelvis. Use a large loop of band. See also the exercises in chapter 10; they do not require the band to be attached to anything but your own body, which can be helpful when warming up on stage or where there is no suitable place to attach the band. Wear a thick sock or a kneepad around the ankle if the band rubs against the Achilles tendon. Most often the problem can be solved by repositioning the knot in the band at the top of the foot. If you are using a yellow or red Thera-Band, this may not be a problem.

The open loop exercises are also beneficial for developing balance and coordination. Within a comparatively short time they address many important conditioning concerns for the dancer. Performed with few repetitions, this exercise series can be used as a warm-up; with many repetitions, it constitutes a complete conditioning routine if you incorporate some upper body movement. However, attention to alignment and movement initiation is more important than the amount of repetitions or the level of resistance of the band.

The next six exercises provide a lot of information on how to make the leg exercises more valuable for improving technique. Don't try to absorb all this information at once. Instead, focus on one concept each week of training. Brushes, battements, tendus, and jetés are common training elements in ballet, modern, jazz, and other dance forms. They train the dancer to move one leg in space while the other creates a stable base for this movement. The coordinated action of supporting and gesture leg greatly influences your technique.

A dancer needs to learn about transferring weight from one leg to the other efficiently and effortlessly. Efficiency means that you make no unnecessary adjustments to transfer weight. Dancers tend to lift the pelvis on the side of the gesture leg even before they tendu, battement, or jeté à la seconde. Many say that they are doing this to be on the leg, or lifted. Obviously no one wants to sag or be pulled down. But being *lifted* is not a specific enough image, and what happens most often is that the dancer tightens his hip joint (see also Franklin 1996a, pages 93 and 98–102).

Unnecessarily lifting one side of the pelvis causes the muscles that connect the pelvis to the femur to shorten and be overactive. The tensor fasciae latae, the gluteus medius and minimus, and the deep rotators are most affected, becoming shorter and tighter than necessary. On the side of the gesture leg, the muscles that connect the pelvis to the rib cage are shortened from the lateral flexion of the spine caused by the one side lifting the pelvis. The superficial hip flexors are overused to brush the leg to the side, as opposed to emphasizing the iliopsoas muscle group. As a result, the dancer uses the same pattern of tilting the pelvis when she transfers weight, causing the pelvis to move back and forth between a lift of the right and left side of the pelvis. This pattern limits the technical progress the dancer can make, and it causes strain on the knee and foot.

The following ideas will help you create effortless and technically sound brushes and tendus.

1. Become aware of the anatomy of the pelvis. Visualize the location of the pelvic bones, the sacrum, the pubic symphysis, and the pelvic crest.

2. Keep the pelvic crests level as you move the leg to the front, side or back. If you need to move toward the gesture leg, keep any lifting of the side of the pelvis to a minimum (see also imagery in Franklin 1996b, pages 135–139.)

3. Do not keep the pelvis level by increasing tension, but by moving from the hip joint. Be clear in your mind about the location of the hip joint, and try to initiate the movement from that point without additional effort in the spine or other area of the body. You may need to make some subtle adjustments to the pelvis and sacrum, but let your main focus remain on the hip joint.

4. Feel how the ball at the top of the femur bone can swing freely in the hip joint, and keep the surrounding muscles fluid. In the mind's eye, allow the head of the femur to float within its muscular surrounding.

5. In tendus to the back, allow for a minimal forward anterior tilting of the pelvis. If you feel pressure in the lumbar spine as the gesture leg moves backward, imagine the ball of the femur dropping down on the gesture side as the leg moves to the back. Once you find that you can move the leg into a brush without unnecessary tilting movements, you will feel liberated in the hip joints and it will be easier to feel the ball of the femur. Once you can clearly feel this place, you will have better feedback about the placement of the pelvis and the use of the legs in many movements. Also, the tightness in the hip joints and the surrounding muscles will vanish.

6. When moving the leg from the side (second) position to the back (en arrière) position, you need to subtly change your spinal and pelvic alignment because the ligaments at the front of the hip joint do not allow for much extension (20 degrees if the knee is extended). If you keep the pelvis rigid or tucked under and try to move the leg from side to back, you will hike up the hip on the side of the gesture leg. As you move the leg to the back, allow the pelvis to tilt slightly forward and extend the spine subtly with the moving back of the leg. The pelvis tilts to a greater degree if the knee is bent in an attitude position. The rectus femoris muscle that flexes the hip and extends the knee joints lengthens over the knee and limits extension at the hip as the leg moves from the side to the back position. The spine and pelvis need to adjust to maintain pelvic and upper body alignment. If this is not done, the pelvis will lift on the side of the gesture leg, and the supporting leg will twist.

LEG BRUSH, BATTEMENT TENDU AND DEGAGÉ

In this movement you change from a two-legged to a one-legged movement with the additional challenge of a Thera-Band tied around the ankle. When you first perform this exercise, balancing may be difficult. Adjust the length of the band so that you can prioritize correct alignment over initial strength gains. Using rhythmic music during this exercise gives the conditioning exercises a more dancelike feel.

1. Attach a loop of band about 10 inches above the ground.

2. Step into the loop, and move back until you feel tension. As you progress over several weeks, you can increase the resistance of the band by moving progressively farther away from the point of attachment.

3. Maintain the arms in second position throughout the exercise, or move to an arabesque position in the battement to the back.

4. Start in third position facing the band, which is looped around the left leg (figure a).

5. Battement (brush) the left leg to the front (en avant) (figure b), and return to third position.

6. Battement the left leg to the side (à la séconde), and return to third position (figure c).

7. Repeat the front and side battement moving through third position eight times. Perform the action at moderate speed to feel the leg muscles being active throughout your movement range. If you move too fast, you will not have sufficient eccentric training of the musculature.

8. Rotate the body a quarter turn. Stand the legs in third position. The band is pulling to the left.

9. Perform a moderate-speed battement to the side (à la seconde) with the left leg (figure d), and return to third position.

10. Perform a moderate-speed battement to the front (en avant) with the left leg (figure e), and return to third position.

11. Repeat the side and front battements moving through third position eight times.

a

b

c

d

12. Rotate the body a quarter turn. (You are now facing away from the band.) Start the next movement from third position, with the left leg in back.

13. Battement the left leg to the back (en arrière) (figure *f*). Return to third position.

14. Battement the left leg to the side (figure *g*), and return to third position.

15. Feel the ribs integrating into the spine (figure *h*) to allow the legs more ease in their action and stabilize the torso without increasing tension.

16. In all exercises, maintain a clear sense of the space around you. Feel the width of the chest, and allow the arms to be part of the exercise, even though they are not working as hard as the legs. To maintain the image of space around you, imagine glittering diamonds in the hands, feet, and chest.

17. Visualize the psoas major and adductor muscles anchoring the spine and pelvis to the supporting leg.

18. Perform the action eight times, moving through third position at moderate speed, so that you feel the leg muscles being active throughout your movement range.

19. Remove the band, and test your battement action without its resistance.

20. Perform the sequence on the other side.

h

You may perform the same exercise from fifth position turned out or in parallel, except to the back, where only the turned-out version is feasible with the positioning of the band. The parallel version is highly recommended for modern dancers. Make sure you maintain a truly parallel position when facing the band, ensuring sufficient activation of the inner hamstrings (semitendinosus and semimembranosus muscles) and lengthening of the external rotators. If the leg is always turned out, the outer hamstring (biceps femoris) will increase in strength relative to the inner hamstrings, causing a muscular imbalance, which is not healthy for the knee.

If you feel any of the previous movements twisting the supporting leg, switch to a lower-resistance band, or decrease your distance to the attachment of the band. In time you will gain so much stability in the supporting leg that you will feel imperturbable.

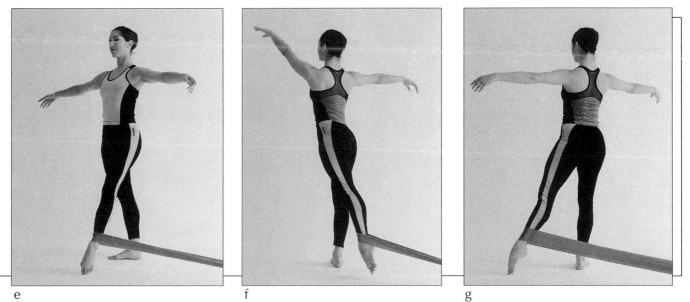

e   f   g

a

b

In this exercise the dancer strengthens the hip flexors, adductors, and the stabilizers of the pelvis and legs while maintaining a relaxed upper body with flowing arms. Achieving a relaxed upper body can be challenging as the supporting leg struggles to maintain its alignment, but the ability to work hard in one area of the body while the other is moving with grace is a skill any dancer should aspire to master. The arm positions described below are suggestions; the dancer is welcome to use a more modern style of arm movements.

1. Face the attachment of the band with the right leg in a battement tendu position and the arms in third position (figure *a*).

2. Move the right leg into a third position plié (figure *b*).

3. Stretch the left leg, and perform a passé retiré with the right leg moving the arms into a rounded position at chest level (figure *c*). Imagine the spine as one long arrow extending from the base of the skull to the floor as you move the leg out. This image will give you a sense of the supporting leg and spine acting as two supports, even when one leg is off the floor.

4. Return to the third position plié, and move the leg forward to a battement tendu position.

5. Feel the symmetry of both sides of the back and the equality of both sides of the rib cage. Allow the ribs to suspend effortlessly between the sternum and the spine. Image the joints connecting the ribs to the spine being soft and easy.

6. Repeat the sequence four times.

7. Rotate a quarter turn, battement the right leg to the front (figure *d*), and then move it into a third position plié.

c

d

e

8. Stretch the left leg, and perform a passé retiré with the right leg (figure e). Make sure the hip joints are level. Don't sacrifice pelvic alignment for enhanced leg turn-out.

9. Move the leg back into third position, and battement to the front.

10. If you are using music, feel it massaging the neck and shoulders. Let the music help support the arms.

11. Repeat the sequence four times.

12. Rotate the body a quarter turn. (You are now facing away from the band.) With the right leg, perform a battement tendu to the side (figure f).

13. Visualize the sit bone of the gesturing leg hanging downward like a bell clap as the leg swings in battement to the side.

14. Move the leg into third position plié.

15. Stretch the left leg, and perform a passé retiré with the right leg (figure g).

16. Return to third position plié, and battement the leg to the side to return to the starting position. As the leg moves out, imagine the action being supported dynamically by the pelvic floor and abdominal musculature. Feel the pelvic floor integrating and the front of the pelvis widening. The pelvic floor musculature shortens, the transversus abdominis lengthens; this is an important if slight action (figure h). Imagine the lower leg turning out.

17. Feel the sliding action of the iliopsoas muscle filaments. This image will take the strain off of the superficial hip flexors.

18. As you move the gesturing leg back in and you plié, feel the support of the transversus abdominis in a concentric action as the pelvic floor muscles lengthen, especially the coccygeus and iliococcygeus musculature. Imagine the lower leg turning in (figure i).

19. Repeat the sequence four times.

f

g

You may perform the fondu battement with a barre nearby so you can stabilize yourself with a hand. As you gain strength and coordination, you will be able to do without the barre.

Some dancers jam the rotator muscles in an effort to turn out. The result is the opposite of their goal: restricted and even painful external rotation. This exercise provides an opportunity to build fluidity and strength into external rotation while balancing on one leg, when it is often hardest to maintain turn-out. A word of caution: Never use the leverage of the floor to increase your turn-out. Turning the feet out more than the hips permit and then using the resistance of the floor to keep the feet in position causes the feet to pronate (inside of the foot drops and tilts the pelvis anteriorly). You react by lifting the inner border of the foot and shortening the abdominal and pelvic floor muscles to lift the front of the pelvis. Both of these actions effectively lock the joints of the leg. The result is eventual back, knee, and foot pain. If this remains your strategy over extended time, you will develop a sickle-shape of the feet through years of forced supination to keep the feet from pronating.

1. Loop a Thera-Band around the lower leg just above the ankle. Adjust your distance to the attachment of the band so that you have some resistance throughout the exercise.

2. Place small towels or soft balls under the arms to release tension in the shoulder and neck.

3. Start with the foot of the gesture leg pointed and in front of the ankle (coupé en avant) facing the attachment of the band (figure a).

4. Slowly move the foot to a battement tendu position (figure b).

5. Move the gesture leg back in a controlled fashion to the coupé en avant position in front of the ankle. Repeat the action eight times.

6. Remove the balls, and perform the movement without balls or a band. Notice especially that you can have a lot of leg power while maintaining relaxed shoulders. Feel the space between the shoulder blades. Feel the back of the hands expanding into space.

7. Now perform the action eight times to the back. Start with the gesturing foot pointed and behind the ankle of the supporting leg (coupé en arrierè, figure c).

a

b

c

d

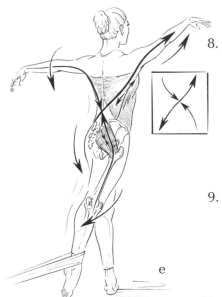

8. Battement to the back, performing an accompanying port de bras (figure *d*). With the arms moving into a third arabesque position, imagine the muscle chains crossing the back to increase your dynamic stability. The muscle chain through the latissimus dorsi, the lumbar connective tissue, the oblique abdominal muscles, and the gluteals lengthens on the side of the arm being stretched forward. At the same time, the chain on the other side shortens (figure *e*).

9. Feel the process of stretching and bending the supporting leg; don't just become aware of it when it is stretched. Feel the action of the muscles during the whole contractive phase to gain controlled strength. In the fully extended position, avoid pushing back the knee of the supporting leg.

10. Visualize the line of force of your quadriceps femoris in the supporting leg. An imaginary plane through this line of force would be aligned with the lower leg and foot.

11. As you did with the supporting leg, tune in to the process of stretching and bending the gesturing leg. Avoid locking the knee into a stretched position. Feel the end of the stretch, then return into the bending of the knee in a continuous flow.

12. To deepen your plié, relax the neck, shoulders, tongue, and jaw. If you become tense, rest, and gently knead the neck muscles. Perform a series of battement fondus with one hand on the neck. Then perform them without the hand on the neck. You may notice that your posture is more upright and that your plié is deeper (see also chapters 4 and 5).

13. Deepen your plié and improve alignment by visualizing the horizontal rotation of the pelvic half and femur. As you go down in plié, feel the pelvic half of the supporting leg rotating inward as the femur counterrotates. The sit bone moves outward as the ASIS moves inward (figure *f*). As you raise up and battement tendu the gesturing leg, feel the pelvic half of the supporting leg rotating outward as the femur counterrotates. The sit bone moves inward, the ASIS outward (figure *g*).

14. As you practice, observe the spine with the mind's eye. Imagine a bright flashlight illuminating the front of the spine, and become aware of minute changes in position (figure *h*).

15. Repeat the sequence 6 times, and increase repetitions to 12 in increments of 1 each week.

16. Perform the movement without the band. Enjoy the feeling of simultaneous strength and relaxation.

You may also exercise with the gesturing leg facing sideways to the band's line of pull. This is an excellent action to improve balance while conditioning the adductor muscle group. Perform the exercise slowly, feeling every moment to gain controlled strength.

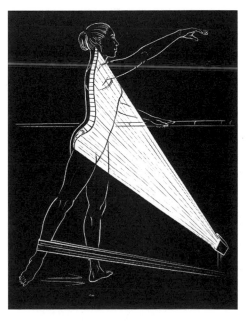

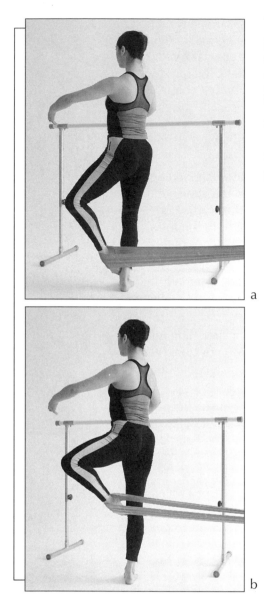

a

b

The following exercise improves turn-out, the strength of the passé, and foot position. To increase turn-out, maintain a sense of sliding in the muscle. Before you begin the exercise, review your awareness of the external rotator action. Place a finger behind the greater trochanter of the femur on the side of the gesturing leg. The greater trochanter is the bony bump at the top and outside of the thigh. As you bring the gesturing foot into a pointed position in front of the ankle of the supporting leg (coupé en avant) and then passé at the knee, you feel the rotators in action behind the greater trochanter.

1. Loop a Thera-Band around the hindfoot and heel so it pulls back against the heel bone.

2. Perform a coupé plié with the gesturing leg in front of the ankle (figure a) with the arms in port de bras.

3. Lift the gesturing leg into a passé while stretching the supporting leg (figure b).

4. Imagine the heel pushing forward against the band. Feel the activity of the adductor muscles on the inner thigh. Imagine the adductors lengthening while the rectus femoris centers the leg in the hip socket (figure c).

5. Repeat this sequence 8 times on each side, and increase to 12 repetitions in increments of 1 each week.

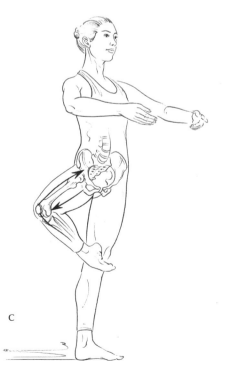

c

This exercise strengthens the internal and external rotators in a balanced fashion. Balanced strength in the rotators is key to avoiding tightness in the hip joints. The exercise emphasizes the eccentric lengthening of the adductors, creating a sense of length and strength in these muscles. Because we are working within the frame dance gesture, the newfound flexibility and control is immediately available.

1. Attach a Thera-Band just above the knee and level with the hip joint with a line of pull parallel to the ballet barre.

2. Face away from the barre, and hold on to the barre if necessary.

3. Adduct the leg into a parallel passé retiré position (figure a).

4. Slowly abduct the gesturing leg into the turned-out passé retiré position (figure b).

5. Repeat the action 12 times, increasing to 20 in increments of 2 each week.

6. Face sideways to the barre with the Thera-Band pulling away from the barre.

7. Adduct the gesturing leg into a parallel passé retiré position (figure c). Abduct the gesturing leg into a turned-out passé retiré position (figure d).

8. As you adduct, feel the widening of the back of the pelvis creating a centering action into the hip sockets (figure e).

9. Feel the lungs balanced equally on both sides of the spine. Imagine them to be soft sponges lathering up against the spine to make your spine feel supported but relaxed (figure f).

chapter 8

Developing Power in the Torso and Arms

The human body is uniquely constructed to give the hands an unparalleled range of movement. The wrists, elbows, and shoulders allow the hands to move with maximum dexterity and provide the hands the ability to adjust to the most delicate tasks. Using the wrists, elbows, and shoulders to move the arms in a coordinated and graceful manner helps center the whole body and is paramount to improving dance technique.

Traditionally, dance classes have emphasized training the legs, but this focus is changing. In some dance companies, dancing on the arms is becoming more of the standard repertoire. Particularly in ballet training, the dancer's arms and torso need to have enough strength for lifts and rapid gesturing in the petit allegro. Developing arm and torso strength not only improves all dance techniques, but also eliminates the common strength imbalances between the upper and lower body (see also chapter 4 on releasing shoulder and neck tension). The arms can function properly only when supported by a strong and muscularly balanced torso and back. Muscle chains that envelop the upper body create the baseline from which you can initiate graceful and powerful arm movement.

Center the Arms

The hand and arm connect to the spine through a complex set of joints. Moving from the center of the body outward, focus on the interaction of the rib joints, the rib cage–shoulder blade joints, the shoulder joints, the elbow, and the wrist joints. If you can feel how the arms interact with the spinal center, you can improve your arm coordination and dance with minimal tension. The following imagery exercises are designed to liberate your arm movements and create a sense of natural lift in the upper spine.

Your coordination depends on where you experience weight transfers. For example, if you take a step, you can experience the interaction of the feet with the floor, or the leg with the pelvis. Depending on what you are aware of, your coordination changes. One of the skills of good technique is to be able to feel a distinction between the more central skeleton and musculature, such as the spine and rib cage, and the outside, or appendicular skeleton. In the case of the upper body, the outside skeleton is the shoulder girdle and arms. By experiencing the shoulder girdle and arms as separate yet balanced and close to the central skeleton, you will create more efficient and tension-free movement.

1. Hold the arms horizontally in front of you or overhead, with the palms facing each other. Feel the weight of the arms resting on the shoulder blades.

2. As you hold up the arms, visualize how weight transfers from the shoulder blades to the clavicles, and through the clavicles to the sternum and first rib. See how the first rib sits snugly in the joint provided for it by the topmost thoracic vertebra.

3. Feel how the weight of the arms rests at the level of the first thoracic vertebra.

4. Now allow the weight of the arms to travel down the spine. This action centers the upper body gestures and relaxes the shoulders. Don't let the weight of the arms rest on the rib cage, because this position depresses the thorax and may lead you to counteract it by increasing neck tension (see figure).

5. Ultimately you may feel the weight of the arm arriving at the base of the spine and in the pelvis. Practice this feeling by standing with equal weight on both legs, and experience the weight shifting in the hip joints as you move the arms.

8.2 FLOATING FIRST RIB

Unlike other ribs, the first rib is rather flat, like the edge of a pizza without the middle part. Visualizing this flat, horizontal surface can help you find balanced action of the arms. Misalignment in the arms can affect the nerves that move the arm. They leave the spine in the neck, hanging down toward the first rib like loose power lines. They travel over the first ribs and under the clavicle out to the arms.

1. Move the arms from a horizontal position in front of you to an elevated position overhead. Now move the arms down to the sides and back to a horizontal position. Try a variety of movements, and notice the upper body alignment and the ease of movement.

2. Place the tips of the middle finger and thumb next to each other at the top of the breastbone (manubrium). You will feel two bony bumps, the joints between the clavicle and the breastbone.

3. Feel the clavicle, and place the fingers just under the joint between the clavicle and the breastbone. This point is easy to feel, because there is a little bump there. Don't be surprised if the area is tender.

4. Put the tips of the fingers of the other hand at the bottom of the neck. You will feel a spinous process that is sticking out more than the others. This is the seventh cervical vertebra. Place the fingertips just underneath that point on the seventh cervical vertebra.

5. Visualize a flat circle in the area between the two hands to create the first rib in the mind's eye.

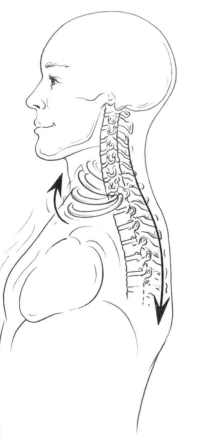

6. Feel this circle hovering between the breastbone and the spine (see figure). Notice the alignment of the first rib. Is it horizontal?

7. Move the spine with the hands still in place, and sense the changing position of the first rib.

8. Let go of your touch, and visualize the first rib floating upward and the spinous processes of the upper spine dropping downward. You may even imagine the shoulder muscles melting down on to a supportive first rib.

9. Shake out the arms, and perform arm gestures. Notice changes in your alignment and ease of movement.

As you have seen in the leg action (see chapter 7), the counterrotation of the bones along their long axis is key to good alignment and balanced muscle action. The arm bones perform a similar movement that you will visualize to create more freedom of movement in the upper body. As you stretch the arm in front of you, the shoulder blade rotates outward, the humerus inward, the lower arm outward, and the hand inward along the long axes. As your retract the arm, the shoulder blade rotates inward, the upper arm bone outward, the lower arm bone inward, and the hand outward along the long axes. Because these movements are subtle, it is difficult to visualize all the actions at once, so focus on one relationship at a time.

1. Hold the right arm in front of you with the joints flexed so that the hand is at shoulder level. Hold the right upper arm bone with the left hand.

2. Slowly move the hand forward as if you were pushing a door. Feel the humerus rotating inward, and visualize the shoulder blade moving in opposition. You can best feel the inward rotation of the upper arm bone when you fully stretch the arm (see figure).

3. As you move the hand back, feel the humerus rotating outward, and visualize the shoulder blade rotating inward.

4. Repeat the arm movement with touch several times. Then hold the right lower arm with the left hand, and repeat steps 2 and 3.

5. Repeat the movement several times, then let go with the left hand, and stretch both arms out to the front simultaneously. You will probably notice a significant difference in length and power between the right and left arms.

6. Practice the same touch-supported movements with the left arm. Once you are finished, try to visualize the action in both arms at the same time. It is helpful to visualize shoulder blades rotating in the same direction as the lower arm bones and the upper arm bones rotating in the same direction as the hand.

7. The analogy of the leg and arm rotations can be extended to the spine. Just as the sacrum nutates when the legs are flexed, you can visualize the part of the thoracic spine between the shoulder blades nutating as the arms are retracted. As you stretch the arms, visualize this area counternutating.

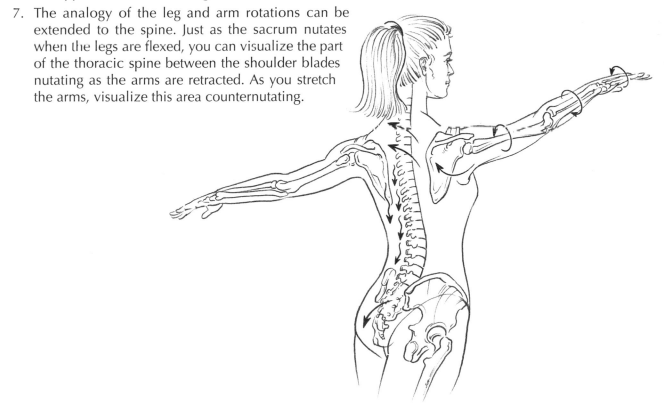

Thera-Band Loop for Upper Body Strength

This upper body series focuses on strengthening and balancing the muscles of the torso and arms. The series is popular among dancers, because it not only increases strength and flexibility, it involves many of the dynamic movements essential to dance training, especially modern dance. You can expand the series to create a complete training for the body by adding some exercises for the legs and feet. Unless otherwise noted, start by performing 8 repetitions of each exercise, and work your way up to 20 repetitions by adding 2 each week.

8.4 ARM OVERHEAD AND BACK

Although this exercise strengthens the muscles that extend the elbow and shoulder, it is mostly designed to increase the flexibility of the rib cage and to open and widen the chest and front of the shoulders. This movement balances the previous exercises that mostly focused on the front of the body. The movement reminds me of a morning wake-up stretch.

a

b

1. Position a Thera-Band in front of you with the palms facing down and the arms stretched. Lift the band overhead while moving the hands farther apart (figure a).

2. As you move the arms up, imagine the individual ribs lifting in front. Add a sense of rotation to the image. The ribs roll up in front as you lift the arms.

3. Depending on your flexibility and comfort, move the hands behind you approximately to the level of the shoulders (figure b).

4. As you move the arms to the back, imagine a water fountain gushing up the back and supporting the head from underneath. Let the back rest on this fountain, allowing the water to flush out any tension in the neck and the base of the skull (figure c). Or feel the breastbone arching forward and spreading out like icing on a cake.

5. Stretch, breathe, rotate the spine slightly for as long as feels comfortable, and move the arms to the front again.

6. As you move the arms forward and downward again, allow the ribs to drop and roll down. The ribs, not the spine, drop and roll down, but the spine can benefit from this downward thrust of the ribs by experiencing more length.

7. Repeat the movement three or four times at a comfortable speed.

c

This exercise warms up the muscles of the torso, especially the spinal extensors and lateral flexors. It improves your ability to arch the back and stretch the diaphragm and the body wall musculature. Choose a green Thera-Band for the first three months of your three-times-weekly practice of this series, then graduate to a blue Thera-Band.

1. Sit on the floor with the legs stretched to the sides at a right angle to each other.
2. Create a large loop of Thera-Band that fits around the soles of the feet and around the back at the bottom of the rib cage. Adjust the band around the back and feet to create a comfortable feeling during the exercise.
3. Loop the band behind the upper back, and drape the lower arms over it. Keep the tension in the band sufficient to carry the arms (figure a); the tension should be moderate, so movements can be performed with adequate resistance without straining.
4. Bend the torso to the left (figure b). Initiate the movement from the center of the body. Allow the force to be generated there while keeping the shoulders and neck as relaxed as possible. Allow the head to swing with the movement. Feel the lumbar spine as your center of power while keeping the movement smooth and continuous.
5. Bend the torso forward, flexing the spine into a long curve (figure c).
6. Continue the circling action of the torso by leaning to the right and maintaining a long curve in the spine, and arch the torso to the back, maintaining a long curve in the spine (figure d).
7. Continue the circling movement on to the left side, and repeat three more times.
8. Discover a comfortable breathing rhythm; it may be helpful to exhale as you arch forward, and inhale as you arch backward.
9. React to gravity, accelerating and slowing down as if you were riding on a roller coaster.
10. Perform the torso circling to the right four times.

The arm lift is the first of several exercises done from the same basic starting position and aimed at strengthening the muscles of the arms and shoulders. It engages the muscles that aid in elevating the arms, bending the elbow, and stabilizing the torso, especially the deltoid, biceps, trapezius, and erector spinae.

a

b

1. Bend the elbows at right angles, and place the hands under a Thera-Band (figure *a*).

2. Lift the arms, pushing against the band with flat hands (figure *b*). If you find the band slides up the back, lean back to increase tension. If the band feels uncomfortable on the arms, use a kneepad or wear a long-sleeved sweatshirt for protection.

3. Take more time to lower the arms than to elevate them. Think *up* for one count, and *down* for three. Imagine two balloons pulling up as you slowly lower your arms.

4. Imagine the muscles performing the action (especially the deltoid) sliding.

5. Explore a variety of breath initiations: Exhale when you lift the arms, and inhale when you lower, or vice versa. As you push up, allow the lower rib cage to widen and the first rib circle to narrow (figure *c*). You may coordinate this image with an inhalation. As you lower the arms, allow the first rib circle to widen and the lower ribs to narrow. You may coordinate this image with an exhalation.

6. Imagine you are pushing the band upward from the pelvic base and sit bones.

7. Lift the arms without the resistance of the band to enjoy the feeling of lightness in the arms. This is a good idea after any of the exercises, because it presents the nervous system with a clear sensation of how effortless movement can be. The nervous system tends to reproduce what it has experienced, so these sensations improve your enjoyment of dance.

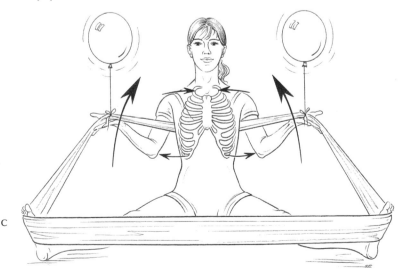

c

As its name implies, this is a classic movement, albeit in a new position, that strengthens not only the biceps, brachialis, and shoulder extensor musculature, but also the spinal extensors and the abdominals to stabilize the torso.

1. Hold the band with the palms of the hands facing upward. The arms are stretched out in front of with a slight downward angle (figure *a*).

2. Flex the elbow joints while moving the elbows next to the chest (figure *b*). Perform the movement in two counts. Imagine the muscle filaments sliding. As you bend the elbow, the flexors slide together. As you stretch the elbow, they slide apart.

3. Extend the elbow joints, and release the arms away from the chest. Perform the movement in four counts so you are taking more time to move the arms out than to pull them in.

4. Now reverse the position of the hands so the palms are facing downward. If this position feels uncomfortable, spread the band so it covers the back surface of the hands (figure *c*).

5. In this position, again flex the elbows in two counts, and extend them in four counts.

6. Let the tailbone release into the floor, and allow the spine to release into length. Think of warm water pouring down the back to flush out any tension.

7. Imagine your exhalation traveling down the back and releasing tension in the ribs and the joints between the spine and the ribs. Feel the breath softening the spaces between the ribs (figure *d*).

8. Roll the shoulders, and shake the arms to relieve any tension before you continue the series with the next exercise.

a

b

c

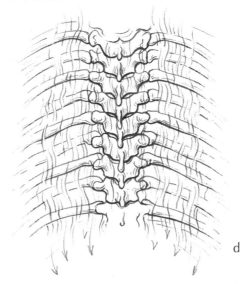

d

8.8 OUTWARD PUSH

This exercise strengthens the rhomboids, deltoids, and horizontal trapezius muscles. It also exercises the muscles that rotate the arm, creates a sense of width in the back and rib cage, and strengthens the muscles that move the wrists and fingers.

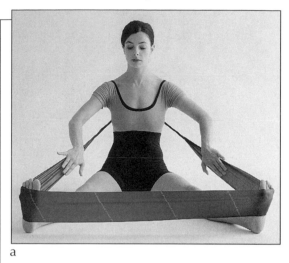

a

b

1. Place the hands on the inside of a Thera-Band, palms facing outward. Make sure the band is unwrinkled and is spread over the surface of the hand (figure a). Position the arms in front of you at a slight downward inclination, and slightly bend the elbows.

2. Push sideways against the band with the hands (figure b), and move the arms back to center. Take three counts to move the arm in, and one count to move it out. This pacing emphasizes the eccentric training of the musculature, creating more strength and a sense of length in the muscles.

3. Feel the back widening as you move the arms to the sides.

4. Imagine the muscles sliding. As you move the arms to the sides, the filaments in the rhomboids and horizontal trapezius slide together, and those in the pectorals slide apart. As you move the arms back in, the filaments in the rhomboids and the horizontal trapezius slide apart, and those in the pectorals slide together.

5. During the movement, visualize the rib heads resting in their spinal joint sockets. Allow the ribs to feel supported in their connections to the front of the body as well. This position helps you maintain a sense of spaciousness within the rib cage and length in the spine (figure c).

6. Enhance this exercise by circling the feet while moving the arms out and in. This simultaneous movement trains your coordination and strengthens the muscles of the ankle and foot.

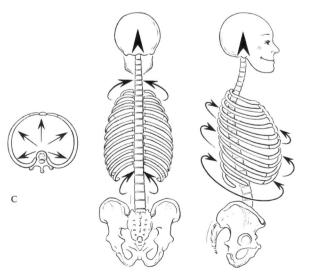

c

By reversing the movement in the preceding exercise, you will strengthen the pectoral muscles and release tension between the shoulder blades. The inward push engages the muscles that stabilize the shoulder joint and the abdominal muscles to create a sense of knitting at the front of the pelvis. The exercise also strengthens the musculature that moves the wrist and fingers.

1. Place the hands such that the palms are facing the outside of a Thera-Band. Spread the band so it covers the whole palm of the hand, and position the arms at a downward angle with the elbows slightly bent (figure a).

2. Move the hands toward each other to push the band toward the midline (figure b).

3. Move the arm back out. Take three counts to move the arm out, and one to move it in.

4. Feel the psoas major muscle lengthening downward to create a sense of grounding while releasing the spine into length (figure c).

5. As you move the hands toward the midline, imagine the transversus abdominis muscles knitting together in the navel area. You can visualize the transversus as a rope or stack of ropes being tied firmly at the front of your body. Notice how this image creates a sense of width in the lower back.

6. As with exercise 8.7, you can enhance this exercise by circling the feet while moving the arms in and out.

a

b

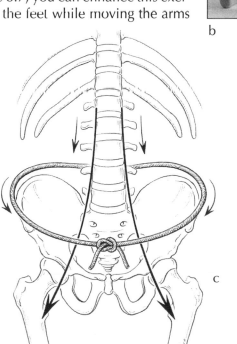

c

This exercise strengthens the muscles that rotate the spine and torso. This includes the inner and outer oblique abdominal muscles and the deep rotator muscles of the spine such as the multifidi, semispinalis, and rotatores. After performing this exercise regularly, you will notice an increased flexibility of the spine in rotation and a sense of lift and power in the abdominal area. This exercise also strengthens your turns and all spiral dance movements.

a

1. Before you begin, check the range of rotation of the torso without the resistance of a Thera-Band.

2. Lace the band over the upper arms, and hold it from above as shown in figure a.

3. Rotate the torso to the right, keeping the head over the pelvis. Maintain the arms in the same configuration relative to the torso to achieve the desired effect on the oblique abdominals. Initiate the rotational movement from the central, core muscles of the body—the pelvic floor, abdominals, intercostals, and scalenes. Often this core group of muscles is neglected for movement initiation in favor of the more superficial muscles. If you can reengage the core, you will find that tension in the superficial muscles melts away.

4. As your reach the end of your range, gently flex the spine to increase the activity of the abdominal muscles. As you flex the spine, feel the belly button moving back to help you create more movement in the lumbar spine.

5. Return to center, and rotate the torso to the other side. Maintain the arms in the same configuration relative to the torso. As your reach the end of your range, gently flex the spine to increase the activity of the abdominal muscles. Make sure that your movement is smooth and continous.

6. Lower the band to the back of the pelvis, and check your rotational flexibility. You may notice significant improvement.

7. Repeat the exercise 4 times to each side, and increase to 20 in increments of 2 each week.

8. Imagine the spindle rotating around its long axis to begin your movement (figure b). This action may not be easy if you are used to initiating with superficial musculature. After a while, you will notice that you can differentiate initiating from the core from initiating from the peripheral muscles. It may be helpful as an experiment to initiate from the shoulder and arm muscles to demonstrate that you will have less rotational range than when you initiate from the spindle core.

b

9. Feel the peripheral muscles releasing tension. Stay relaxed and tension free in the shoulder and neck musculature as you rotate the core spindle. Imagine the trapezius muscle as a sail being billowed by a cool breeze (figure c).

If you are able to stay relaxed in the shoulder and neck, you will have more rotation in the torso and therefore increase your strength over a greater range of movement. Flexibility and freedom from tension allow you to develop your full strength potential in this as well as all the other exercises.

c

The ribs are not considered an active part of movement and are usually relegated to being placed in position or even closed or pushed down in front. Because the body is a dynamic whole, and all joints and muscles (including the rib cage) interact to create movement, the following two exercises can strengthen your dynamic awareness of rib action. This awareness not only improves alignment, breathing, and a sense of relaxation in the shoulders, it centers pirouettes and increases the height of jumps.

The ribs are connected to the spine and sternum through a complex network of more than 150 joints. These joints make subtle adjustments as we move the spine, arms, and legs. If you imagine the rib cage as a static participant in movement, the spine, arms, and legs will lose flexibility and power.

a

1. With a Thera-Band in the hands and the palms facing downward, stretch the arms forward, and lift the band overhead. If this position is difficult, select a band with less resistance, or make a longer loop. Make sure never to place the band behind the neck. You should feel a comfortable level of resistance (figure a).

2. Bend to the left for two counts, keeping the arms stretched and pushing the band out and away from you (figure b).

3. As you bend to the left, think of the right ribs lifting up and the left ribs lowering down. This action is similar to lifting a bucket handle, except that every rib is a bucket handle in its own right (figure b).

4. Return to the center for two counts, and bend to the right for two counts, keeping the arms stretched. As you return to center, visualize the left ribs lifting and the right ones lowering. As you move back and forth, allow this rib movement to become smooth and continuous. This movement increases the lateral flexibility of the spine, especially in the thoracic area.

5. Return to center for two counts, and repeat bending to the left and right four times each. Increase the repetitions to 12 in increments of 1 each week.

6. Because the spine is a series of curves, a sidebend always has an element of rotation to it. Try this exercise with a flexible rod or twig. Bend it, then tilt it to the side. You will notice a rotation along the long axis of the rod. As you bend to the right, imagine the rib cage rotating to the right. Do not actually perform this movement; just imagine it to increase your lateral flexibility. As you bend to the left, imagine the rib cage rotating to the left. If you think of the rib cage rotating in the opposite direction, you will feel as if the spine is locked.

b

a

b

c

You started the exercise series with an upper body circle. You will now perform another such circle, but with the arms stretched out. This position strengthens not only the muscles of the torso, but also those of the arm and shoulders. This exercise creates a wonderful sense of central support for your arm movements.

1. Sit with the legs stretched at a comfortable angle to each other.

2. Place a Thera-Band under the pelvis, and reduce its length so you can have comfortable resistance with the band in the hands stretched over head (figure a).

3. Make a circle to the left by laterally flexing and rotating the spine (figure b). Initiate the movement from the navel center, and feel the activation of the abdominal muscles and the support of a flexible lumbar spine.

4. Reach forward and downward until the hands nearly touch the floor (figure c).

5. Continue the movement to the right.

6. Return to the starting position, and repeat the movement three more times on each side.

7. To create a sense of resilient support without tension, think of the arms as supported by the lungs. The left arm is supported by the left lung, and the right arm by the right lung (figure d). Feel the shoulder and neck muscles melt as the lungs take over the support of the arms.

d

This exercise strengthens the adductor group of muscles, which is important for stability in dance, especially when balancing on one leg. Dancers learn how to stay as centered as possible when they lift one leg off the floor as in a passé retiré movement. Beginners tend to move way over to the side of the standing leg and balance there, which is fine for everyday use, but not for dance, where weight needs to be transferred from leg to leg with minimal sideways deviation. It is important to remember that this exercise does not replace training the nervous system to control balance—this happens mainly through doing the actual movement—but laying a strong foundation will speed up that process. This exercise will feel quite intense, especially if you are at the beginning stages of conditioning. If the adductors feel exhausted after eight repetitions, start practicing this series regularly.

a

1. Loop a Thera-Band around the feet and back.

2. Lie on the left side of the body, and place the right foot and right hand on the upper strand of band, holding it down against the floor.

3. The left foot is now in a loop of band, ready to be lifted upward. Keep the upper loop of the band around the shoulders (figure a); don't let it slide down the back. In the beginning, arranging the band this way may be a challenge, but after a few practice sessions it becomes second nature. You may want to practice with a mat or towel underneath you for more comfort.

4. Now lift the left foot and leg upward against the band, keeping the foot parallel to the floor.

5. Imagine that an elastic thread is pulling the lifting leg upward. No effort is required on your part; the elastic is taking care of the work for you (figure b).

6. Lower the leg down to the starting position. Take two counts to move down, and one count to move up.

7. Send the breath into the adductors. Imagine the breath providing a continuous flow of fresh oxygen to keep the muscles energized. Imagine the color red filling the muscles for renewed energy.

8. Turn over to the right side, and repeat the movement with the other leg.

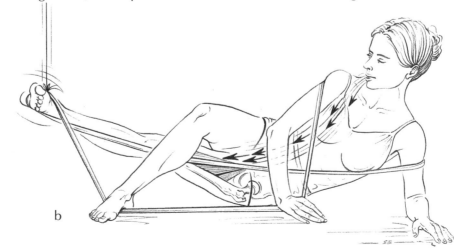

b

Now you will exercise the muscle group that opposes the action of the adductors—the abductors. The abductors are also important for stability when you stand on one leg. Because standing on one leg is common in dance, these muscles are often overworked. They may also feel strain if you elevate the leg with the help of the abductor muscles instead of the iliopsoas. In modern dance and jazz, the leg can be lifted to the side in parallel, placing the abductor in direct demand. These factors may contribute to tension in the area of the hip joint. It is therefore important to keep breathing and to send as much relaxing imagery to the muscles as possible during the abductor strengthening exercises.

You may wonder whether you should strengthen an overworked muscle in the first place. In this case, the rationale for strengthening is to increase muscle endurance to support the demands of dance. Also, the elastic rebound provided by the band may increase circulation to the muscle.

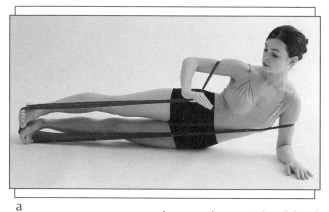

a

1. Lie on the left side with a Thera-Band looped around the feet as when you were sitting, only reduce the length of band between the feet to increase the level of resistance (figure a).

2. Lift the right leg up against the band. Lower the right hand against the band.

3. Lower the leg to the starting position. Take two counts to move down, and one to move up.

4. Imagine the breath melting all tension out of the abductors while you exercise.

5. Move the mind's eye and sensation to the bony surfaces at the outside of the ilium and greater trochanter where the abductors attach. Glide an imaginary ice cube over these surfaces to keep them cool while you exercise. Feel the muscular layers (gluteus medius and minimus) softening and melting toward the bone.

6. Imagine a large spring between the feet. This spring pushes the leg up without any effort from you. Let the imaginary spring do all the work, while the leg simply responds to its movement (see figure b).

7. After the exercise, tap the muscles that feel tight, make sure you release all tension before you roll to the other side, and repeat the exercise with the other leg.

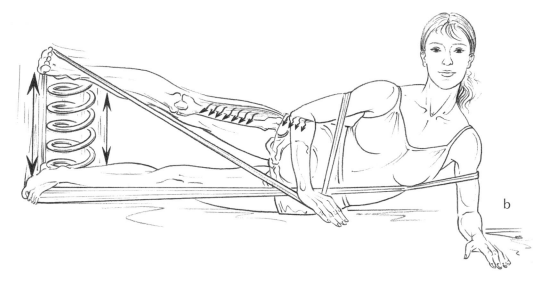

b

The next part of the exercise series (exercises 8.15 through 8.18) is both demanding and fun. If you have arrived at this point and still feel vigorous and ready for more, continue on with the following exercises. Otherwise, practice the series up to this point for three weeks before continuing.

SAILING THROUGH THE AIR: SECOND POSITION SPLIT   8.15

The second position split also exercises the abductors, but it engages both legs at the same time. This exercise calls for brain activity similar to that required in the performance of a second position leg split while leaping. The nervous system is the key component in performing a movement. Without its organizational skills, all the strength in the world won't make you perform a leaping split. Because it is difficult to do a regular split jump with any consistency 20 consecutive times while a band is tied to the legs, you will reverse the body's position, so the legs will be in the air while you perform a shoulder stand. This position should feel reasonably comfortable and will in no way strain your neck if you are to perform it.

1. Move into the shoulder stand position with the hands supporting the pelvis. Start from a supine position, bend both legs and lift them off the floor. Support the lower back firmly with both hands. Always use care when moving into or out of a shoulder stand position.

2. Loop a Thera-Band around the back and feet. Hold on to the band with the hands so it does not slide off the back (figure a).

3. Split the legs, moving them to the sides at equal distances from the center (figure b).

4. Move the legs back in. Take two counts to move the legs in, and one count to move them out.

5. Perform the movement both in parallel and turned-out positions.

6. It may be difficult to focus on imagery while you are in this unusual position. If you can manage to visualize yourself performing a split jump, your nervous system will soak up the information and provide you with an improved second position split jump.

7. If you prefer an anatomical image, imagine the muscles on the inside and back of the legs from the sit bones to the heels lengthening as you move the legs to the sides.

8. Engage the reliable elastic string image, and imagine the elastic pulling the legs to the sides effortlessly.

9. Start with 4 repetitions, and increase to 12 in increments of 2 each week.

a

b

Now focus on the classic split position with one leg to the front and the other to the back. Again, you are close to exercising the actual muscular configuration you need when you do an actual jump. There are so many muscles involved in the jeté split action that you could fill the page with their names. Again, if the action feels uncomfortable to the head, shoulder, or neck, don't do it.

a

b

1. From a shoulder stand, prepare to split the legs to the front and back. Turn out both legs, and flex the feet to allow a Thera-Band to be looped around the heels and stay in place. The first time you get in to this position, you may have to experiment with adjusting the band (figure a).

2. Split the legs, moving the left leg toward the face and the right leg to the back (figure b).

3. Visualize performing a jeté en l'air. Imagine sailing through the air, and feel the whole sequence from beginning to end, including an elegant landing.

4. Move the legs back in. Take two counts to move the legs in, and one count to move them out.

5. Switch the configuration of the legs, so the right leg moves forward and the left leg moves backward. The pelvis functions as an elastic plate consisting of a right pelvic half, a sacrum, and a left pelvic half. This plate can twist along its transverse axis slightly to store and release energy for walking and jumping. When the right leg moves forward and the left moves backward, the right top corner of the plate moves to the rear and the left top corner to the front, causing the plate to twist. As the leg positions reverse in walking, but more rapidly in consecutive jeté leaps with alternating legs, the plate twists back and forth, storing and releasing energy. Such elasticity helps the body to save muscle energy. One reason a jeté feels easier on one side than the other is because the plate twists more easily in one direction. To avoid joint pain from imbalance in the iliosacral joints, the plate should twist to the same degree in both directions. Think of the pelvic halves supporting and providing push for the movement of the legs. Imagine the right pelvic half increasing the movement range of the right leg, and imagine the left pelvic half increasing the movement range of the left leg.

6. Take plenty of time to come out of the position by rolling down on the back.

7. Start with 4 repetitions, and increase to 12 in increments of 2 each week.

This exercise is called Verena's split and rock because the model for this exercise series spontaneously performed this movement after finishing the series. It certainly is a natural exercise for dancers, because it stretches the adductors and helps to release hip and back tension.

1. Continue from exercise 8.16 by resting supine and moving the legs to the sides in wide second position stretch.

2. Rock the pelvis back and forth, and allow the legs to swing up and down in response to this movement. Do what feels comfortable to achieve a stretch and release.

3. As you rock back and forth, feel the muscles of the lower back melting into the floor, and keep the shoulders relaxed.

4. Feel the muscles on the inside of the leg, the adductors, stretching into length like taffy, and push out into space with the feet.

3. Engage the quadratus lumborum and psoas major muscles, then initiate lateral flexion of the spine as the pelvis rocks.

NATURAL LIFT—HEAD FLOATS UP 8.18

This exercise is the last in the series. It will get you ready for the standing position by increasing the tone in the muscles that create lift through the torso and especially the spine. In this way, you can dissipate discomfort remaining from the shoulder stand exercises. The exercise will leave you with a feeling of floating upward and great lightness in the head and spine.

1. Place enough length of a Thera-Band under the pelvis that you have a moderate amount of tension in the band when you place the remaining loop over head.

2. Slowly flex the spine for four counts while maintaining a feeling of length in the back.

3. Slowly extend the spine for four counts while being careful to keep the head well aligned. Do not allow the head to jut forward.

4. Remove the band, and enjoy feeling the head floating up!

5. Repeat the exercise four to six times at a comfortable speed.

6. After doing this exercise, you will have the experience of effortless lengthening of the spine. You may, however, add several ideas to increase the benefits of the movement:

   • Maintain a sense of length between the tail and the top of the head throughout the exercise. Exhale as you flex the spine, and inhale as you extend the spine.

   • Push the sit bones into the floor, and reach up with the head to maximize the distance between the top of the head and the pelvic floor.

   • Think of pushing the head through the band as you move up.

   • Imagine muscles sliding in the errector spinae muscles of the back: As you roll down, they slide apart. As you roll up, they slide together. Imagine muscles sliding in the rectus abdominis muscle: As you roll down, they slide together. As you roll up, they slide apart.

   • Imagine the ribs rotating downward as you flex the spine, and imagine the ribs rotating upward as you roll back up.

   • You may find it helpful to roll the back on balls for a few minutes. Then perform a simple dance step with a new feeling of length in the spine.

chapter 9

Improving Turns, Jumps, and Turn-Out

In this chapter you will take a closer look at three of dancers' main functional concerns: jumping, turning, and increasing turn-out. Beyond the physiological and anatomical limits of every dancer, having insights on how to coordinate movement and change one's body image can go a long way to improve these big three. My focus in this chapter is to help you improve technique and dance safely at the same time. Higher jumps, more turns, and better turn-out should not be exchanged for a dancer's health.

Fearless Turning

Even dancers who turn well are always seeking to improve the number and aesthetics of their turns. When you learn how to turn well, it can be so much fun that you can get attached to doing it. For these reasons, one can often feel the tension level rise in the room when a dance class moves along to turning practice.

Some dancers seem to make progress in every other aspect of their dancing but their turns. This is the sign of a problematic movement pattern that has become well established from years of practicing poor habits. In many cases it is easier to help a beginner than it is to help an advanced student whose habits are more firmly set and harder to change.

At this point the emphasis we placed on strengthening with a focus on alignment, movement initiation, balance, and imagery throughout the previous chapters pays off. I often observe strong dancers who utterly fail at pirouettes. If strong muscles pull the body in the wrong way, they are useless for turns. The dancer with a clearer image of his body, even if he has less strength, muscle per muscle, will be more successful. The same holds true for jumps and turn-out. I have encountered situations in which just about every dancer in a dance school has knee, foot, or lower back problems from forcing their turn-out. Using sheer muscular force to increase turn-out simply creates rigid joints, alignment problems, and a loss of flexibility. Instead, you should achieve turn-out by releasing tension and understanding how the joints of the body interact to create maximum flexibility. With jumps as well, it is not just sheer force, but alignment, imagery, and sense of rhythm that make all the difference. Increasing strength only makes sense if it is placed at the service of a mind and nervous system that can guide the body's action with safety and precision.

Without good alignment, performing multiple turns is not possible. You can always manage one or two with decent alignment and a good sense of rhythm and spotting. Spinal alignment is the first place to look for problems. If the spine is aligned, joints throughout the body are balanced. Also, the spine is both the support and area of attachment for many organs, muscles, and connective tissues. In this way, changes in the spinal alignment will transfer to every part of the body and vice versa.

When you have trouble turning, scan the following areas of the body to improve spinal alignment:

1. Let the spinous processes release. Imagine them dropping and melting downward. Visualize the processes above each other in the same sagittal plane (see figure in exercise 6.16).

2. Notice the balanced alignment of the left and right joints of the jaw (temporomandibular joint), the left and right joints between the head and the top of the vertebrae (atlanto-occipital joint), and the left and right joints between the ilium and sacrum (iliosacral joint). Become aware of the state of these joints and how they relate to each other, and trust the nervous system to start you on the path of better alignment (see also chapter 5).

3. Imagine the equal arrangement of the paired organs (the lungs, kidneys, and large intestine) within the torso.

4. Notice the position of the pelvis. If it is tilted forward or tucked (posterior tilt), it will throw off your balance when turning. Notice whether the pelvic crests are on the same horizontal plane and whether their alignment in this plane changes as you go from preparation into the turn.

5. Imagine the alignment of the brain and spinal cord as a soft axis (see figure). After you have laughed off the novelty of the image, the awareness might add a new quality to your turns.

6. In the preparatory phase for pirouettes, think of the central axis' plumb line grazing the front of the cervical and lumbar spine.

9.2 UNCLENCHING THE JAW

Many dancers tighten the neck and clench the jaw when they perform a pirouette. This may sound exaggerated, but observe a class and you will see it happen. Seeing other dancers clench may be one of the best ways to recognize and stop this pattern in yourself.

1. Perform a pirouette with a clenched jaw, then perform one with a relaxed jaw. You may notice that the tight jaw makes turning difficult. The position and tension level of the jaw are key to the alignment of the spine. Also, a tight jaw tends to make the neck inflexible.

2. Put one finger in each ear opening, and push the fingers forward. As you open and close the jaw, feel the action of the joints (figure *a*). The jaw joint has a disc (as does the knee), which divides it into an upper and lower part. The disc improves the range and stability of the joint. By imaging the soft, elastic disc, you can create a sense of smoothness and relaxation in the jaw. Imagine the disc resting on the joints as a lazy lizard (or the animal of your choice) resting its belly on a warm rock.

3. Put the fingers just in front of the ears, and move the jaw to feel the action of the joint. It may be painful to touch if you have been tense in this area.

4. As you open the mouth wide, think of the disc sliding forward and downward. You can imagine the disc being a slippery raft gliding on a river (figure *b*).

5. As you close the jaw, imagine the disc sliding back up (reverse the river; all is possible with imagery if it helps you).

6. Move the fingers forward half an inch, and slide them vertically down the side of the jaw. You are now massaging the masseter, one of the strongest muscles of the body for its size. Massage all the way down to the lower rim of the jawbone. Think of the masseter melting down as you seek out and soften tension spots in the muscle (figure *c*).

7. After relaxing the jaw, repeat the pirouette, and notice changes in the mobility of the neck and the alignment of the head. Turns feel different with a tension-free jaw, so do not be surprised. Notice also the increased sense of rhythm in the head and neck. Tension makes it hard to experience rhythm.

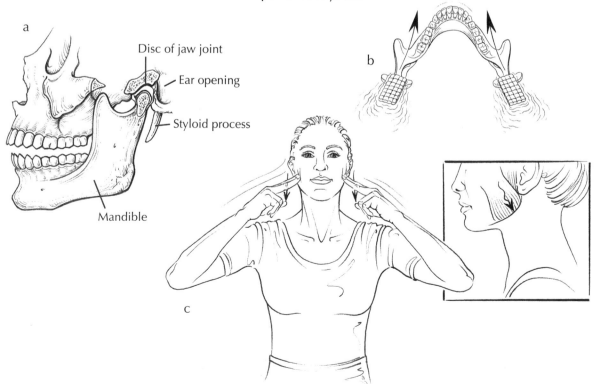

Disc of jaw joint

Ear opening

Styloid process

Mandible

Excess tension, even in the tongue and mouth, throws you off center as you turn. If you tighten this area, the neck muscles will also be tight, making it difficult to spot with the eyes.

1. Squeeze the tongue and the muscles of the face, and rotate the head to the left and right. Then relax the face and mouth and do the same. You have increased range with a relaxed face and tongue. Notice the changes in the neck muscles.

2. Tighten the tongue and face, and try to perform a turn.

3. Move the tongue around in the mouth, stretch it out as far as you can, and shake out your facial muscles. Push the tongue against the floor of the mouth and against the hard palate several times.

4. Imagine the tongue resting on the floor of the mouth. While you do this, visualize the neck lengthening (see figure). Notice whether you can feel the connection between the length in the cervical spine and a relaxed tongue.

5. With shoulder tension it is difficult to sense the alignment of the upper spine. Lift the shoulders, and exhale as you drop them slowly downward and think of the cervical spine lengthening. Repeat this movement three times. Notice whether the tongue seems to want to add tension to the event. Do not let it happen.

6. Try the turns again with relaxed tongue, jaw, and shoulders. Even if you are not successful initially, you will begin to notice the connection between your turns and tension in the mouth and tongue.

Unless specifically requested by a choreographer, it is not a good idea to contract (flexion of the lower spine) when you turn. This practice often finds its origin in the faulty execution of the plié. The problematic patterns include posteriorly tilting (tucking) the pelvis and pulling the tailbone forward (counternutation). (Review exercises 5.7 and 5.8, pages 93 to 94)

1. Pay attention to the movement of the sacrum, tailbone, and sit bones as you move from preparation to turn. Are you tucking the tail? Are you clenching the pelvic floor? These are sure signs of tucking. Allow the pelvic floor to change its configuration but not to tighten up as you relevé onto the supporting leg.

2. Imagine the sit bones being levitated by a flying carpet as you move from the preparation into the turn. The sit bones remain level on the carpet.

3. Watch the lumbar spine as you move from preparation to turn. Do you notice a significant amount of flexion? Stabilize the lumbar spine for turns, but do not flex or extend it.

4. Imagine the shoulder blades dropping and being pulled down gently by the ascending part of the trapezius.

5. As you turn, feel the lungs rotating around the heart, and don't let the heart drop back behind the lungs as you turn.

6. Think of the bones at the base of the skull. Imagine them forming a plate, just like the ones Chinese acrobats spin on long poles. Think of the spine as the pole, and allow the head to spin around on the pole without creating any disturbance of the pole's alignment.

Sensing both sides of the body equally goes a long way to improving pirouettes. The equal momentum (speed, force) of the body halves, not just their alignment, is important.

1. As you turn, think of the pelvic halves revolving around the sacrum like a revolving door with the sacrum at its center.
2. Imagine the bones under the eyes, and let the eyes rest on these bones. As you turn, allow the floors under the left and right eye to be level.
3. Feel the equality of both sides of the back. Feel the equality of both sides of the rib cage.
4. Keep the arms level with each other. If you have trouble feeling horizontal in the arms, imagine a water balance placed between the left and right elbows. The air bubble at its center should remain centered as you turn.
5. Visualize the rectus series of muscles (see figure). Think of both sides of the rectus abdominis having equal length, from the right pubic bones to the right ribs, from the left pubic bones to the left ribs. Imagine the median sagittal plane transversing this muscle. This image will help center the spine for better turns.
6. Feel the equal length and rhythm of both sides of the neck as you turn.
7. When you spot, think of the face being photographed from the front, twice for two turns, three times for three turns, four times for four turns. The picture being made shows an aligned face.

Rhythm is all important in turns. Once you have established a balanced tension-alignment relationship, use your auditory imagery to hear yourself turning. Hear the music to which you are turning, or create an inner rhythm and connect it to your alignment imagery. Rhythm and alignment are the winning combination for successful turns.

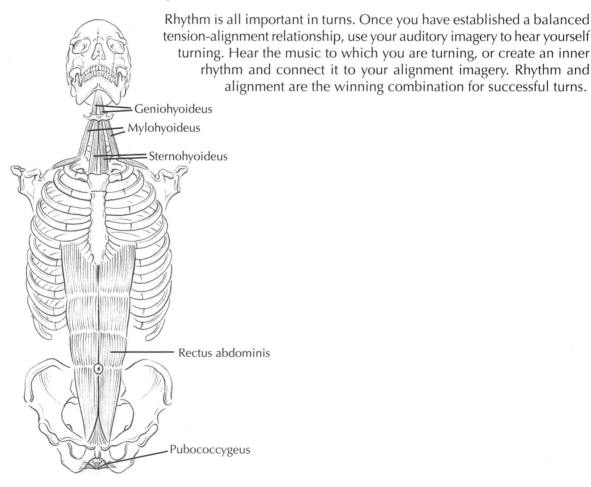

Geniohyoideus

Mylohyoideus

Sternohyoideus

Rectus abdominis

Pubococcygeus

Jumping Higher With Less Effort

Jumping is fun, especially once you notice that you need much less effort than you thought necessary. This feeling is achieved by using the full elasticity of the body, optimal alignment, rhythms, and finely tuned muscular control. Besides the following exercises listed, you will find ideas throughout this book that will help you with your jumps. Of great value are the alignment and pelvic floor exercises in chapter 5, the foot exercises at the beginning of chapter 7, and the relevé exercises in chapter 10.

MUSCLE TEAM PLAYS FOR BETTER JUMPS   9.6

When landing from a jump, focus on the eccentric (lengthening) action of the leg muscles. Feel the lengthening of the gluteals and the hamstrings. This lengthening gives you more stability and reduces the pressure on the knees. Also, feel the lengthening of the muscles of the calf as you land from small jumps. If you do this regularly in training, your landing will become smoother, and you will develop better coordination.

As with turns, for powerful jumping, alignment is key. If you are not aligned, a lot of force will be wasted by compensatory tension.

1. Practice feeling an equal push from both legs in pliés to prepare for balanced jumping from two legs (see figure).

2. Do not provide force for jumping by bending the upper body forward and backward. Feel the upper body completely relaxed, yet vertically bouncing on a giant spring, the legs.

3. Perform jumps while focusing on the breath. Don't do anything specific; just let yourself breathe. This focus greatly improves your endurance and your power. Any holding of the breath tightens the joints.

9.7   TRAVELING LEAPS

The human body is built for efficient movement; it is good at conserving energy. In a sense the body consists of a combination of swinging pendulums that exchange, but do not waste energy.

1. When you push off the floor for a traveling leap, imagine the body as an inverted pendulum swinging from the point of push-off (see figure). The head is the weighted end of the pendulum swinging around the foot. Use this image to increase the length and ease of your jumps.

2. As you take off from the floor, imagine the head swinging out into space.

3. In forward leaping action, feel the push-off foot connecting to the whole body. Feel the action of the pushing leg creating force that embraces the whole body.

4. The flying carpet image can provide excellent support for traveling leaps. As you perform a sideways leap with the legs stretched out to the side (grand jeté à la seconde), as is commonly seen in jazz dance, imagine the pelvis being carried along by a supporting force such as the flying carpet.

9.8   JUMPING WITH TENSION-FREE FORCE

When you jump, your *strength* should be added to the jump, not *tension*. If the shoulders are rounded and tense, it is difficult to jump high or do jumps that involve turns. The more you can relax the shoulders, the more centered you will be. Try this during your next jump:

1. Feel the rib cage in balanced alignment. Differentiate the first rib and clavicle to release tension in the upper chest.

2. Keep the neck free and released. Feel the head resting on the top of the spine while you jump. If you can achieve this feeling, you will develop more control and have more leg power.

3. Try jumping with a relaxed jaw, then with a clenched jaw. If you can relax the jaw while jumping, you gain more leg power. Your net jumping power is your power minus internal resistance, or tension. Image the jaw and tongue dropping, creating length in the spine (see figure).

4. Do not let the leg and arm movements distort the spine. Think of the arms and legs moving freely without disturbing the elasticity of the legs and spine.

5. Imagine a partner pushing you upward just a bit further as you reach the highest point of your jump.

The diaphragm greatly influences the height and elasticity of your leaps. Rarely do you see a dancer who has a sense of flow, space, and elasticity in his rib cage. With an aim to reduce extra movements, dancers may have been told to hold the rib cage in various ways. These instructions, however well intentioned, tend to make the ribs less elastic and inhibit the action of the diaphragm, which is attached to the rib cage. The following exercise is designed to give you an idea of the helpful elastic support of the diaphragm and rib cage for jumping.

1. Perform a few jumps (sautés) in place focusing on the rib cage and diaphragm.
2. Hold the belly in to impede the breath, and perform a few jumps. Notice changes in the elastic rebound of the legs and the whole body.
3. Jump once again, and inhale as you land. Notice how stable you feel as you land.
4. Jump up and down once. Exhale as you land from the jump, and think of the diaphragm relaxing. How stable do you feel on landing? You may feel more grounded if you exhale on landing from a leap.
5. Rest for a moment, and visualize the diaphragm as an elastic structure, like the surface of a trampoline.
6. Perform a series of jumps. Imagine the diaphragm being elastic, reacting to the body's movement. Allow the diaphragm to bounce up and down with your motion.
7. When you land, the diaphragm counters the downward movement by moving up on your exhalation (figure a).
8. When you leap up, it counters the upward movement by moving down on inhalation. This action helps stabilize your leap and gives you more thrust, because the body is employed as a complete elastic system (figure b).
9. Rest for a moment, and rub the area just below the sternum, where the abdominal muscles begin and the diaphragm is attached to the front of the body. Perform a series of jumps while feeling the elasticity of the diaphragm. Notice how the leg action is influenced by the bounce of the diaphragm.

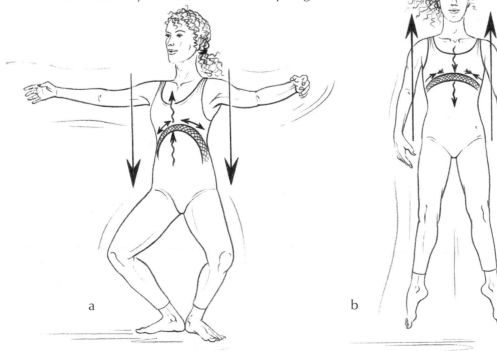

a   b

Discovering Your Elasticity

Bones, tendons, ligaments, and fasciae are all connective tissue. All connective tissue is made up of structures that are like miniature ropes and elastic wires. This includes connective tissue surrounding and creating the shape of cells. Cartilage, for example, is a type of connective tissue that needs to resist pressure in joints, so it contains proteins that are able to contain water and help cartilage act like a tough water cushion.

Ligaments and tendons contain the most common protein in the body, called collagen. Collagen is an extremely tough fiber, capable of resisting a pull that equals 10,000 times its own weight. This reminds us of the amazing abilities of the human structure, always a good thing to do when we are so often focused only on our shortcomings. Another common fiber in tendons and ligaments is called elastin. As its name implies, it is rather elastic, more so than collagen. Together they make tendons and ligaments elastic, yet very tough.

Connective tissue in and around muscles forms tendons at each end of a muscle and links them to the bone. In that sense, muscle does not move bone; it moves connective tissue (the tendon), which moves the bone. This sequence is advantageous, because the link is elastic and can store some of the power produced by the muscles.

The elasticity of tendons helps to create the bouncy feel of jumps. If the tendons are not sufficiently elastic, the muscles work harder to compensate. Certain ligaments and connective tissue sheets are connected to muscles, making them more dynamic in their function. The gluteals and the tensor fasciae latae on the side and back of the pelvis connect to a large expanse of connective tissue that attaches to the thigh bone and reaches all the way down beyond the knee joint. This connective tissue helps to maintain the optimal position and tension of the thigh muscles.

When you are landing from a leap, much of the energy is stored in the tendons of the body, foremost the Achilles, connecting the heel bone to the calf muscles. This is the largest tendon of the body, and it stores the elastic energy generated by the muscles for reuse in the next jump.

1. Perform a few jumps, and get a sense of the elasticity of the Achilles tendon connecting the calf muscles with the heel bone.
2. Sit down, and place the right Achilles tendon between the left thumb and second finger. Gently massage the tendon up and down, from the heel bone to the beginning of the muscle belly. This action should not hurt; if it does, consult a qualified medical practitioner, because you may have some inflammation in the tendon.
3. Press the tendon rhythmically while you visualize jumping on the right leg.
4. Stand up, and perform a few jumps on the leg that had its tendon touched, then on the other leg. You may notice an astonishing difference in the ability to jump.
5. Now imagine jumping on two legs that are more like the left one, and realize how much elastic power you have been missing out on.
6. Sit down, and repeat the exercise with the left Achilles tendon.
7. Once you have experienced both sides, make a firm commitment to build Achilles tendon elasticity into your body image.

In the following exercise you will touch the patellar ligament between the patella and the shin bone. You will try to feel the subtle changes that happen through your touch and notice how this exploration affects your leaps.

1. Perform a few jumps while focusing on the front of the knees.
2. Sit down, and place one finger on the lower rim of the patella, the kneecap, and the other on the bump on the top of the shin bone. This place is called the tuberosity of the tibia, and it is the point of attachment for the quadriceps muscle.
3. Focus on the ligament spanning the space between your touches. Imagine that it is an elastic band that can actively support your jumping.
4. Massage the patellar ligament from the patella down to the shinbone. Squeeze it gently in the rhythm of the jumps you intend to do.
5. Remove your touch, and support your weight on the leg you have worked with. Perform a plié, then bend and stretch the knee. Do the same with the leg that you have not touched, and notice the difference.
6. Perform some jumps on the touched leg and then on the other leg, and notice the difference in knee elasticity.

Other ligaments that store elastic energy when you are leaping include the Y ligaments (in front of the hip joints), the ischiofemoral ligaments (at the back of the hip joints), the sacrotuberous ligaments (connecting the sacrum with the sit bones), the spring ligament of the foot and, to a lesser degree, all the ligaments of the spine, knee, and foot.

Once you have developed a feeling for the elasticity of the tendons in jumping, it is helpful to imagine the whole body acting as a elastic unit. The body, from a connective tissue point of view, may be viewed as an interconnected mesh of semi-elastic fibers.

1. Many connective tissue sheaths in the body communicate forces between muscles, bone, and even nervous system structures (figure *a*).

2. Even the cells of the body contain structures called the cytoskeleton, made up of rapidly adjustable microtubules. Microtubules together with microfilaments form a web that maintains and alters the shape of the cell.

3. The skeletal-ligamentous arrangement as well as the cytoskeleton remind me of tensegrity structures. Tensegrity structures are made of interconnected tensile (elastic) and compression members (spacers). Tensegrity structures are very light and robust and distribute the forces they receive to all their parts.

4. When leaping, practice thinking of yourself as a total elastic structure; think of yourself as having the ability to receive and distribute force without losing central organization.

5. Imagine the elasticity happening everywhere in the body. This is not slumping elasticity, but one that maintains its shape while it absorbs and recycles the absorbed forces.

6. Feel the spinal curves deepening resiliently as you land, and rebounding into increased length as you jump up (figure *b*). Visualize and do not pantomime the image, or you will not have the desired result.

7. As you land from a leap, feel how the bottom of the foot spreads to break your fall. Allow the elastic recoil of the foot to provide force for your next jump.

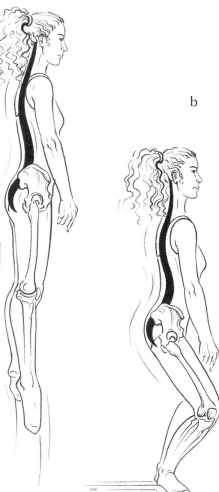

b

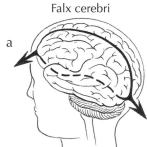

Falx cerebri

a

Plantar fascia

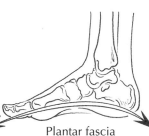

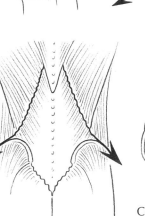

Central tendon of diaphragm

Fascia thoraco-lumbalis

Increasing Turn-Out the Healthy Way

Now you will look at some simple methods to increase your turn-out without causing any damage to the tissue or straining muscles.

A dancer's maximal turn-out is limited by the structure of her bones, joints, and connective tissue. Some dancers obviously have better bodies for turn-out than others, but most dancers are not using their full turn-out potential. Reasons for this include the following:

- Excess muscle tension caused by incorrect muscular coordination. It reduces the freedom of movement in the hips. The most powerful external rotator of the hip joint is the gluteus maximus. Because it also extends the hip joint, it is not a good candidate for external rotation when the hip is flexed, such as in an attitude en avant position. Focus on the deep rotators (see following text) and accessory muscles, such as the sartorius, to create the desired result.

- Alignment problems (excess forward tilt of the pelvis) causing the hips to be limited in outward rotation.

- Not practicing hip joint rotation in dance class. I have often observed dancers who may believe they are turning out the leg when they are mostly twisting the pelvis. Hip joint rotation remains limited, because the brain never learns about pure movement of the hip joint.

- Being able to maintain turn-out while dancing. You may be very mobile in the hip and yet unable to maintain turn-out because of lack of strength and coordination in the appropriate muscles. Tightness in the muscles that oppose turn-out may also be causing this situation. These muscles are the tensor fasciae latae, the gluteus minimus, and the anterior fibers of the gluteus medius.

- Too much tension in the muscles that turn out the leg. To function well, the muscles of external rotation must be able to lengthen and shorten to their full range. Focusing solely on the shortening aspect is a problematic approach that causes tension. Most often self-touch and imagery can work wonders to release these areas.

- Forcing turn-out twists the knee and foot excessively, causing the pelvis to tilt forward, the knee to be pushed forward, and the feet to roll in (pronate). This misalignment causes an imbalance and strain in the muscles and ligaments supporting these structures and leads to injury. The dancer's compensations—forcing the knee back and using tension to lift the front of the pelvis and the inner border of the foot—cause further technical problems. This pattern is difficult to change, because dancers are so used to it and do not want to turn in to the correct position.

Ideally, turn-out should be achieved in the hip joint with little participation of the joints of the lower limb (figure 9.1, a and b).

Figure 9.1, a and b The safest way to achieve optimal turn-out is by initiating the movement from the hip joints.

Here are five main ways to improve rotation and turn-out, some of which were discussed in earlier chapters:

1. Review the joint rhythms of the leg and pelvis. Once these are clearly visualized and felt, the joints and muscles will discover their natural maximum range of movement, which is always greater than range achieved through tension and force (see chapters 5 and 7).

2. Release excess tension in all the muscles of the hip joint, especially the adductor, abductor, and internal and external rotator muscles with ball rolling exercises, imagery, touch, and stretching (see also chapter 4).

3. Perform exercises for the iliopsoas and external rotators to create more force and length in these muscles (see also chapter 6).

4. Strengthen turn-out with Thera-Bands, and balance this strength to create equal turn-out (see chapter 7).

5. Strengthen turn-out through leg–pelvis coordination and pelvic floor awareness (see also chapter 5).

Releasing the Deep Rotators

The six deep rotators are key muscles for dancers. They are the obturator internus and obdurator externus, the superior and inferior gemelli, the piriformis, and the quadratus femoris. They are important both for turn-out and pelvic alignment, and they need to be strong without being tense. If they are tight, they will tilt the pelvis forward, decreasing and limiting turn-out. The lower back is then strained in an effort to turn out and lift the front of the pelvis (see iliopsoas, chapter 6). Except for the quadratus femoris, which is an adductor, the deep rotators can also assist abduction of the leg depending on the elevation.

Tightness in the deep rotators predisposes the hip joint to arthritic changes, because the legs tend to remain somewhat turned out, even during daily activities. If this is the case, the ligaments of the hip joint remain somewhat slack, and the lack of stability may contribute to increased wear and tear of the joint. Pay special attention to the piriformis (see following text), because it is the strongest of the six rotators.

One of the hallmarks of good technique is being able to experience weight transfer in the hip joints. It enables you to use the pelvis as a center of power that can hardly be felt when the rotators are tight. Once the deep rotators are released, your plié is deeper, the pelvis is more aligned, your balance improves, and leg power, also in the turned-out position, is fully available to you. Rather than just stretching these muscles once they are tight, use them with a sense of length and ease. Simply increasing the awareness of the area immediately adds to the available flexibility.

The focus of this exercise is the piriformis and obturators, because they are important for adjusting the weight transfer from pelvis to legs. The obturators and the piriformis attach to a groove (fossa) just inside of the ridge of the greater trochanter at the top of the femur bone. This detail is important, because visualizing softness in this groove helps to release tension in these muscles.

The obturator internus travels around the sit bone to the front of the pelvis, attaching to an area called the obturator foramen. The obturator externus attaches to the same place, only its route is shorter. It travels under the hip joint to the outside of the obturator foramen. The externus also acts as an elastic support for the hip joints, like a hammock stretched beneath it. The obturators are difficult to visualize both in their location and action, but it is well worth spending the time to embody their function.

Besides being external rotators of the femur, the contracting obturators tilt the pelvis forward when the legs are fixed on the ground (closed-chain position; figure a).

1. Walk the fingers up the outside of the left leg until you feel a bony prominence, the greater trochanter. Don't confuse the trochanter with the pelvic crest, which is further up.

2. Touch the left greater trochanter with the left hand, and the sit bone of the same side of the body with the right hand to visualize the first half of the path of the internal obturator. Massage these points gently with circular motion of the fingers, while you think of the obturators' route from the trochanter around the sit bone to the inside of the pelvis.

3. Image the muscle flowing from the trochanter downward to the sit bone and then to the front of the pelvis, like a river (figure b).

4. To complete the inner obturator visualization, move the left hand to touch the left pubic bone. Focus on the part of the obturator after it has traveled around to the sit bone and flows into the inside of the pelvis.

5. Visualize the end of the obturator spreading like a river delta as it attaches to the obturator foramen.

6. Compare left and right hip flexion and rotation, and repeat the touch on the other side of the body.

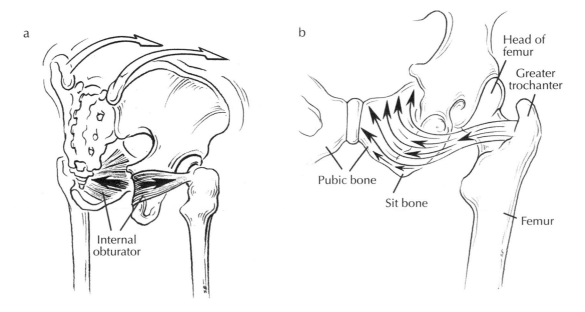

a

b

Head of femur

Greater trochanter

Pubic bone

Sit bone

Femur

Internal obturator

The external obturator runs under the hip joint from the groove on the inside of the trochanter to the outside of the obturator foramen. As it passes under the hip joint, it also forms connections with the hip joint capsule, a dynamic aid to hip stability (see figure).

1. Visualize the outer obturator by touching the trochanter and the part of the pubic bone that descends to the sit bone on the same side.

2. Again, think of the flow traveling from the trochanter to the sit bone. Imagine the muscle sagging like a hammock as it travels under the hip joint.

3. Once you are able to visualize these muscles, turn the leg in and out (medial and lateral rotation in the hip joint). Embody the sliding of the filaments in the obturators. As you turn out, they slide together. As you turn in, they slide apart.

4. If you visualize these muscles with great sensitivity, you may be able to increase your turn-out to an astonishing degree. Do not imagine shortening in the muscle; just think of easy sliding of filaments.

5. As you turn out, also focus on the tensor fasciae latae, an internal rotator and abductor of the leg. Touch the ASIS, and slide the fingers downward an inch or two and slightly to the back to feel this muscle. Massage the tensor fasciae latae while you image the muscle melting down the front and outside of the pelvis.

6. Before you work on the other side, compare the right and the left legs so you can appreciate the results of your effort.

7. Lift your right leg into a passé. Turn the leg in, and imagine the obdurators sliding apart. Turn the leg out, and imagine the obturators sliding together.

8. Once you have exercised both sides, perform a plié and think of the outer obturators shortening and lengthening without tension beneath the hip sockets. Also try extensions in second position while thinking of the obturators. Let the greater trochanter drop to the back and downward to get an easy contraction of the obturators. If you master this skill, you will have more turn-out with less effort in the upper thigh.

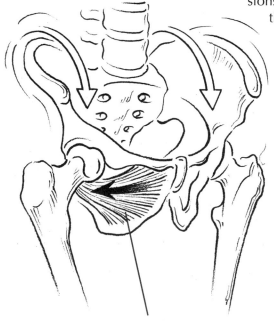

External obturator

You have already touched the piriformis in the previous exercise. But it is valuable to pay separate attention to this muscle. The piriformis, which means pear shaped, runs between the greater trochanter and the front of the sacrum. As it runs between the top of the leg and the sacrum, it coordinates the movement of these two bones. If one of the piriformis muscles is tighter than the other, the sacrum is subject to a twisting force, and the joint between the ilium and sacrum (iliosacral) may feel painful. The sacrum is the base of the spine and should be well aligned. If a dancer gestures more frequently with one leg than the other (as is often the case), he will create a one-sided strength pattern in the piriformis. This pattern should be balanced out of the body with awareness imagery and conditioning exercises.

1. Place most of the body's weight on the left leg. Keep the right foot on the floor with the leg slightly abducted.
2. Touch the greater trochanter on the right side of the body.
3. Slide the fingers to the top of the trochanter and then to its back edge.
4. Visualize the piriformis running between the trochanter and the sacrum.
5. Turn the leg in and out, and notice the bulging of the muscles around the fingers. As you turn the leg in, the gluteus minimus and the tensor fasciae latae (internal rotators of the leg) are felt bulging in the front of the fingers. As you turn out, the gluteus maximus is felt mostly behind the fingers.
6. Massage the area between these two bulges to contact the piriformis. Rotate the leg in and out, and see whether you can feel deep muscle activity under the fingers. This activity is difficult to feel if you lift the right foot off the floor, because the gluteals bulge and cover up any chance to feel deeper muscles.
7. Once you have completed your touch-discovery, compare leg extension (développé à la seconde) on the left and right, and repeat your exploration on the other side.
8. Go for a walk, and think of the legs swinging from the sacrum through the piriformis. If someone comments on your new ease of walking, be prepared to lecture on the benefits of piriformis awareness.

This exercise teaches never to force your turn-out. Muscle freedom, not strain, increases turn-out. Also, tight muscles cannot develop strength and will not be able to maintain turn-out during movement.

1. Place a ball under the right side of the pelvis between the greater trochanter and the sit bone. (Information about rolling balls is included in the references and resources listing at the end of this book.) You need to rotate the pelvis to the right to be able to do this. Adjust the body until you feel comfortable. It may take a bit of practice to get the ball in the right place and still feel comfortable in the rest of the body (figure *a*).

2. As you roll over the ball slowly, imagine the muscles melting. Breathe into this area. Imagine the breath having the power to dissolve all tension.

3. As a variation, use two balls, one under the pelvis and the other under the outside of the thigh, just above the knee. You can now release tension both in the lateral pelvic and thigh muscles (figure *b*). Adjust the position of the ball on the outside of the thigh with the hands, and roll under various areas of the outside of the leg.

4. Increase or decrease the pressure on the balls depending on the state of the muscles.

5. Initiate movement from the right pelvic half, turn the leg in and out, breathe, and move slowly.

6. Imagine the muscles melting over the ball. Breathe into the knots you encounter and dissolve them with the breath.

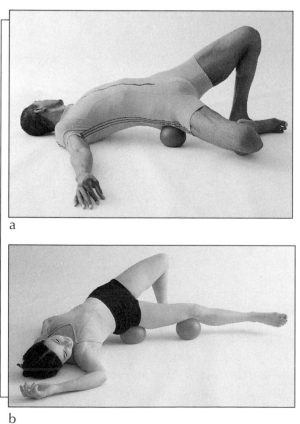

a

b

7. Practice for about five minutes on one side. Before changing sides, take a moment to stand up and perform a plié and développé extension with each leg. You may notice a significant difference in the ease of motion and amount of turn-out between sides. Also practice balancing on one leg and notice the stability of the knee.

8. Brush the leg to the front and turn the leg in and out. You may have increased both the range and fluidity of the in-and-out motion. Notice the rest of the body as you do this. Can the action be focused in the hip joints, while the rest of the body stays undisturbed? Or do you tense up certain areas as you try to turn out?

9. After you have completed both sides, perform some more pliés in second position to integrate the new range into the nervous system's movement guidance system.

10. Visualize the muscles around the greater trochanter. Focus on the groove (fossa) on the inside of the trochanter, and see the muscles melting to increase the depth of your plié without disturbing pelvic alignment.

You will now use movement and visualization to create a smooth lengthening action of the deep rotators. In the following exercise it is important to pay attention to the positioning of the legs, because the muscles change their function depending on the amount of hip flexion. As you have seen in chapter 4, the piriformis acts as an internal rotator if the leg is flexed more than 60 degrees in the hip joint, and as an external rotator at less than 60 degrees of flexion. To optimally lengthen the muscle, we need to switch from external to internal rotation during hip extension. This exercise also helps to release tension in the hip flexors, notably the iliopsoas (see also chapter 6).

1. Place two balls under the pelvis.

2. Keeping the right foot on the floor, lift (flexion in the hip joint) the left leg, turn it out, and abduct it in the hip joint (figure a).

3. Slowly lower the left foot to the floor (extension in the hip joint) while turning the leg in and adducting it (figure b).

4. Visualize the piriformis muscle lengthening. Imagine the distance between the sacrum and the greater trochanter increasing as the foot lowers toward the ground.

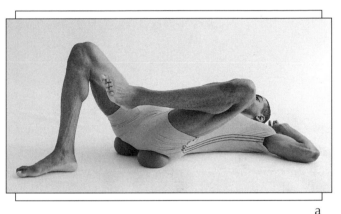

a

5. Lift the foot off the floor, and bring the leg back into the starting position by flexing the hip, abducting and rotating the leg outward.

6. Repeat the movement cycle five times.

7. Before you switch sides, remove the balls, stretch the legs out on the floor, check your external rotation, and perform a few hip flexions, développés, or leg kicks to experience the benefits of the exercise. Note the degree, but also the quality of external rotation.

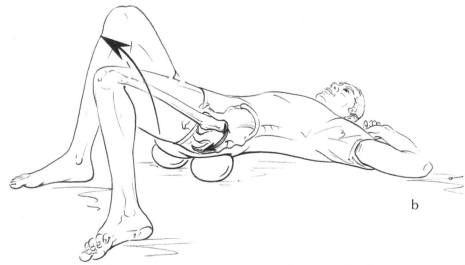

b

9.18   STRETCHING THE PIRIFORMIS

Contracting the piriformis turns the leg out in standing, but abducts and turns the leg in when you elevate it over 60 degrees. I have frequently observed in dancers that when this muscle is not diligently stretched, the leg turns in as it is elevated, and the abductors (gluteus medius) instead of the iliopsoas come into play to create higher leg elevations. Because this action causes the greater trochanter to push against the side of the pelvis, a dancer cannot lift the leg very high to the side in abduction. To compensate, the dancer lifts his pelvis on the side of the gesturing leg. For ballet this is not acceptable, and it is not a good strategy for any dance form because it throws your supporting leg out of alignment and endangers the knee. To lift the leg in abduction as seen in some jazz and modern dance styles (e.g., Horton Technique), you need to consciously keep the knee of the supporting leg over the foot.

1. For this stretch you need a ballet barre or some elevated surface. Place the side of the left foot on the surface, fully turn out the hip joint, and bend the knee just over a right angle.

2. Move the leg toward you on the barre to increase the adduction of the left hip joint.

3. Lean the torso forward and turn it to the left. You may now start to feel the stretch at the side and back of the left pelvic half. Depending on your individual configuration, you may also feel a stretch in the back or other areas A stretch does not feel the same for everybody, because we all have a different length and shortness in our muscles.

4. Breathe as you go deeper, and use the hands to tap the areas of tension. This tapping increases circulation, which helps to release tension. Stay in the stretched position for one minute, then lift the torso up and rest for a moment.

5. Go back into the stretch, drop the left knee, move the torso over to the left, and adduct the left leg. Breathe, and visualize the piriformis lengthening for one minute as you relax the shoulders (see figure).

6. Come out of the stretch, and rest. You may repeat the stretch a third time if you wish.

7. Before doing the other side, perform a second position plié, and notice the difference in turn-out and knee alignment. The right knee will drop forward relative to the left. But the most interesting comparison is the extension: First perform a développé with the left leg, and notice the ease of movement, turn-out, and height of the leg. On this side the iliopsoas muscle is helping to achieve the elevation. Now perform a développé with the other leg. You may notice that the leg is more turned in, and the muscles on top of the hip joint feel bunched. These muscles are the abductors that are overworking with less iliopsoas support.

8. Repeat the exercise on the other side.

If the turn-out muscles are straining to keep your external rotation intact, the hip joints will feel tight. This tightness is because the gluteus maximus, the most powerful external rotator, is a hip extensor. Logic tells us that if you contract the most powerful hip extensor in an effort to increase turn-out, you cannot flex the hip well. A dancer will flex his hip joints anyhow, but with strain (and pain) in the legs.

The rolling balls will now massage the adductors and, depending on our position, the inner-most quadriceps (vastus medialis), tensor fasciae latae, and sartorious muscles. Move carefully and slowly, as the adductors may be very tight, even if you have been stretching diligently. Never roll the ball under an area of acute pain or recent injury. The balls may however be useful for releasing tension in muscles and scar tissue related to an old injury.

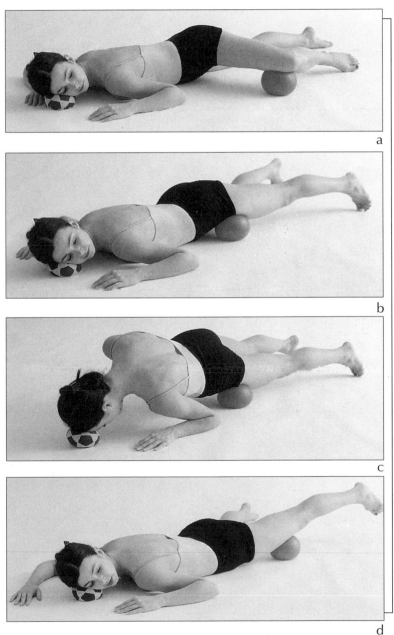

1. Lie prone with the left leg angled off to the side. You may place a soft ball or a pillow under the head for more comfort.

2. Place one ball under the inner thigh of the same leg, but not directly under the knee (figure *a*).

3. Search, discover, and release points of tension. Keep breathing; you may encounter some hefty knots.

4. Slightly turn the thigh in and out, and initiate movement from the pelvic half of the same side.

5. Move the whole body downward to slowly roll the ball upward along the inner thigh toward the hip joint.

6. Release tension in the area at the top of the leg (figure *b*).

7. Rotate the body to reach the muscles at the outer edge of the upper thigh and pelvis (figure *c*).

8. Move the body further up to massage the muscles at the front of the thigh and around the hip joint (figure *d*).

9. After having released tension points to your satisfaction, stand up, and notice the difference in turn-out in extension as well as in second position plié between the rolled leg and the other.

10. You may notice that the leg that has been worked on is much less prone to dropping inward into a turned-in and adducted position. Turn-out is maintained with less effort.

a

b

c

d

Pelvic Floor and Turn-Out

The pelvic floor is related to turn-out through its close proximity and connective tissue relationships to the muscles of the upper leg. An inelastic pelvic floor inhibits the movement of the pelvic joints, which in turn reduces the flexibility of the joints of the whole leg. A strong and elastic floor will not only create more turn-out, it will help the dancer to maintain turn-out in difficult dance steps.

9.20 PELVIC FLOOR EXTENSION

This exercise is quite challenging but very valuable for coordinating the pelvic floor and leg muscles. It helps to increase the strength for leg elevation and turn-out in extension.

1. Lie supine with two balls supporting the pelvis. You can do the exercise without the support or with a rolled towel. The balls make the exercise more comfortable and easier to perform.

2. Place the heels together; the legs are turned out, abducted, and flexed at the hip joint. Dorsiflex the feet at the ankles (figure a).

3. Stretch the legs up at an angle of about 70 degrees. Think of pushing against the air with the soles of the feet.

4. Initiate the movement from the pelvic floor and adductor musculature. Imagine a line of force extending from the sit bones to the heels. The abdominal muscles actively support the pelvic floor effort.

5. Move the legs to the sides into an abducted position (figure b).

6. Bend the knees, and flex the hip joints, keeping the feet flexed as well (figure c).

7. Repeat the action four times, each time exhaling as you stretch the legs out. Increase the repetitions to eight in increments of one over a four-week period. To increase the workload on the abdominal muscles, you can lower the legs to a 45-degree angle. Do not attempt this variation until you have exercised the iliopsoas and transverse abdominal musculature for at least three weeks, or you will arch the back (see chapters 5 and 6).

8. Stand up and perform an extension to the side, and notice the changes in alignment and turn-out. Don't feel surprised if you feel a bit wobbly after this exercise, especially if you are at the beginning of conditioning the adductors and the pelvic floor.

The adductor magnus adducts, extends, and medially rotates the hip joint. Creating a sense of length in the adductor magnus increases turn-out while improving stability. The muscle connects the back of the sit bone to the back of the femur (short head) and to the top inside of the knee (long head).

1. Feel the bump above the inner side of the knee, the medial femoral condyle.

2. Just above this spot you can detect a tendon. It feels like a thinner version of the Achilles tendon. Massage this tendon up along the inside of the leg, as far as you can feel it. It eventually blends with the big muscle mass of the adductor magnus.

3. Then touch the right sit bone and the adductor tendon attachment simultaneously, and visualize the length of the adductor magnus.

4. Now stretch the right leg forward in a turned-out position with the heel flexed. Image the adductor magnus flowing outward from the sit bones toward the inside of the knee. This image will probably not work as well on the untouched side.

5. Perform a plié, and in the downward move imagine the adductor magnus to be a sail pushed to the front by wind blowing from behind you. This image helps increase turn-out by promoting the correct movement of the femur.

6. Repeat the touch on the other side.

ADDUCTOR MAGNUS AND PELVIC FLOOR   9.22

In the following exercise (adapted from Bonnie Bainbridge Cohen), you will engage both the adductor magnus and the pelvic floor simultaneously.

1. Lie in a supine position with two balls supporting the pelvis. Engage the pelvic floor and adductor magnus to bring the legs together.

2. Stretch the legs out to the sides, and visualize the pelvic floor and adductor magnus musculature. Think of the adductor magnus as the continuation of the pelvic floor.

3. Bring the legs back together by engaging the pelvic floor and adductor magnus (see figure).

4. Slowly lower the legs, and think of the eccentric lengthening action of the adductor magnus and pelvic floor musculature. Visualize the muscle filaments sliding apart.

5. Repeat the adduction of the legs by initiating in the pelvic floor and letting the power travel down the inside of the legs to the adductor magnus. Exhale as you do this.

6. Repeat the exercise no more than six times when you begin to practice. Increase the number of repetitions to 12 in increments of 1 over a six-week period.

7. Stretch the legs to the sides, and notice your flexibility.

8. Stand up, and notice the state of your turn-out in a second position plié and extensions. If the legs are shaking, this is a sign that the pelvic floor and adductors are in dire need of conditioning.

Now that you have extensive knowledge of how to improve turn-out, let's finish with a focus on the parallel position. Standing with the legs and feet in true parallel is important in many dance forms, and it is just as challenging as turning the legs out. Modern dancers who have trained with a lot of ballet often have difficulty achieving a parallel position; they are always slightly turned out. Also, it is highly recommended that ballet dancers practice the parallel position, because it helps to improve the sense of centered leg movement.

One of the key muscles to be aware of in creating parallel position is the tensor fasciae latae you encountered earlier. The tensor fasciae latae is connected to the powerful iliotibial band (ITB), which runs down the side of the leg. The tensor fasciae latae flexes, abducts, and internally rotates the hip, and can assist in extending the knee through the ITB. One of its jobs is to help stabilize and center the heads of the femurs in the hip sockets, which is important in all dance forms. It influences the position of the upper leg muscles through the fascia, a connective tissue sac surrounding these muscles. In her book *The Hidden You,* Mabel Todd describes the tensor fasciae latae as a postural muscle that "aids the support of the lower spine, that part of the spine which must lend power to *direction and control of movement.*" She points out: "The tightening of the fascia latae prevents any one muscle from overworking to the extent of seriously jeopardizing the safety of the thigh and knee joint." (Todd 1953, page 57). Some dancers experience an uncomfortable snapping over the greater trochanter because of tightness in the ITB and tensor fascia latae (iliotibial band syndrome). Related knee and lower back pain may also exist.

1. Visualize the tensor fasciae latae attached to the front upper and outer part of the iliac bone. It descends to attach to the iliotibial tract and ends about mid-thigh (figure 2). Through the iliotibial tract, it can send its influence all the way down to the lower leg. It helps to flex, abduct, and internally rotate the hip joint and extend the knee joint.

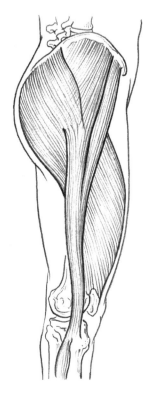
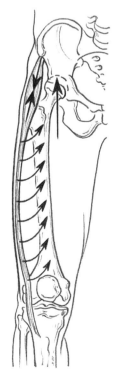

2. Massage the muscle on the right side. To localize the bulge of this muscle flex, abduct, and internally rotate the hip joint. Place the body's weight on the left leg, keeping the right foot on the floor. Begin at the upper attachment and massage down to the upper front and outside of the leg.

3. Swing the right leg front and back in parallel, and imagine the tensor fascia latae pulling on the sleeve surrounding the thigh muscle with the goal of centering the femur head in its socket. Imagine the tensor fasciae latae moving the muscle bulk toward the midline (see figure b).

4. Stand on the right leg, and notice the stability of your parallel position. Stand on the left leg, and compare the two feelings.

5. Repeat the movement with the left leg. Stand in parallel on both legs, and perform several pliés with a sense of the action of the tensor fascia latae in support of focusing the heads of the femur into their sockets. Imagine the tensor fasciae latae acting as the guiding force in achieving this goal together with its partner, the iliopsoas. Both muscles are weak internal rotators, but when their forces combine, they create a sense of parallel leg action.

chapter 10

Thera–Band Centre Workout

T he Thera-Band centre workout is a complete body conditioning routine for dancers. The movements are derived from ballet and modern technique to provide a close match between the building of strength and flexibility and the movement patterns required for dance. The keys to success in the following exercise sequence are good alignment, relaxed breathing, and correct movement initiation.

Preparing for the Sequence

Ideally, you should wear tights or long pants so that you will not be bothered by the Thera-Band occasionally rubbing against the legs. Select a band that is at least three yards (about three meters) long. To determine whether you have the correct length of band for your height, place the center of a Thera-Band on the head. It should be long enough to touch the floor on both sides of the body.

Create a fairly large loop on one end of the band, and make a knot (figure 10.1a). You may have to experiment with the size of the loop that best fits the foot. Place the loop over the foot, and make a figure eight with the band to create a second loop (figure 10.1, b and c). Pull the second loop up over the foot so the knot faces upward. The band should not be too tight on the foot, or it will constrict the flow of blood. On the other hand, if it is too loose, it will slip off during the exercises.

During the following exercises, keep your awareness on the whole body, not just the part that is resisting the band. Even when you are working with a specific image to support the exercise, always tune part of your attention to whole-body awareness. Success in this exercise sequence requires proper alignment. You will strengthen muscles to support the position and movement you are doing, so if you are not well aligned, muscles will gain strength to support this faulty alignment, which is not good for your dance technique. Every exercise description includes movement instructions as well as imagery pointers to keep you aligned.

a

b

c

Figure 10.1, *a* through *c* To prepare for the Thera-Band workout, create the right size loop in the band and tie a knot.

Initiate all movements with minimal tension, and breathe freely. Build strength for movement, not tension. Watch how you hold the band, as this is often a source of tension. Hold it tightly, but without tension. If you feel strain and tension, you are using a band that is not long enough or that has too much resistance. Increase the length and use a lower-resistance band until you can perform the exercises without excess tension.

How you think during the exercise is a crucial part of the training. Use imagery and awareness of the breath to stay focused on the movement. Feel transitions clearly, move smoothly, and think of the band as a friend, not an opponent.

You may perform this sequence daily as a warm-up or cool-down before or after class or rehearsal. However, to use it for conditioning, practice the sequence at least three or four times a week. Once you have learned the individual exercises, try to do them in sequence. When you move up to a higher-resistance band, begin again with four repetitions for the first week, six the second, and eight the third.

Begin practicing with a medium- to low-resistance (red or green) Thera-Band. After one month of regular practice graduate to the blue Thera-Band, and after two months you may use the black, and then the silver for conditioning purposes. For warming up don't go beyond the blue Thera-Band. But you should always return to using a lower-resistance band under the following circumstances:

- You feel that the band you are using offers too much resistance to do the exercise with good alignment while remaining free of tension.
- The band does not feel sufficiently elastic to you.
- You are using the exercise sequence as a warm-up or cool-down.
- You have not practiced the sequence for over a week.
- You are recovering from an injury.

Perform each exercise first with the right leg. Then when you have completed the sequence, repeat each exercise with the left.

The back hammock is not actually part of the Thera-Band workout, but it warms up the back and relaxes and deepens the breath for the following exercises. The exercise also lubricates the joints between the ribs, relaxes the muscles between the ribs and the spine (intercostals), and creates a sense of width in the back.

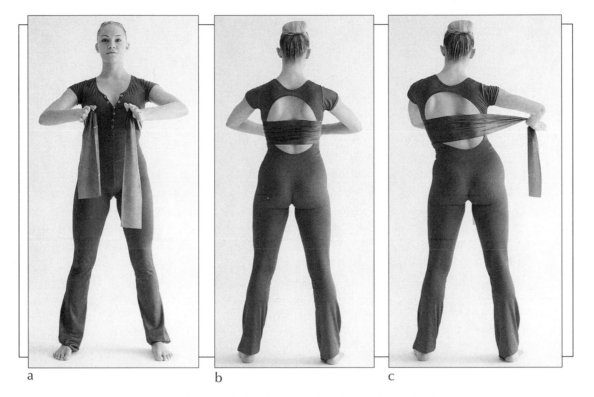

a   b   c

1. Place a Thera-Band behind the back and hold each of the loose ends with the arms bent at the elbows (figure *a*).

2. Bend the spine, and rest the back into the band as if it were a hammock (figure *b*). Relax the neck and jaw, drop the shoulders, and exhale as you let the back rest into the hammock.

3. Push the arms forward, and extend the spine to get out of the hammock again. Repeat this sequence four times.

4. Move the arms to the right, and push the ribs to the left into the band (figure *c*). Then move the arms to the left, and push the ribs to the right into the band. Repeat this sequence four times.

5. Imagine the many joints of the ribs and spine being lubricated by rich synovial fluid: the spinal joints, the joints between the sternum and rib cartilages, the joints between the ribs and the spine, and all of the joints of the body.

6. Circle the rib cage to the right within the band, moving the arms in opposition to the movement of the rib cage to create a constant tension level in the band. Repeat, circling toward the left.

7. Imagine that the lungs are mobile within the rib cage and they are slipping within the ribs like a giant bar of lathery soap (figure *d*).

8. Let go of the band, and appreciate the newfound feeling of width in the back, depth of the breath, and limberness of the spine.

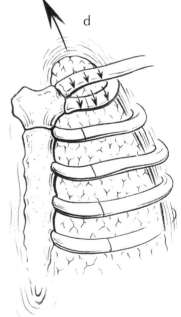

d

a

This exercise marks the beginning of the Thera-Band centre workout, and it is aimed at strengthening the body using a plié position including an upward arm action. It emphasizes the quadriceps, gluteal, and triceps eccentric and concentric strengthening as well as coordinated leg and arm action. The primary lateral flexors of the spine, the oblique abdominal muscles, the longissimus, and iliocostalis muscle of the spine are also strongly engaged in the second part of the exercise.

1. Attach a Thera-Band to the right foot, and start in second position plié while holding the band in both hands with the elbows at right angles (figure a).

2. As you move upward, push the band upward with both arms (figure b).

3. As you move downward in plié, bend the arms, resisting the band with minimal tension. Let the band push you down.

4. Compare the feeling of pushing with the arms to that of pushing the band from the legs and feet. Notice whether the latter feels as though it takes less effort, and you may experience how much a simple image can change the way you perform a movement.

5. Visualize the floors of the body in horizontal alignment (pelvic floor, diaphragm, first rib, base of skull; see figure b). Feel the feet connect to the pelvic floor, and experience the pelvic floor supporting the legs. This image allows you to drop the shoulders and feel the push of the arms connected to your base of power. Feel the thrust of the feet and legs transferring to the pelvic, diaphragmatic, and first rib floors.

6. After doing four to eight repetitions, add a sidebend to the left as you come up from the plié.

b

7. Pull the belly button inward toward the spine as you bend to the side. Notice how flexible the spine feels. Now breathe freely, and bend to the side again. Do you notice an increase in flexibility? The idea of approximating the belly button and spine restricts the breath and limits flexibility. If you restrict the action of the abdominal muscles by holding them, you have less lateral flexion because they are actively involved in producing lateral flexion. The belly button postural strategy results in less strength, because it reduces the ROM. If you have less ROM, the muscles do not contract and release over the same distance, resulting in less training effect. If pulling in the belly feels stronger to you, then you may be confusing tension with strength for movement.

8. Repeat the sequence 8 times, increasing to 16 times in increments of 2 each week.

The contraction with spiral exercises trains all the muscles of the torso, specifically the abdominal muscles and the spinal lateral flexors, extensors, and rotators. The contraction spiral improves the simultaneous initiation of the tail and head and improves the coordination of spine and leg movements.

1. Stand with the feet in a wide stance, and hold the upper arms out to the sides (figure a).

2. Turn to the left by pivoting the feet on the floor (figure b).

3. Straighten the arms, bend the knees and raise the right heel, and adjust the legs and feet so the knees remain over the feet.

4. Place the Thera-Band over the right shoulder and back just to the right of the spine.

5. Curve the spine, and turn the head slightly to the left and downward. Pull the band down in front of you.

6. While bending the spine, initiate the movement simultaneously from the tail and head, and feel the spine bend smoothly and equally along its whole length. Allow the lumbar spine to drop back, and let the sit bones and tail move forward (figure c).

7. Push the left knee forward until you feel the right thigh (quadriceps) actively contract.

8. Imagine a spiral action from head to tail through the upper body, bringing the right shoulder closer to the left hip.

9. Return to the starting position, and repeat the exercise four times. Increase to eight repetitions in increments of two each week of practice.

a

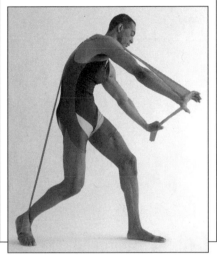

b

c

STRENGTHENING THE TURNING MUSCLES: ROTATING ORGANS

a   b

This upper body rotation strengthens the muscles of the torso, arms, and back. The oblique abs and spinal rotators (multifidi and rotatores) are engaged in a way that is important to dance and that supports turns. The obliques lack strength in many dancers, and dance-specific conditioning exercises are rare for this muscle group. The exercise also increases the rotary flexibility and alignment of the spine.

Once you are well acquainted with this exercise, perform it right after exercise 10.3 to create one continuous movement that engages just about all the muscles of the body.

1. Stand with the feet in a wide stance, hold the arms out to the sides with elbows bent and a Thera-Band looped over the hands (figure a).

2. Raise your arms, rotate the torso (not just the arms) to the right, and push against the band with the right arm (figure b). As you rotate, visualize the head aligning vertically over the pelvis, keep the shoulders dropped, and above all, breathe! If you relax the shoulders and neck, you will notice a significant improvement in the degree of your rotation.

3. As an experiment, lift the shoulders, and notice how it impedes the rotation of the spine.

4. Adjust the feet to the changing position of the pelvis so the knees remain aligned over the feet (figure c), and keep the head and shoulders over the pelvis.

5. When rotating to the right, visualize the right deep spinal muscles lengthening. When rotating to the left, visualize the left deep spinal muscles lengthening.

6. Organ imagery is supportive of any rotary movement. Imagine the kidneys or any of the paired organs rotating around the spine. Visualize the lungs floating around the spine, and breathe into the kidneys. If you can feel the movement originating in the organs rather than in the superficial muscles you will increase the range of your rotation, thereby enhancing the expressive possibilities of the spine.

8. When you have reached maximum rotation, return to the starting position.

9. Repeat the sequence four times, and increase to eight repetitions in increments of one each week of practice.

This exercise strengthens and stretches the lateral flexors of the spine as well as the muscles of the arms and shoulders. It helps create coordinated torso and leg action and a feeling of moving out into space. This exercise is ideal for keeping a dance feel during conditioning.

a   b   c   d

1. Start with a plié in second position, holding the Thera-Band at the same level in both hands (see exercise 10.3, figure *a*).

2. Push the band up, and stretch the legs (figure *a*). Focus on pushing the band away from you and moving the limbs into space.

3. Cross the right leg behind the left (figure *b*), and bend the spine to the left. During the initial phase of the exercise, make sure you don't hyperextend the back as you bend to the side.

4. Circle the band over the head with the right arm, and place it across the left upper arm, directly above the left elbow (figure *c*).

5. Lift the left shoulder; and push forward against the band with the left arm (figure *d*). Imagine the spine lengthening and the shoulder muscles sliding.

6. Lift both shoulders and the right heel, and push the band higher. (Obviously the left arm is working harder as it is pushing against the band).

7. Lower the shoulders and heels.

8. Return to the original position by stepping to the right with the right leg and moving the band back over the head in a semicircular swing.

9. To keep the upper body in fluid motion, visualize sliding joints between the organs. Image the lungs sliding over the heart in the sidebend (figure *e*). In the sidebend to the left, the right lung slides up, and the left lung slides down. Notice how this internal perspective creates a more fluid feel in the superficial musculature.

10. Repeat the sequence four times. Increase to eight times in increments of one each week of practice.

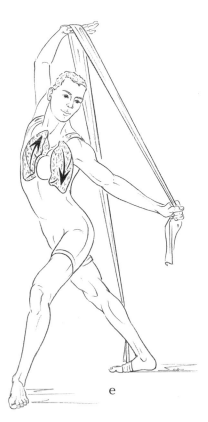

e

From the previous exercise, continue directly into this exercise, the backward extension, which may be challenging for your balance and spinal alignment. This exercise strengthens all the limbs, especially the supporting leg, and it helps you gain a feeling of an elongated spine in arabesque position.

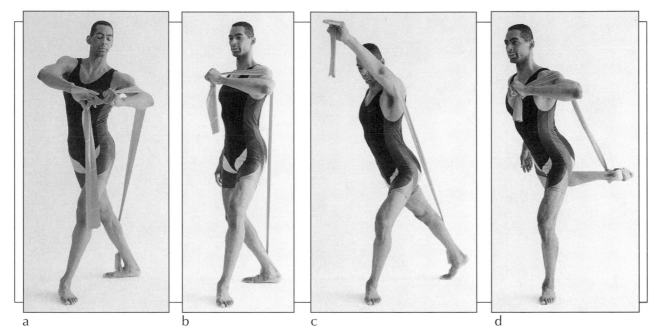

a   b   c   d

1. Begin in the crossed leg position with the Thera-Band in the left hand. Adjust the length of the band. It should not be so short as to strain the arm and shoulder (figure *a*).

2. Shift your weight to the left leg. Bring the band up and over the left upper arm (figure *b*).

3. Extend the right leg and the left arm, and feel the length of the spine. Raise the right heel off the floor (figure *c*).

4. Return to the starting position, and repeat the sequence 8 times, increasing to 16 in increments of 2 each week of practice.

5. Tilt the upper body forward, and balance on the left leg. Extend the right leg behind you in an arabesque-like position.

6. Bend the standing leg, the extending leg, and the arm holding the band (figure *d*).

7. Push the band to the front with the left arm and to the back with the right leg. Stretch the supporting leg (figure *e*). Make sure the back does not arch, and keep the head aligned with the spine.

8. Bend and stretch both legs and the left arm eight times, maintaining a clear sense of spinal alignment. Increase to 16 repetitions in increments of 2 each week of practice. Let the right arm rest at the side.

9. Imagine the connection between the head and tailbone, and feel it lengthen as you extend the arms. You may exhale as you lengthen the spine.

10. Notice the position of the pelvis. Keep both halves of the pelvis equal, and feel the spine balanced between the two sides of the body. Feel the spine being supported from underneath, especially in the lumbar area.

e

The following exercise is excellent for strengthening your extension without sacrificing alignment. The supporting leg works hard and will improve its ability to balance the whole upper body when landing from a jump onto one leg. The gluteus maximus and medius and the quadriceps and calf musculature are strongly engaged throughout this exercise.

1. Continuing directly from step 11 in exercise 10.6, switch the band to the left hand, and drape it over the left elbow (figure *a*).

2. Place the left arm in second position, and keep the elbow lifted against the band.

3. Place the pointed right foot in a coupé position close to the ankle, with both knees bent (figure *a*). The band should not be too taut. Use the left arm to adjust the band's length during the exercise.

4. Move the right leg to second position while stretching the supporting leg (battement fondu à la seconde). Lift the extended leg between 45 and 90 degrees depending on your capacity. You may lift the leg higher than shown in figure *b*.

5. Use only very light resistance of the band against the extending leg.

6. Visualize the sacrum and tailbone as a weight pulling the spine into aligned length (figure *c*). This pull creates more space between the individual vertebrae and releases the spine downward. This image is applied to greatest effect when you are stretching the legs. When bending the legs, imagine the tail becoming lighter to increase hip flexibility.

7. Feel a current, flow, or sense of release down the gesture side of the spine and sacrum. This feeling helps to keep the spine aligned and increases hip flexibility, which you will notice when you practice an extension after removing the band (figure *d*).

8. Feel the sliding filament action in the muscles of the supporting leg. It is especially beneficial to feel the sliding in the muscles at the back of the supporting leg (hamstrings). Notice how this feeling changes your alignment and improves your balance.

9. Repeat the sequence 4 times, and increase to 12 repetitions in increments of 2 each week of practice.

a

b

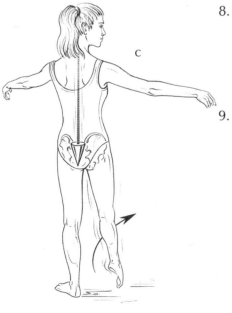

c

d

STRONG ALIGNMENT FOR BATTEMENT FONDU EN AVANT

This exercise is another opportunity to build strength into good alignment. The result is a clear and stable extension to the front and better balance. The exercise also strengthens the adductors in their role as hip flexors.

a   b

1. Continuing directly from the previous exercise, bend both knees, and point the foot at the front of the ankle in a coupé position (figure *a*).

2. Move the gesturing leg to the front while extending the supporting leg (battement fondu en avant; figure *b*).

3. On the side of the extending leg, visualize the downward sloping and grounding effect of the large intestine to give you a clearer sense of creasing in the hip joint. Imagine the large intestine acting as a counterbalance to the gesturing leg.

4. Feel the lower spine and cervical spinous processes being gently pulled to the rear by soft threads as you bend the supporting leg. This feeling will help you to maintain a lengthened spine without tension.

5. Visualize an equal distance between the bottom of the rib cage and the pelvic crest on both sides of the body (figure *c*).

6. Bend both the legs to return to the starting position.

7. Repeat the sequence 8 times, and increase to 12 repetitions in increments of 2 each week of practice.

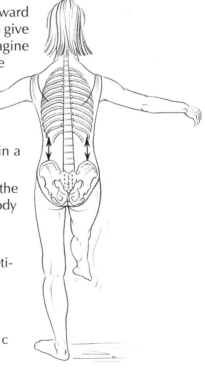

c

Continuing from the previous exercise, this optional exercise provides an excellent opportunity to create aligned strength for extensions to the back. The exercise also strengthens the hip extensors and spinal muscles and helps to create higher extensions to the back. Omit this exercise the first month of practicing the Thera-Band workout, because exercise 10.5 serves these needs for the first month.

In all leg actions and extensions to the back, alignment and correct movement initiation pose a challenge. Good alignment and coordination go a long way to prevent the aches and pains in the upper and lower back plaguing so many dancers. Most often the pelvis on the side of the gesturing leg is hiked excessively, causing a twist in the spine, distorting the supporting leg and making balance and turns in arabesque difficult. In most dancers, extensions to the back are accompanied by tension in the shoulders and the neck, reducing the flexibility of the back.

1. While pointing the foot at the back of the lower leg near the ankle and bending both knees, place the left arm in front of the body.

2. Plié and extend to the back (fondu battement en arrière).

3. Return to the starting position.

4. Visualize a well-aligned and dynamic sacral action with both upper corners of this triangular bone approximately on the same level. To create alignment, think of balanced movement into the new shape. The pelvic halves rotate forward and in opposition to the leg bones that are turning out. This rotation keeps the back free and flexible and allows you to lift the leg higher. The shoulder blades drop in response to the lifting of the arms. Think of the sacrum and tail as the continuation of the extended spine. Imagining the sacrum and tail as flexible and mobile vertebrae, which they once were, creates additional mobility in the spine (figure *a*).

5. The breastbone may be considered the spine of the front of the body. It is composed of seven sternebrae, which are fused in the adult with the exception of the junction between the manubrium and the body of the sternum and the xiphoid process and the body of the sternum. To increase the flexibility of the upper spine, imagine that the breastbone consists of individual vertebrae that are as mobile as a string of pearls.

6. Imagine the paired organs of the body balancing the two halves of the body (figure *b*). Imagine the lungs placed equally on both sides of the spine.

7. Visualize the kidneys and ascending and descending colon helping to balance the spine.

8. Repeat the exercise 4 times, and increase to 12 repetitions in increments of 2 each week of practice.

9. Alternately perform fondu extensions to the front, side, and back, and repeat four times. Increase to eight times in increments of two per week of practice.

a

b

10.10　SECOND POSITION PLIÉ AND RELEVÉ

This exercise strengthens and deepens the plié in second position and is a classic example of how you can gain strength and flexibility from one exercise. The results after only one series are usually a welcome surprise because of the reciprocal release of the muscles that oppose a deep plié. (The muscles that oppose the primary working muscles are lengthened by signals from the nervous system.) The exercise lengthens the adductors, creates more elasticity in the pelvic floor, and strengthens turn-out. Further benefits include a stronger relevé and a clearer sense of moving the torso vertically in second position relevé.

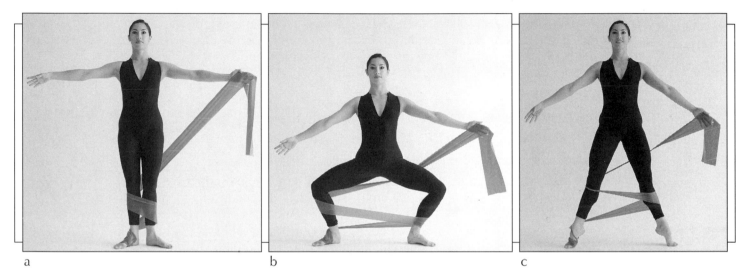

a　　　　　　　　　　　　　　　　b　　　　　　　　　　　　　　　　c

1. Loop the band around the back of the right lower leg and then around the front of the both lower legs (figure *a*).

2. Hold the band with the left hand. Be ready to adjust the tension during the exercise. The band should be loose enough to allow you to widen the legs to a comfortable second position.

3. Turn out the legs in a comfortable first position. Feel the relaxed stacking of the vertebrae of the spine. Widen the pelvic floor, and allow the muscles of the back of the leg (adductors and hamstrings) to release outward toward the knees.

4. Slide the right leg out to the side, and move into a second position plié (figure *b*). Feel a deep creasing in the hip joint, with the knees floating up as the pelvis moves down. Exhale as you slide out into second position. As you slide into second position plié, feel the back of the pelvis widening, spreading out to allow for a natural increase in turn-out. Visualize the femur externally rotating in response to the release at the back of the pelvis.

5. Relevé in second position (figure *c*).

6. Return to the plié, and slide the right leg back into first position.

7. Visualize all the muscles that attach to the front of the pelvis and can potentially pull the front of the pelvis downward (rectus femoris, sartorious, tensor faciae latae). While performing a plié, notice whether you feel any of these muscles tugging on the front of the pelvis to pull it down. Think of these muscles lengthening and letting go of the front rim of the pelvis. Notice the increased flexibility of the hip joints.

8. Repeat the sequence eight times.

Fourth position is even more challenging than second for your sense of vertical action in a relevé. This exercise is also an excellent opportunity to practice pelvic alignment as you move through space.

1. From first position, perform the same sliding plié action as in exercise 10.10 into a fourth position front (en avant). As you slide into fourth position, maintain the verticality of the upper body. Try to create the aligned movement with one action, and avoid lots of piecemeal corrections as you go along. Relaxed shoulder and neck muscles are essential for a sense of verticality.

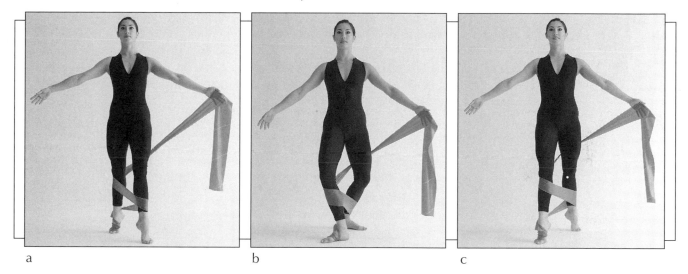

a　　　　　　　　　　　b　　　　　　　　　　　c

2. Perform a relevé in fourth position front (figure a).
3. Perform a sliding plié to a fourth position back (en arrière) (figure b). Allow your weight and flow, not excess force, to create the plié action. Don't focus on pushing against the band. This may cause unnecessary tension.
4. Perform a relevé in fourth position back (figure c).
5. Imagine the legs moving through a soft substance such as whipped cream (figure d). Feel the knees actually penetrating this substance.
6. Repeat the sequence four times.

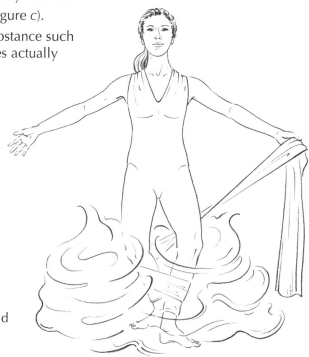

d

STRENGTH AND SPEED FOR LIGHT, DELICATE, POWERFUL FEET

This exercise imparts a great lightness to your battement and brushing actions. It strengthens the musculature of the toe and the arch of the foot. The muscles of the leg and foot are prepared for quick action for frappés or jazz dance styles that require a rapid and coordinated action of the foot and leg.

1. Lift the band above the right knee and place the lower loop below the left knee. Adjust the length of the band to allow you to move the right leg with some resistance in the battement action.

2. Perform a turned-out tendu, with the leg extended forward and the toes and ball of the foot on the floor. Lift the heel, sensing the arching of the foot.

3. Push the toes down rapidly, lifting the foot just a few inches off the floor, and extend the toes fully (figure a). Push the tips of the toes against the floor to initiate the lifting of the leg, keeping the action light and delicate yet explosive. Imagine the toes telescoping into length. (Don't claw them inward.) Imagine pushing the floor downward with the toes.

4. Rapidly lower the ball and toes back onto the floor. Move the leg to the side (second position), with the toes and ball of the foot on the floor (figure b).

5. Push the toes down rapidly, lifting the foot off the floor. Repeat this action 16 times in second position (figure c).

6. Move the leg to the back (en arrière), with the toes and ball of the foot on the floor.

7. Push the toes down rapidly, lifting the foot off the floor (figure d). Repeat this action 16 times to the back.

8. Repeat the action to the side (à la seconde) 16 times, then repeat the action in all directions 16 times.

9. If you are doing the series for the first time, now remove the band for a moment, and try the movement without it. You will be happily surprised at the lightness, ease, and speed of your movement!

10. Feel the feet being under water, working against the water's resistance (figure e). The bottom center of each foot is able to suck the water in, and the extension of each foot causes water to squirt forcefully out of the tips of each toe.

a

b

c

d

11. Don't let the leg and foot movement wiggle the pelvis or cause reverberations through the whole body. This is a sign that the action is not centered in the hip joint. Practice maintaining your alignment in a dynamic way by being aware of where the movement should happen as opposed to keeping the body steady through tension. Think of moving the leg from the hip socket while the pelvis and torso remain calm.

12. When you move the leg from the side to the back position, the sacrum will tilt forward, slightly increasing the arch of the lower back. If this slight increase in the tilt is inhibited, the hip joint will not be able to accommodate the movement of the leg to the back, and the pelvis will lift on the side of the gesturing leg. If the pelvis remains lifted for the battement action to the back, the spine will twist, causing muscular imbalance.

e

ANKLE RELEVÉ   **10.13**

The ankle relevé develops your arch and increases the strength of the ankles and calf muscles. It trains the calf muscles in a predominantly eccentric fashion. This training results in softer, more controlled landings from leaps, deeper pliés, and more stability in relevé.

1. Start in second position plié (see exercise 10.10, figure b).
2. Without shifting the pelvis, lift the heels off the floor (see figure). Feel the toes spreading on the floor like pancake batter. Feel the width of the lower back and pelvis. Imagine the tailbone lengthening to the floor.
3. Slowly return the heels to the ground.
4. To maintain turn-out, think of both knees being pulled to the sides by imaginary strings. Move the heels up and down, slowly pushing on imaginary springs (see figure). Breathe freely, and drop the shoulders. Keep the action fluid. You may experience a slight trembling in the musculature; this will pass as you gain more strength.
5. Repeat the sequence eight times.

This exercise creates well-aligned, strong attitudes and higher leg extension. It strengthens the supporting leg for all positions of the gesturing leg and is an opportunity to improve pelvic alignment for leg lifting actions. As in the previous exercise, this is a three-part exercise with movement to the front, side, and back in a turned-out position. The exercises can also be performed in a parallel leg position, which encourages balanced development of the leg muscles. The following description and photos show the turned-out variation.

1. Support with the right leg, and gesture with the left (figure *a*). While you place the tip of the left foot on the floor, bend the right knee.
2. Lift the left leg against the resistance of the band (figure *b*).
3. Lower the leg slowly; don't let it drop.
4. The hamstrings need to lengthen to perform an attitude position to the front. The hamstrings, primarily the biceps femoris, are connected by the ligaments and connective tissue of the lower back to the latissimus dorsi muscle forming a musculo-ligamentous chain from the upper arm to the knee (see chapter 7). As you lift the left leg, visualize the lengthening of the chain extending from the right upper arm down the back, over the sacrum and sit bone to the knee. As you lift the right leg, visual-

ize the other diagonal chain lengthening. Notice whether you feel a difference between the chains on the left and right sides. This feeling may indicate an imbalance in the position of the pelvis. It is also beneficial to visualize both chains simultaneously and independent of which leg is being lifted.

5. Place the tip of the left foot on the floor at the right side of the body (second position), and bend the knee.
6. Lift the left leg into attitude position (figure *c*).
7. Feel a release of compression around the tailbone. Create a widening space around the tail, and feel the neck as soft and flexible. Notice how this feeling increases the flexibility of the hip joint.
8. Slowly lower the leg.

a

b

c

d

9. Think of the tailbone as a miniature pendulum, swinging slightly backward as you lift the leg and slightly forward as you lower it. This image supports the small, necessary adjustments of the sacrum in response to leg movement. Make sure to image this and not to do this action.

10. Imagine the muscles resting on the bones as you move the leg through space. Now focus on the lightness of the bones: Think of the fact that a million new cells are being born in the bone marrow every minute. Use this image to feel alive, light, and immensely creative in your limb movements.

11. Now place the tip of the left foot on the floor at the back of the body, and bend the knee.

12. Lift the left leg to the back in attitude position (figure d).

13. Slowly lower the leg.

14. Create alignment through balanced flexibility. Instead of tensing the back muscles with the increasing resistance of the band, focus on where movement needs to happen to keep the back upright and free of tension. Allow the space between the vertebral bodies to widen in front, and feel the sliding of the facet joints between the individual vertebrae.

15. The hip joint allows for only about 25 degrees of extension. Attitude and arabesque require lifting the leg significantly higher, requiring changes in the position of the pelvis and spine. This movement must be done in a balanced and coordinated fashion.

16. For the middle back to be flexible, it is important to be aware of the relationship between the diaphragm, lungs, and upper abdominal organs. Often dancers hike the pelvis, in turn twisting the back to achieve attitude, and causing discomfort in the back.

17. In the middle back, where tension often builds in the arabesque, visualize the diaphragm sliding back on the upper abdominal organs. Imagine both sides of the back working equally (figure e).

18. Repeat the exercise 6 times to the front in a turned-out position, and increase to 16 repetitions, increasing by 2 each week.

19. If you are doing the series for the first time, you may want to remove the band for a moment and try the previous movement without it to feel the difference.

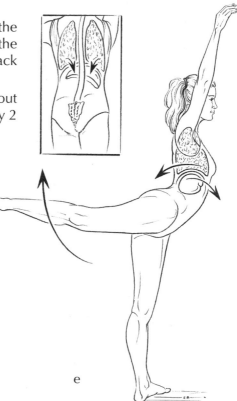

e

a

The following exercise trains your balance and may be quite challenging. Include it only after you have practiced the Thera-Band workout sequence for one month. The supporting leg may be exhausted from the previous exercise and may not have enough strength to continue without causing tension in the rest of the body. This tension will reduce the benefit of the exercise.

1. Place the band under the right leg.
2. Lift the right leg into attitude position and the band overhead, holding it with both hands (figure a).
3. With the right leg in attitude position, turn on the left leg solé (hopping with very low repeated lifting of heel).
4. During the attitude rotation, feel the whole shape moving as a unit. Avoid turning the arms and then adding the torso and legs, or vice versa. This movement distorts the shape and is not beneficial for the joints. Before you start turning, get a clear sense of your position, and move this position around with the action of the supporting leg (figure b). Keep the shoulders and neck relaxed, and think of the whole body, every limb, relying on the centered power of the supporting leg. Keep the movement slow, but in a continuous rhythm, and turn out the supporting leg with the knees aligned over the feet. (Dance the leg into turn-out; don't think of forcing it there).
5. Imagine the shoulder blades resting on the back. Think of them as leaves resting on the rib cage. Feel these leaves floating on the back, with a nice air cushion between them and the rib cage. You can use this image in all positions where the leg is raised to the back to keep the muscles surrounding the shoulder blades relaxed.
6. It may not be helpful to think of pulling up to create balance. Although the intention inherent in this image is correct, the effort to pull up usually results in increased tension and distortion, causing the dancer to lose his balance (or at least his grace and flow of movement). Lift and balance are created with respect to biomechanical principles by allowing the weight to flow down through the torso, spine, and supporting limb(s). This distribution of weight causes an increased counterthrust experience, resulting in more lift than with pulling up.
7. Once you experience this spontaneous lift through counterthrust, as opposed to the artificial lift through pulling up, you will have a better understanding of how to create balance. The problem is that many dancers are so used to pulling up that they will not even allow themselves to try other options, even if they have been failing at balance for years.

b

This exercise is a workout that challenges balance, flexibility, and strength, but the effort is well worth it. Even after the first try you will notice an increased height and ease of motion in your high leg kicks (grand battement). All the muscles of the pelvis and leg are engaged, especially the hip joint musculature. The exercise also increases the active ROM of the hip joint.

a   b   c

1. Stand on the loose end of a band, leaving two to three feet of band between the gesturing foot and the supporting foot. You know you have the right band length when the leg has reached a 45-degree angle and you experience some resistance from it. Make sure the band is flat you can firmly place the foot on top of it.

2. With the right leg, perform a grand battement to the front against the resistance of the band (figure a).

3. Grand battement to the side against the resistance of the band (figure b).

4. Adjust the band with the left hand so the loop around the legs is a bit tighter for movement to the back (figure c).

5. Grand battement to the back against the resistance of the band (figure d).

6. Perform steps 2 through 5 four times increasing to eight times in increments of one per week.

7. Feel the head balancing on top of the spine and the spine supporting a centered head. This will free your neck, allowing your leg to go higher (figure d).

8. In battement to the back, imagine the psoas major and the crura of the diaphragm lengthening. The crura are two little legs of the diaphragm that connect it to the spine. Try to feel both sides of the psoas and the crura lengthening equally to increase the arch of the back without harming the lower spine (see also chapter 6).

9. You may also perform four battements turned out and four battements in parallel in each direction. Another option is to keep the leg in the lifted battement position and bounce it upward against the resistance of the band 16 times in each position.

d

PENCHÉ BOUNCES FOR RAPID ELEVATION: NAVEL CONNECTION LIFTS THE LEG

a

Depending on your level of conditioning, the following exercises may be a challenge to perform and should be attempted only once you have practiced the previous exercises for at least one month. Nevertheless, they are popular exercises among dancers. I have taught them because they are so helpful for improving penché and arabesque positions.

1. Stand on one end of a Thera-Band, the other is still attached to the foot.

2. Move the gesturing leg into the penché arabesque position and place both hands on the floor.

3. Bounce the gesturing leg against the band 16 times (figure a).

4. Move the leg into second position and bounce it against the band eight times (figure b).

5. Think of pushing from the center of the belly (navel) into the floor with your hands and up through the gesturing leg into space. Imagine that the push helps to lift the gesturing leg higher. Make sure the neck and jaw stay free of tension, and keep breathing regularly.

6. Take the leg down very slowly, and place both feet firmly on the floor.

7. Slowly move back to the upright position. If you lift the upper body too fast, the blood flow will not have enough time to readjust to erect posture, and you may feel faint for a moment.

8. Shake out the legs, and compare the arabesque of the right and left legs.

b

Enjoy this stretch to finish up the Thera-Band work-out. Increase the flexibility of the hip joint and spine, and improve your balance at the same time.

1. Using a Thera-Band, pull the leg into an arabesque position.

2. Pull on the band to increase the elevation of the gesturing leg (figure a). Do not overstretch. The position should never feel painful. Remain in the position for about 30 seconds.

3. Imagine yourself as a fountain with the water gushing up through the supporting leg and spreading out into space to create the shape of the upper body (figure b).

4. Slowly lower the leg

5. If the knees are hyperextended (as the dancer in figure b illustrates), make sure that you do not push them back any further in an effort to maintain balance. Engage the quadriceps of the supporting leg to compensate for a hyperextended knee.

a

b

Repeat the series with the other leg. I suggest using your favorite music to perform the Thera-Band workout. Ask another dancer to perform the series with you, and perform a conditioning duet. Share and enjoy the process of becoming a better dancer.

References and Resources

Thera-Band® products may be purchased at www.Thera-Band.com or by calling (800) 321-2135 in the United States or (330) 633-8460 outside the United States.

The exercise balls mentioned in the book can be obtained by writing to
Institut für Franklin-Methode
Brunnenstrasse 1
CH-8610 Uster
Switzerland
e-mail: info@franklin-methode.ch
To order the balls in the United States, e-mail pinhasiamos@hotmail.com.

Albrecht, K, and R. Gautschi. 2001. Dehn'Dich Gesund! *Mobile Praxis.* Magglingen, Switzerland: BASPO.

Albrecht, K. S. Meyer, and L. Zahner. 1997. *Stretching, das Expertenhandbuch.* Heidelberg: Karl F. Haug Verlag.

Alter, M.J. 1996. *The Science of Stretching.* Champaign, IL: Human Kinetics.

Chopra, D. 1993. *Ageless Body, Timeless Mind.* New York: Random House.

Clark, B. 1963. *Let's Enjoy Sitting-Standing-Walking.* Port Washington, NY: Author.

Clark, B. 1968. *How to Live in Your Axis—Your Vertical Line.* New York: Author.

Clark, B. 1975. *Body Proportion Needs Depth—Front to Back.* Champaign, IL: Author.

Cohen, B. 1994. *Sensing, Feeling, and Action: The Experiential Anatomy of Body-Mind Centering.* Northampton, MA: Contact.

Dowd, I. 1990. *Taking Root to Fly.* Northampton, MA: Contact.

Epstein G., MD. 1989. *Healing Visualizations.* New York: Bantam.

Feldenkrais, M. 1972. *Awareness Through Movement.* New York: Harper Collins.

Fleck, S., and W. Kraemer. 1997. *Designing Resistance Training Programs.* Champaign, IL: Human Kinetics.

Franklin, E. 1996a. *Dance Imagery for Technique and Performance.* Champaign, IL: Human Kinetics.

Franklin, E. 1996b. *Dynamic Alignment Through Imagery.* Champaign, IL: Human Kinetics.

Franklin E. 2002. *Relax Your Neck, Liberate Your Shoulders, The Ultimate Exercise Program for Tension Relief.* Highstown, NJ: Princeton.

Franklin E. 2003. *Pelvic Power: Mind/Body Exercises for Strength, Flexibility, Posture and Balance for Men and Women.* Highstown, NJ: Princeton.

Gotheiner, Z. 2001. Interview with author. November 15.

Grossman, G., and V. Wilmerding. 2000. The effect of conditioning on the height of dancer's extension in à la seconde. *Journal of Dance Medicine and Science* 4(4), 117–121.

Hather, B.M., P.A. Tesch, P. Buhanan, and G.A. Dudley. 1991. Influence of eccentric actions on skeletal muscle adaptations to resistance training. *Acta Physiol Scand* 143, 177–185.

Hawkins, A. 1991. *Moving from Within*. Pennington, NJ: A Capella.

Holmes, P.S,. and D.J. Collins. 2001. The PETTLEP approach to motor imagery. *Journal of Applied Sport Psychology,* 13(1), 83–106.

Juhan, D. 1987. *Job's Body.* Barrytown, NY: Station Hill.

Keeleman C.S. 1985. *Emotional Anatomy.* Berkeley, CA: Center Press.

Kendal F., and E. McCreary. 1983. *Muscle Testing and Function,* Baltimore: Williams and Wilkins.

Liederbach, M. 2000. General considerations for guiding dance injury rehabilitation. *Dance Medicine and Science* 4(2), 54–65.

Matt, P. 1993. *A Kinesthetic Legacy: The Life and Works of Barbara Clark.* Tempe, AZ: CMT Press.

McGill, S. 2002. *Low Back Disorders.* Champaign, IL: Human Kinetics.

Molnar, M., and J. Esterson. 1997. Screening students in a pre-professional ballet school. *Dance Medicine and Science* 1(3): 118–121.

Moran, A. 1999. *The Psychology of Concentration in Sports Performers: A Cognitive Analysis.* East Sussex: Psychology Press.

Moyers, B. 1993. *Healing and the Mind.* New York: Doubleday.

Nagrin, D. 1994. *Dance and the Specific Image.* Pittsburgh: University of Pittsburgh Press.

Neumann, N. 2002. *Kinesiology of the Musculoskelettal System.* St. Louis: Mosby.

Norkin, C., and P.K. Levangie. 1992. *Joint Structure and Function.* Philadelphia: F.A. Davis.

Olsen A. 1991. *Body Stories: A Guide to Experiential Anatomy.* Barrytown, NY: Station Hill.

Page, P. and T. Ellenbecker. 2003. *The Scientific and Clinical Application of Elastic Resistance.* Champaign, IL: Human Kinetics.

Pert, C. 1999. *Molecules of Emotion: The Science Behind Mind-Body Medicine.* New York: Simon & Schuster.

Pease, B., and A. Pease. 2001. *Why Men Don't Listen and Women Can't Read Maps.* London: Orion Books.

Richardson, C., G. Jull, P. Hodges, and J. Hides. 1999. *Therapeutic Exercise for Spinal Segmental Stabilization in Low Back Pain.* Edinburgh: Churchill Livingstone.

Roberts, T.D.M. 1995. *Understanding Balance.* London: Chapman & Hall.

Rolland, J. 1984. *Inside Motion: An Ideokinetic Basis for Movement Education.* Urbana, IL: Rolland String Research Associates.

Shell, C.G., Ed. 1986. *The Dancer As Athlete.* Champaign, IL: Human Kinetics.

Schiebler, T., W. Schmidt, and K. Zilles. 1997. *Anatomie.* Berlin: Springer-Verlag.

Smith R.E., J.T. Ptacek., and E. Patterson. 2000. Moderator effects of cognitive and somatic trait anxiety on the relation between life stress and physical injuries. *Journal of Anxiety, Stress, and Coping,* 13: 269–288.

Southwick, H., C. Michelina, and C. Ploski. 2002. Snapping hip syndrome in the adolescent ballet dancer: Potential causes, clinical findings, and treatment outcomes. Paper presented at the 12th International Meeting of the International Association for Dance Medicine and Science, New York, NY USA.

Sweigard, L. 1978. *Human Movement Potential: Its Ideokinetic Facilitation.* New York: Dodd, Mead and Company

Todd, M. 1937. *The Thinking Body.* New York: Dance Horizons.

Todd, M. 1953. *The Hidden You.* New York: Dance Horizons.

Vaganova, A. 1969. *Basic Principles of Classical Ballet* London: Dover

Van den Berg, F. 1999. *Das Bindegewebe des Bewegungsapparates verstehen und Beeinflussen.* New York: Georg Thieme Verlag.

Volianitis, S., Y. Koutdakis, and R. Carson. 2001. Warm-up, a brief review. *Journal for Dance Medicine and Science,* 5(3), 75–78.

Westcott, W. 1996. *Building Strength and Stamina.* Champaign, IL, Human Kinetics.

Index

Note: The italicized *f* following page numbers refers to figures.

About the Author

Eric Franklin has more than 25 years' experience as a dancer and choreographer. In addition to earning a BFA from New York University's Tisch School of the Arts and a BS from the University of Zurich, he has studied and trained with some of the top movement imagery and conditioning specialists around the world and has used this training as a professional dancer in New York.

Franklin has shared imaging techniques in his teaching since 1986. While a faculty member of the American Dance Festival from 1991 to 1997 he began developing dance-specific conditioning exercises for students. He taught again at the ADF in 2003 and regularly teaches conditioning for dance at schools and universities throughout the world including New York University School of the Arts, the Royal Ballet School, and the Laban Center in London. In 1998 he introduced the first dance conditioning methodology to mainland China.

Franklin is author of *Dynamic Alignment Through Imagery* (1996), *Dance Imagery for Technique and Performance* (1996), *Relax Your Neck, Liberate Your Shoulders* (2002), and *Pelvic Power* (2003). He coauthored the bestselling book *Breakdance* (1984), which received a New York City Public Library Prize in 1984. He also has published several books in German. He is a member of the International Association of Dance Medicine and Science and founder and director of the Institute for Franklin-Method in Uster, Switzerland.

Franklin lives near Zurich, Switzerland, with his wife, Gabriela, and their three children.

Eric Franklin regularly offers workshops and teacher trainings—open to anyone—on the topics covered in this book. You may find out about upcoming events by visiting his web page at www.franklin-methode.ch. Or you may write to him at the following address:

Institut für Franklin-Methode
Brunnenstrasse 1
CH-8610 Uster
Switzerland
e-mail: info@franklin-methode.ch

Thera-Band®
Systems of Progressive Exercise

Exercise Bands

IF IT DOESN'T SAY Thera-Band IT'S NOT AUTHENTIC

Thera-Band® EXERCISE BANDS
Extra Heavy Resistance
Contents: One Roll
50 yards or 45,7 meters

Thera-Band® EXERCISE BANDS

Thera-Band Exercise Bands

For more than 25 years, Thera-Band® has been the world's leading brand of progressive elastic resistance products for professional rehabilitation and home fitness. Thera-Band exercise bands are low-cost, portable and versatile resistance products for building upper and lower body strength and increasing flexibility. Endorsed by the American Physical Therapy Association, they are recognized worldwide as the original System of Progressive Exercise.

For a dealer near you call 800-321-2135

The Hygenic Corporation
1245 Home Avenue, Akron, Ohio 44310 USA
330-633-8460   800-321-2135   Fax 330-633-9359
www.Thera-Band.com   www.Thera-BandAcademy.com

Thera-Band GmbH
Mainzer Landstraße 19, D-65589 Hadamar, Germany
Phone +49-6433-9164-0   Fax +49-6433-9164-64
www.Thera-Band.de

Exercise Bands

6-Yard Dispenser Box

20010	Tan / EXTRA THIN
20020	Yellow / THIN
20030	Red / MEDIUM
20040	Green / HEAVY
20050	Blue / EXTRA HEAVY
20060	Black / SPECIAL HEAVY
20070	Silver / SUPER HEAVY
20080	Gold / MAX

50-Yard Dispenser Box

20110	Tan / EXTRA THIN
20120	Yellow / THIN
20130	Red / MEDIUM
20140	Green / HEAVY
20150	Blue / EXTRA HEAVY
20160	Black / SPECIAL HEAVY
20170	Silver / SUPER HEAVY
20180	Gold / MAX

6-Foot Cut Lengths in Retail Display Box

20400	Exercise Bands, Light (yel, red, grn)
20410	Exercise Bands, Heavy (blu, blk, sil)

Latex-Free Exercise Bands

25-Yard Dispenser Box

20320	Yellow / THIN
20330	Red / MEDIUM
20340	Green / HEAVY
20350	Blue / EXTRA HEAVY
20360	Black / SPECIAL HEAVY

6-Foot Cut Lengths in Sealed Bag

20391	Light Pack (yel, red, grn)
20392	Heavy Pack (grn, blu, blk)